MORE F

WALK
Perth
OUTDOORS

CW01456685

DEPARTMENT OF CONSERVATION AND LAND MANAGEMENT

Published by: Dr Syd Shea, Executive Director, Department of Conservation and Land Management, 50 Hayman Road, Como, Western Australia 6152
Managing Editor: Ron Kawalilak
Editor and Compiler: David Gough
Editorial Assistant: June Ellis
Features: John Hunter and David Gough
Design and Production: Sue Marais
Cover Photography: Guy Magowan (front), David Gough (back)
Illustrations and Location Maps: Gooitzen van der Meer
Mud Maps*: Louise Burch
Marketing: Estelle de San Miguel
Printed in Western Australia by: Scott Four Colour Print

*The mud maps and text are based on information provided by CALM staff and volunteers.

Acknowledgements:
To the many CALM staff in the Swan Region; local government parks and recreation staff; and the many volunteers, including 'Friends' groups, who took time to walk and describe each of the walks contained in this book.
To St John Ambulance Australia for First Aid information.
To Bob Cooper Outdoor Education for bushcraft and safety information.
Thank you all for your support in this project.

© 1994. ISBN 0 7309 6806 5

All material contained in this book is copyright and may not be reproduced in print or by any electronic media except with written permission from the publishers.

Department of Conservation and Land Management

Foreword

Welcome to *More Family Walks in Perth Outdoors*.

Like its companion publication, *More Family Walks in Perth Outdoors* contains 52 walks, one for every week of the year. These new walks are ideal for families of all ages and levels of fitness, and most of them can be completed in just a few hours. They have been tried and tested by CALM staff and volunteers, who have combined their knowledge and individual feelings into their descriptions of the walks.

More Family Walks in Perth Outdoors is another in the popular series of 'Perth Outdoors' books about our capital city and its natural surroundings. *Perth Outdoors: A Guide to Natural Recreation Areas in and Around Perth* was published in 1992 and *Family Walks in Perth Outdoors* was published a year later. Together with this book, they aim to help and encourage WA's residents and visitors alike to enjoy the State's wonderful natural assets.

I believe that this book will be just as successful as our first book of walks and that we will see even more people out there enjoying Perth's great outdoors.

Syd Shea
EXECUTIVE DIRECTOR
Department of Conservation and Land Management

Contents

INTRODUCTION

MORE FAMILY WALKS IN PERTH OUTDOORS

FEATURES

COMMON BIRDS OF PERTH OUTDOORS

INDEXES

Introduction

ABOUT THIS BOOK

Welcome to *More Family Walks in Perth Outdoors*.

Walking is good for you and your family. It is one of the least expensive forms of excercise and one of the most beneficial. It can ease stiffness, improve cardiovascular fitness, reduce stress, help control weight and is especially beneficial if done regularly. Walking is probably the single most important form of physical activity for many people and it's enjoyable too.

More Family Walks in Perth Outdoors contains 52 walks, one for every week of the year. The walks are ideal for families and most of them can be completed in a couple of hours or so. They are intended to provide interest, variety and exercise, while informing you about your natural surroundings. Readers would also find it useful to have a copy of the *Perth StreetSmart Directory* or *Perth UBD* when travelling to the starting points of the walks.

Like our first walks book, *Family Walks in Perth Outdoors*, the 52 walks described in this book are listed first by geographical location (Hills, North, River and South) and then alphabetically by name within those regions. This is a similar structure to the book *Perth Outdoors: a Guide to Natural Recreation Areas in and Around Perth*. Each walk is numbered and the number is used in the indexes at the back of the book. There are two indexes: alphabetical, and by length.

The mud maps that accompany each walk are designed to provide a rough guide to the direction the walk takes and to show some of the physical features—granite outcrops, large trees, bridges, streams etc—that will help reassure you that you are still on the right track. By doing this, we hope to instil and maintain a sense of adventure, where you find your own way along the walk rather than being 'guided by the hand', as it were.

Stage-by-stage descriptions are also provided for each walk. These include some of things you might see along the way, such as the physical features mentioned above or certain plants, trees, birds or other animals found in the area, or historical information about the route of the walk or the area through which it passes. Some descriptions also give directions where the route may not be clear. However, we don't give too much away, so there are still things for you to discover as you find your way around.

The majority of walks listed in the book have carparks and picnic facilities at the start, at the end or somewhere nearby. Some have toilets, water and other facilities close by.

Distances and travelling times from Perth GPO are approximate, and walk times are based on taking a leisurely stroll rather than a brisk walk.

The walk grades are given only as a guide to how difficult or strenuous each walk might be and do not reflect how safe it is. They are as follows:

* **Grade 1** - Short, easy walks suitable for people of all ages and fitness levels.
* **Grade 2** - As Grade 1, but usually longer than three kilometres.
* **Grade 3** - Suitable for people with a moderate level of fitness and will generally be between three and about eight kilometres in length.
* **Grade 4** - As Grade 3, but will have steps, steep slopes or short uneven stretches that may be loose or slippery underfoot.
* **Grade 5** - Long or strenuous walks, usually more than about eight kilometres and suitable for experienced or fit walkers. Trails may be unmarked in places and go over steep, slippery or uneven surfaces.

Additional information, such as 'some steep sections', is given where this might be useful in helping you choose your walk.

While every effort has been made to ensure that the information provided in this book is accurate, no responsibility can be taken for any changes made since the walks were surveyed, or for the state of repair of any walk, as this is subject to weather and usage. When walking in the bush or along established trails, it is important to tread carefully and keep an eye open for potential hazards.

Your safety is our concern, but your responsibility.

WALKING IN PERTH OUTDOORS

Walking through natural bushland is a pleasurable experience. To be surrounded by the sounds, colours, smells and different types of life forms in and around Perth is both enlightening and exhilarating. Few capital cities are blessed with such a variety of natural areas right on their doorsteps.

The natural environment of Perth is made up of four distinctive natural communities, or ecosystems:

- ❖ the forests and woodlands of the Darling Range and Scarp;
- ❖ the woodlands of the Coastal Plain;
- ❖ the wetlands of lakes, streams, rivers and estuaries; and
- ❖ the coast and marine environments.

These distinctive natural communities are characterised by the soil type, landform and dominant plant life. The plants, animals, insects and other invertebrates, micro-organisms, rocks, soil, water, aspect to the sun and resultant microclimate all combine in subtle ways within each community to make each walk different. Wherever you choose to walk within a natural community you can see both the common characteristics and the specific details that make each place special.

The Forests and Woodlands of the Darling Range and Scarp

The Darling Range is the tilted edge of a huge plateau that is the foundation of this part of Western Australia. Here, some of the oldest rocks on Earth are exposed. The granites, gneisses and quartzites are more than 2 500 million years old.

The overlying mantle of orange-red laterite rock formed about 10 million years ago, when wetter and more humid conditions than those of today leached minerals from the soil to form and insoluble hard crust. Jarrah trees, with their stringy grey-black bark, are predominant. Jarrah forest, with its low understorey of wildflowers and groves of balgas (blackboys), is a definitive image of the Darling Range, particularly when back-lit by the sun in the early morning and late afternoon.

The western extremity of the Darling Range is the Darling Scarp. Standing 200 metres or so above the coastal plain, it is the distinctive feature of the Perth horizon. The scarp exposes the huge granite rocks, which over time, have weathered to form clays that favour the white-trunked wandoo trees.

The Woodlands of the Coastal Plain

The forested foothills below the Darling Scarp spill onto the coastal plain. Here, the less fertile sands support woodlands of banksia, sheoaks, stunted eucalypts of jarrah and marri, and, where creamy-grey limestone is exposed, groves of tuart. Shrublands and wildflower heathlands form the understorey. In the wetter areas, paperbarks proliferate. Without landform features, we most often take these woodlands for granted. In spring and early summer, the trees, shrubs and heathlands display their presence with a profusion of flowers.

A complex of sand dune systems is aligned roughly parallel to the coast. These were formed during the past two million years from wind-blown beach sand deposits along previous shorelines of this coastal plain.

The coastal woodlands are a distinctively different community from that of the forests of the range. Compare the rocks and gravels of the range with the sands of the plain; the tall trees of the forest with the shorter-trunked, deep-crowned woodland trees and shrublands on the plain.

The Wetlands of Lakes, Rivers, Streams and Estuaries

The apparent uniformity of the coastal woodlands is broken by urban developments and the wetlands of the coastal plain, which include the Swan and Canning Rivers and the chains of lakes to the north and south of the Swan.

The presence of wetlands is indicated by paperbark woodland, which is tolerant of wet conditions. The mostly smooth-barked and tall flooded gums, along with paperbarks, fringe watercourses and make walking alongside them an often pleasant and tranquil experience.

The many freshwater lakes, dotted throughout the coastal plain, appear like scattered jewels from vantage points through surrounding woodlands of banksia and paperbarks. These wetlands provide important habitat for waders and other waterbirds.

The Coast and Marine Environments

The Perth Coast is a powerful line of demarcation between the coastal plain and the marine environment. Rocky limestone outcrops and sweeping white sand dunes with a plant cover of wattles and other shrubs, beautifully compliment the blue-green waters of the Indian Ocean. Beneath the waves there is a seascape of limestone ledges, walls, caves, reefs and islands that provide habitat for a wonderful diversity of marine life.

WALKING SAFELY

There are basically two forms of bushwalking: strolling along an existing walktrail in a park, reserve, forest, bushland area or along the riverbank, or trekking through wild bush elsewhere. This book deals primarily with the first.

However, all natural areas should be approached with some degree of caution; for example, slippery or uneven surfaces. Walking along tracks, trails and firebreaks is relatively safe, but you should still be alert to potential hazards. Most of the information in this section is common sense, but additional bushcraft, safety and First Aid information have been included in the unlikely event of someone in your party being injured or getting lost.

Please take note of the following:

❖ Wear sturdy but comfortable shoes or boots. Training shoes may be suitable, but care should be taken when crossing uneven or slippery surfaces like mossy rocks. In these cases, it is desirable to wear boots that give some support to the ankles. Always wear good quality, fairly thick, cotton or wool socks.

❖ Long socks or long trousers, such as jeans or canvas drill, will give some leg protection against prickly vegetation or biting insects. A long-sleeved shirt will help protect you from sunburn in the summer and a woollen sweater or fleecy sweatshirt will help keep you warm in the winter. It is preferable to dress in layers of light clothing.

❖ Wear a hat for protection against the sun or rain, and take a light raincoat.

❖ Wear a sunscreen with a minimum sun protection factor (SPF) of 15+.

❖ Keep your things in a light haversack or day pack, to keep your hands free.

❖ If you are making an extended or difficult walk, tell at least two reliable people and advise them when you've completed it.

❖ Take a First Aid kit and insect repellent, as well as any prescribed medications.

❖ Walk in a party of two or more people for safety. If you are injured, you will need someone who can summon help. Five is the ideal minimum.

❖ Make sure you have adequate water *and remember to drink it!* Take at least one litre per person on most days and at least two litres on hot days.

❖ Take care not to trample sensitive areas such as moss-covered rock, sand dune plants or steep slopes.

If you become lost:

❖ Try to retrace your steps until you reach the last recognisable place on the map. Remember to look for your own footprints.

❖ If you cannot retrace your steps, follow a track; it will usually lead to some habitation. Alternatively, head for the nearest high point and climb to the summit. You might then be able to see roads and areas of habitation.

❖ If you are still lost and you have run out of water, remember that animal trails always lead to water. Walk in the direction in which the trails converge into one. Watch out for flocks of birds, they fly rapidly towards water and more slowly when travelling away from water after drinking.

❖ When replenishing drinking water from natural or artificial water sources, you must purify the water either by boiling it or by using a chemical purifier such as Puritabs™.

FIRST AID

Walking in the bush in Perth Outdoors is rarely hazardous. Nevertheless, walkers should be aware of possible problems. The following section deals with the things you need to know in the unlikely event of one of your party being injured.

First Aid Kit

Your first aid kit should contain the following basic essentials:
Antiseptic cream
Antiseptic swabs
Band Aids™
Butterfly wound closures
Dressings (sterile)
Elastic bandage for sprains and snake-bite treatment
Paracetamol
Scissors
Tweezers

Snake bites

Although many species of snake inhabit the areas dealt with in this book, it is extremely rare that you will see one, let alone be bitten by one. Snakes sense the vibration of approaching footsteps and tend to flee into the undergrowth. If you are unlucky enough to be bitten, here is what you should and should not do.

Assume **ALL** snakes are venomous, and take the following action:

DO NOT panic: Try to remain calm, lie down and immobilise the bitten area.
DO NOT wash the wound: Venom left on the skin will help doctors identify the snake and administer the appropriate anti-venin.
DO NOT apply a tourniquet: Take out the snake bandage and bind, not too tightly, along the limb starting at the bite area, then bandage down the limb and continue back up the entire limb over and above the bite area. This will help prevent the spread of the venom through the body. Do not remove the bandage.
DO NOT elevate the limb or attempt to walk or run: Movement will encourage the spread of the venom through the body. Immobilise the limb with a splint. Lie down and keep still until help arrives.

DO NOT attempt to catch the snake: Identification of the snake species can be obtained through samples of the patient's blood or urine, and from venom around the bite area. If the species of snake still remains uncertain, a poly anti-venom may be used, which is suitable for treatment of all venomous snake bites.

Spider Bites

Our most common potentially dangerous spider is the red-back spider (*Latrodectus hasseltii*), which is usually associated with buildings, but also lives quite happily in bush and parkland areas. Red-back spiders are often found under logs or leaf litter, or at the base of clumps of vegetation. It is the female spider that is dangerous (the male spider's fangs are too small pierce human skin).

Treatment for a spider bite is as follows:

❖ No special First Aid need be applied because the venom from a red-back spider bite is very slow acting. Using a bandage will localise the venom, causing the pain to intensify at the bite area.
❖ Transport the victim immediately to medical aid. Apparently, serious illness does not develop for at least three hours and anti-venom is readily available if required.
❖ Children and the infirm are most at risk from red-back spider bites.

Sprains and Broken Limbs

Although most of the walks in this book are along existing, well-walked trails, some have uneven or loose surfaces along the route. Where possible, these have been indicated in the text, but you should always tread carefully as areas can become loose or uneven after heavy rain or very dry periods. If you or a fellow walker trips and sprains or breaks a limb, you should take the following action.

With **sprains** apply the 'RICE' technique:

R - REST and reassure the casualty.
I - ICE: Apply an ice pack, or cloth soaked in cold water, for 20 minutes. It may be reapplied every two hours for the first 24 hours.
C - COMPRESSION: Bandage the sprain firmly.
E - ELEVATE the sprained limb and support the injury.

Remember to avoid both heat and massage.

If the limb is **broken** and the casualty is conscious and breathing freely, take the following action:

DO control any bleeding.
DO rest and reassure the casualty.
DO immobilise the fractured limb with splints and slings in the most comfortable position and check the blood circulation past the last bandaging point. Be sure to handle the casualty carefully.
DO NOT pull on any fractures.
DO NOT give the casualty anything to drink.
DO NOT force or straighten fractured joints.

The First Aid information provided here is very basic. It is desirable for at least one member of your party to have some First Aid experience. St John Ambulance Australia publishes First Aid manuals and runs a variety of First Aid courses. For more information contact your nearest St John Ambulance Centre.

WHAT YOU NEED TO KNOW

Bushwalking

You can bushwalk in two ways: by using walktrails or trekking through wild bush. While the first is usually safe and relaxing, the second could do environmental damage and put your life at risk.

The walks in this book follow either formalised walktrails with signage and occasionally surfaced tracks, or well used and informally established tracks through bushland, parks or riverside areas. Some of the walks cross or form part of the Bibbulmun Track. This is a 650 kilometre long-distance walk track from Kalamunda, in the Darling Range east of Perth, to Walpole, on the south coast.

Camping

While out walking you may see possible sites for a future camping expedition.

As more people head for the bush, greater pressures are put on our natural resources. In an effort to protect our environment, visitors may only camp at designated camping sites—usually marked with a sign in national parks, regional parks, State forest or bush areas. Please leave no rubbish or other traces of your visit.

Camping fees are charged in some areas and the funds raised help to pay for the facilities and services provided.

Dieback

Some areas of forest and woodland have been infected by a soil-borne fungus (*Phytophthora cinnamomi*) that attacks the root systems of trees, shrubs and wildflowers. The disease is known to attack at least 900 plant species and many, such as banksias and dryandras, die very quickly. The fungus travels over and through the soil in water, attaching spores to roots. The rot sets in immediately.

The fungus is carried in soil or mud that sticks to boots and shoes, and the wheels, mudguards and underbodies of vehicles. When the soil or mud drops off, the fungus immediately contaminates the new area and multiplies. There is, as yet, no known cure.

Some areas in national parks and State forest are closed to vehicles to prevent dieback being carried into or spread through them. These areas are largely uninfected. You may enter on foot but you must not take vehicles, motorbikes, horses or any form of wheeled transport into these areas. When walking through infected areas, help stop the rot by not straying from the track. Observe the signs and give our plants a chance.

Entry Fees ($)

Entry fees are charged to some national parks, regional parks and reserves. Where a charge is made, it is indicated by the symbol ($). The funds raised help to pay for the facilities and services provided.

Fire

Fire is a good servant but a poor master. Bushfires are a real danger, particularly during the dry summer months.

Please note these points:

- ❖ Always use the fireplaces provided. Better still, bring your own portable stove.
- ❖ Open fires are not permitted in national parks.
- ❖ Build a stone ring in State forest if no fireplace exists, or dig a shallow pit to contain the embers.
- ❖ Clear all leaf litter, dead branches and anything else that may burn from and area of at least three metres around and above the fire. This also applies to portable stoves.
- ❖ Never leave a fire unattended.
- ❖ Make sure the fire is completely out before leaving. Use soil and water to extinguish the embers, and bury the ashes.

On certain days during the year the fire forecast is 'very high' or 'extreme'. A total fire ban exists on these days. Local radio stations broadcast fire risk warnings, but please check with Shire authorities, the tourist bureau, or the nearest CALM office for advice on the fire situation.

Firearms

No offensive weapon is to be brought into any conservation or recreation area.

Fishing

Fisheries' regulations apply in all areas, but you should also check with the ranger in any national park. Trout and redfin perch have been stocked in inland waters near Perth. Marron fishing is a seasonal activity by permit only. We'd like you to come back, so help conserve fish numbers by taking only enough for your immediate needs.

Granite outcrops

Several walks in this book cross or pass close to granite outcrops. Granite outcrops, often termed 'living rocks', are unique sanctuaries for many species of plants and animals. Exploring granite outcrops is a fascinating experience, but the environment is extremely fragile. Moving a rock, disturbing a plant or carelessly placing a foot can cause irreparable damage. Please do not stray off the tracks that cross granite outcrops.

Native plants and animals

In order to protect the environment, please do not disturb any native animals, and do not pick the wildflowers. Rocks, vegetation or old logs should not be removed, as these are often the homes of small creatures that depend on such habitat for their existence.

Pets

Pets are not permitted in national parks, nature reserves and water catchments. Many other shire-controlled parks, reserves and beaches have similar restrictions. If you are not sure whether dogs and/or other pets are permitted at the place you intend to visit, please leave them at home.

Rubbish

Place all litter in bins provided. If there are no bins, take your litter home with you. When camping or walking in the bush where there are few, if any, facilities, bury organic waste at least 30 centimetres deep and at least 100 metres from any waterway, picnic area or campsite.

Vehicles

Normal road rules apply in all recreation and conservation areas. To protect wildlife habitat and the environment from erosion and dieback disease, please keep to formed roads and designated tracks at all times. Be sure to lock your vehicle if it is left unattended.

Water

Most creeks and rivers in Western Australia are dry during summer months. When you are out and about take your own drinking water. If you do have to use water from the few permanent water points, it should be boiled before use, or purified using a commercially available purification product.

Water Catchments

These special areas are reserved for water and vegetation protection. Because of this, there are restrictions on various recreation activities in certain areas. Check with the WA Water Authority.

REMEMBER

❖ **Be careful:** Stay on paths and help prevent erosion. Your safety in natural areas is our concern, but your responsibility.

❖ **Be clean:** Take your rubbish out with you. Don't use soap or detergent in rivers or streams; they kill the aquatic life.

❖ **Be cool:** Light fires only in fireplaces. Bring your own portable gas stove. Take notice of all fire weather forecasts.

❖ **Protect animals and plants:** No firearms please. Pets are not permitted in national parks and in some other areas. Check before you bring your dog or cat.

❖ **Stay on the road:** Follow signs and stay on the designated roads. Normal road rules apply.

The Hills   Walks 1 - 9

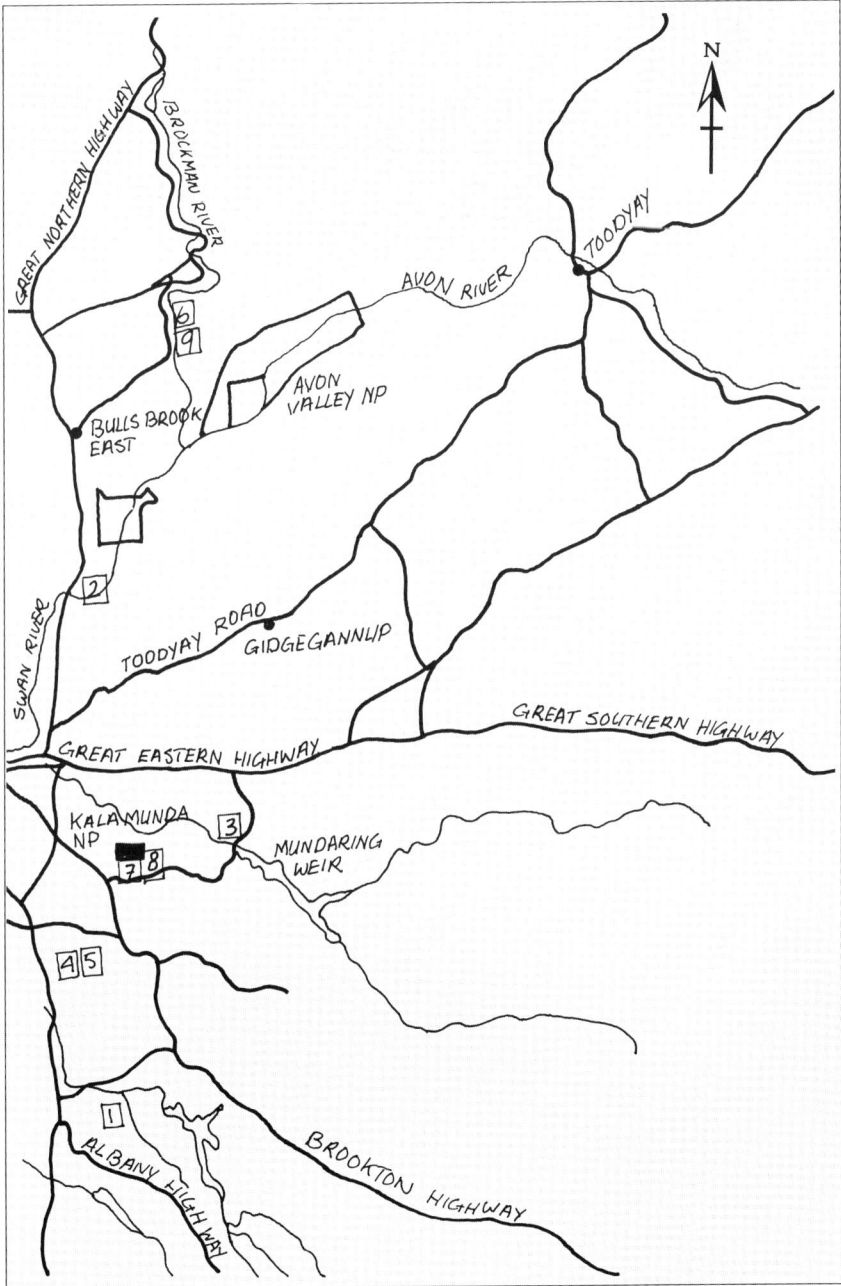

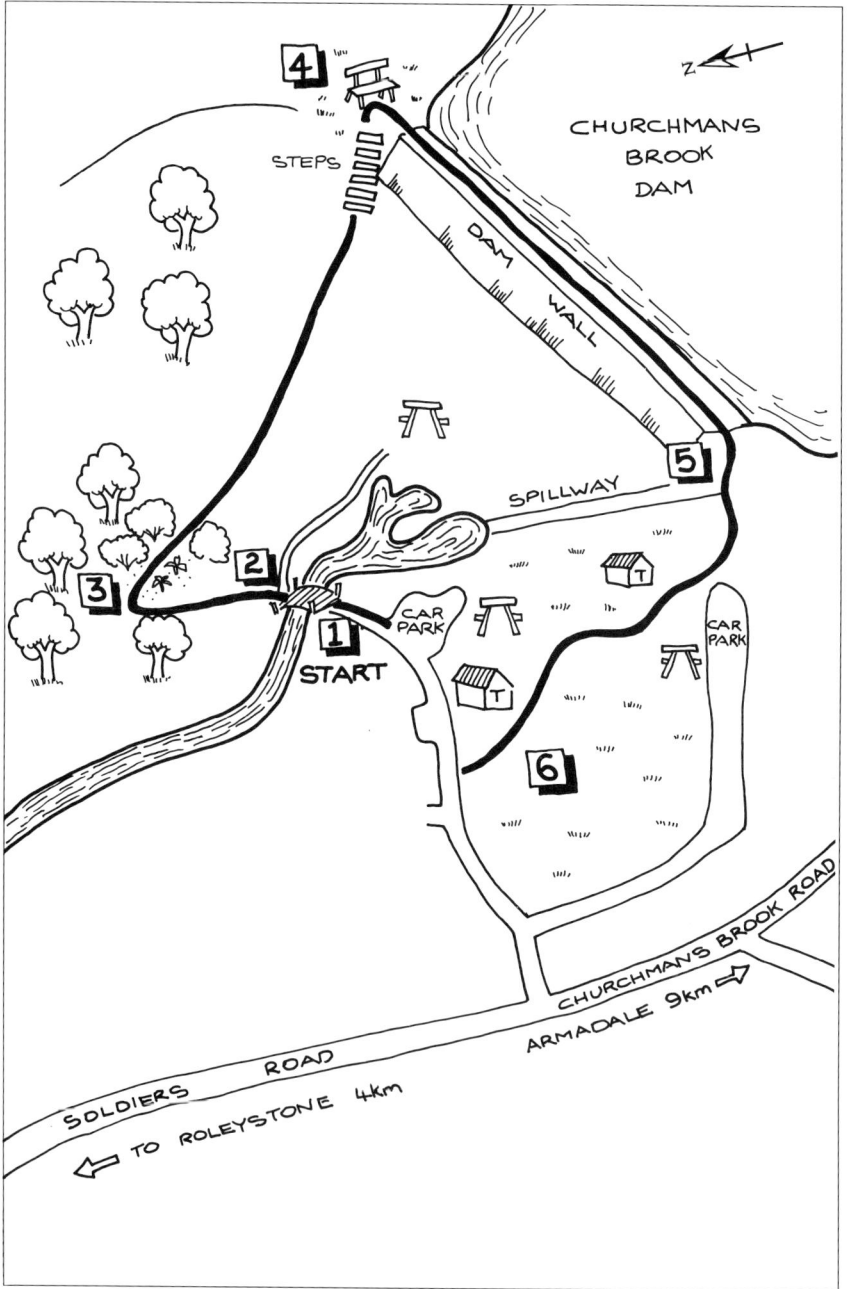

N

CHURCHMANS
BROOK
DAM

4

STEPS

DAM WALL

SPILLWAY

5

T

3

2

CAR
PARK

1
START

CAR
PARK

T

6

CHURCHMANS BROOK ROAD

ARMADALE 9km ⇨

SOLDIERS ROAD

⇦ TO ROLEYSTONE 4km

Churchmans Brook Trail

Churchmans Brook Reservoir

Length: *1 kilometre loop*
Grade: *3*
Walk time: *30 minutes*

Perth's first earthwall dam was completed here in 1926. The WA Water Authority has provided five picnic areas with views of the dam, open woodlands, jarrah forest and pines. This walk goes up the hillside a little way, then cuts across the dam wall and back to the recreation area. **Dogs on leads are permitted.**

1   From the carpark, take the bridge over the small artificial lake, where there are often many ducks.
2   Straight ahead is a walk sign and path leading into mixed jarrah-marri forest. Follow the path for 100 m to open space, where there are more BBQs.
3   Immediately to the right, follow the gentle slope through a very pleasant stretch of forest. The understorey includes coral vine, wattles and ferns.
4   About 200 m further on, steps lead to a level clearing with a seat. Here, you can enjoy views of the reservoir and forest beyond. Walk across the dam wall and look down at the gardens and picnic areas below.
5   At the far end of the dam wall, the spillway can be seen on the right. On the left, a little further on, is a pleasant grassed BBQ area. Follow steps to the 'Village Green'.
6   The 'Village Green' is a large grassed area with a playground, and is ideal for families with children. After spending some time here, wearing the kids out, continue downhill and back to the carpark.

June Ellis

Where is it?: *23 km south-east of Perth*
Travelling time: *40 minutes via Brookton Highway and Soldiers Road*
Facilities: *Picnic areas, BBQs, tables, water, toilets*
On-site information: *Walk sign*
Best season: *All year, spring for wildflowers*

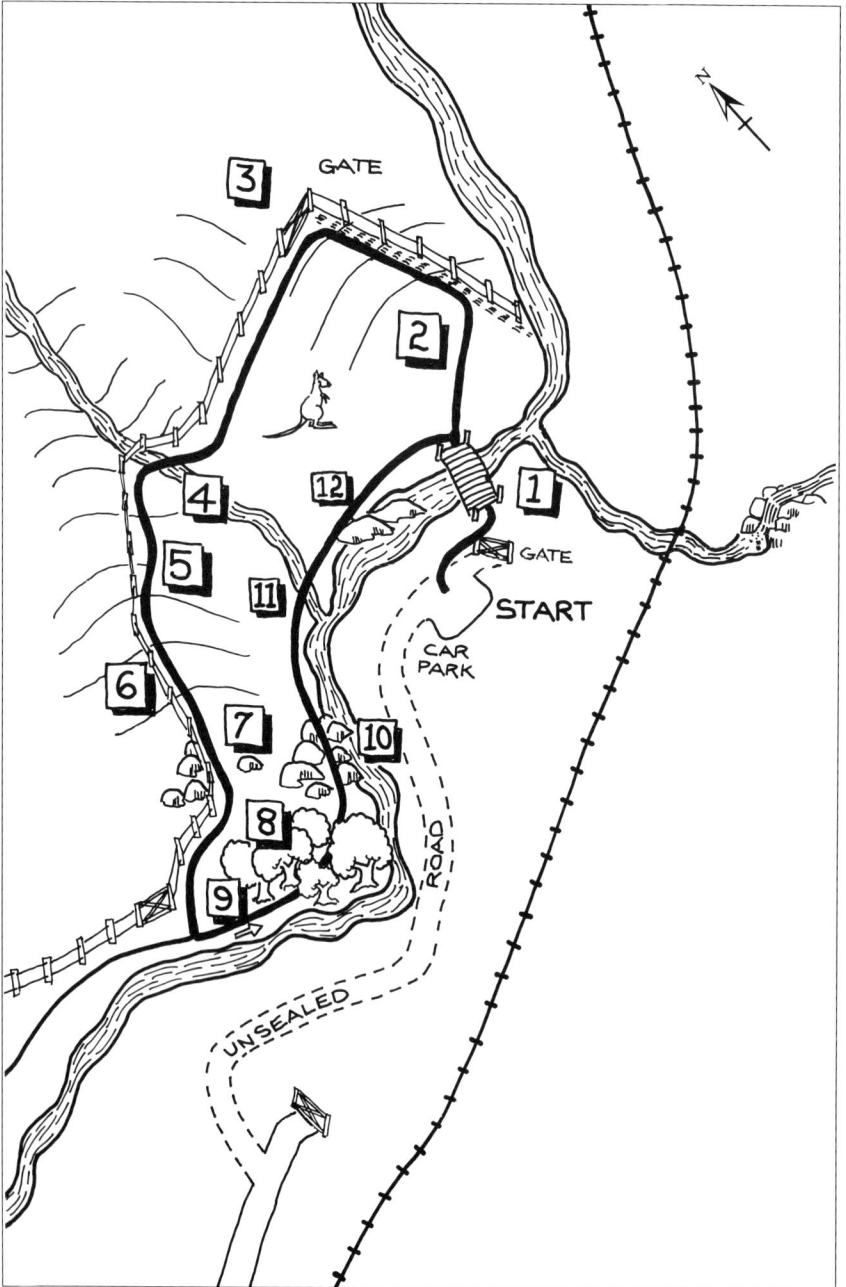

Hillside Trail

2

Bells Rapids

Length: *3 kilometre loop*
Grade: *4 (some steep sections)*
Walk time: *1 hour 30 minutes*

This walk features spectacular views of the upper Swan Valley, wildflowers in spring, birds and animals all year round, and torrents of rushing water after winter rains. It is in two sections: the upper section runs through wandoo, balgas (blackboys) and heath vegetation along a ridge on the lower slopes of Mt Mambup; whereas the lower section follows the river through paperbarks, zamias and grasses.

Granite outcrops at various points along the way make this an interesting and varied walk at any time of the year.

1   After parking at the end of the unsealed access road, walk down a gradual slope towards the river and cross the footbridge to the northern bank. Turn right and head upstream.
2   You will shortly see a fenceline and firebreak that runs uphill. Follow the fenceline up a steep rise.
3   At the top of the rise is a gateway. Turn left here and follow the fenceline as the trail runs gently downhill. From here you can see the footbridge below and, if you are walking in early morning or late afternoon, you may see kangaroos along the ridge and on the upper slopes.
4   After following the fenceline to the right, the trail dips into a shallow gully and crosses a seasonal stream that runs from the higher slopes down to the river. Turn left shortly after crossing the gully and continue following the fenceline.
5   This section rises fairly steeply to the highest part of the walk. In winter, there are spectacular views across the valley to a waterfall on the southern slopes.
6   This is the highest part of the walk. You can see along the Darling Scarp and to the airport in the distance.
7   The trail runs down a gentle slope passing granite rocks.
8   As you turn the bend of the ridge you can now see the Perth city skyline for the first time: the buildings of the central business district rising starkly from the flat coastal plain.
9   As you reach the bottom of the slope and another gate, walk towards the river and pick up the bridle track that runs along the river's edge. Turn left and head upstream through thickets of paperbarks.

10 After following the bend of the river you will come across large granite rocks on both sides of the trail and running into the river itself. Climb over the rocks and continue along the riverbank.

11 Here, you will cross the same small seasonal stream that you crossed higher up the slope. Look uphill to see the gully rising beyond the ridge where you walked earlier.

12 Just before arriving back at the footbridge, note the extensive granite rocks that have been worn flat by the rushing winter waters.

David and James Gough

Where is it?: *30 km north-west of Perth*
Travelling time: *1 hour via Great Northern Highway and Cathedral Avenue*
Facilities: *None*
On-site information: *None*
Best season: *All year, except very hot summer days*

FUNGI

When out walking in Perth Outdoors, make sure you remember to look for those forms of growth that are often forgotten or out of sight in the bush, namely the fungi.

These weird, wonderful and often delicate forms are probably the least well-known plant species and therefore, at any time, you just may be the discoverer of a new species. Early winter is the best time to observe fungi, but as long as there's moisture and a food source such as rotting material, there will be fungi.

A fungus has numerous web-like feeding threads throughout the material that it is living on. At a certain time it grows a fruiting body in the form of a toadstool, mushroom or puffball, so that it can grow and disperse millions of tiny spores, which will develop into new fungi.

Some fungi are parasites, taking nourishment from living things. *Phytophthora cinnamomi* is one which causes dieback disease in trees and wildflowers. Unlike mushrooms and the like, *Phytophthora cinnamomi* produces spores from microscopic structures which move in water and 'attack' the root system of its host.

Other common fungal parasites are the rusts, which cause brown splodges on grass leaves and black patches, which spread and kill young kangaroo paw plants.

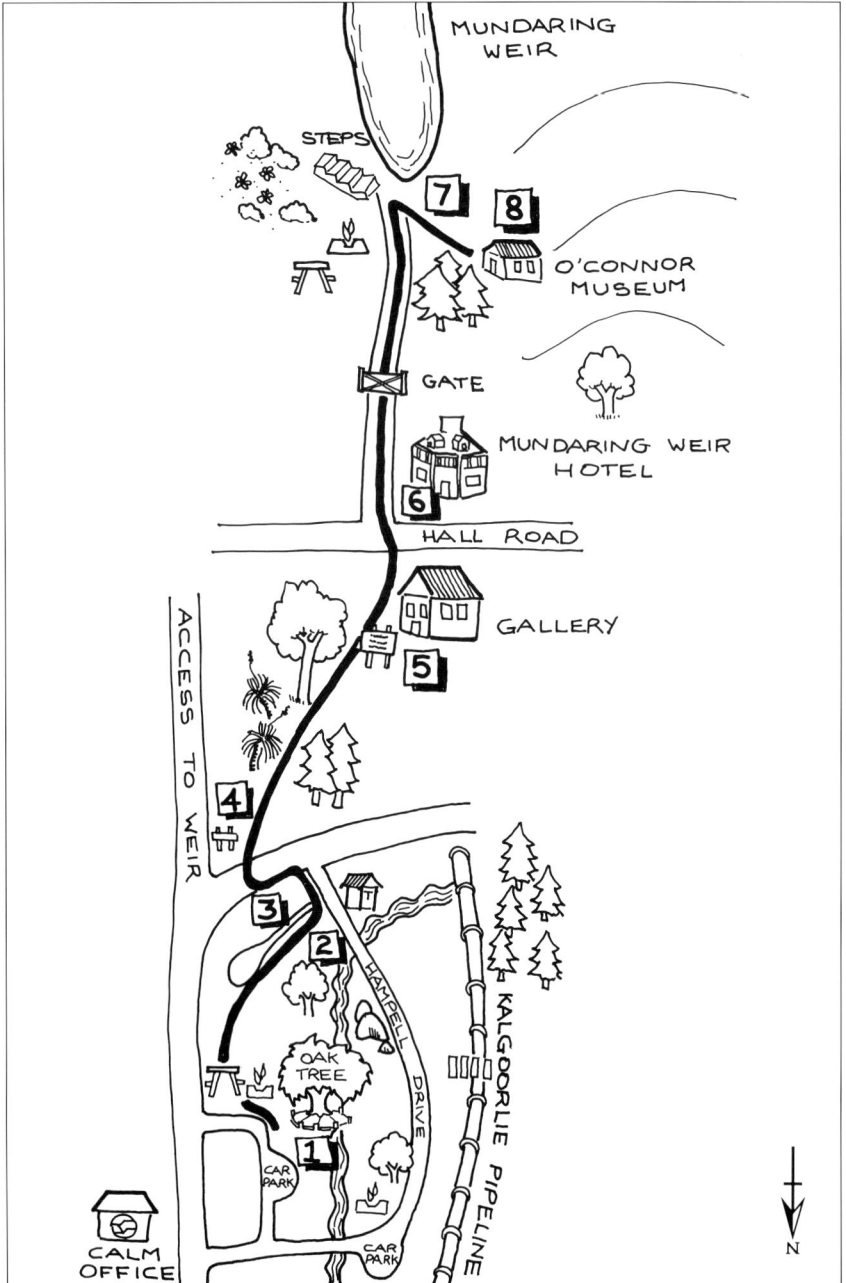

MUNDARING
WEIR

STEPS

7 8

O'CONNOR
MUSEUM

GATE

MUNDARING WEIR
HOTEL

6

HALL ROAD

GALLERY

5

ACCESS TO WEIR

4

3

2

OAK
TREE

1

CAR
PARK

CALM
OFFICE

HAMPELL DRIVE

CAR
PARK

KALGOORLIE PIPELINE

N

Kattamorda Heritage Trail

Stage 2—Fred Jacoby Park to Mundaring Weir

Length: *3 kilometres return*
Grade: *1*
Walk time: *1 hour 15 minutes*

The Kattamorda Heritage Trail is 27 kilometres long, starting at Mundaring and ending at Bickley Reservoir. This stage of the trail begins at the popular Fred Jacoby Park in The Hills Forest and ends at the O'Connor Museum.

1   Fred Jacoby Park is large with open grassed picnic areas. A major attraction of the park is the high spreading English oak tree, planted in 1870. The Heritage Trail sign is located between the oak tree and Mundaring Weir Road. Head south, pass another carpark and walk to Hampel Drive.
2   At Hampel Drive is an information shelter. Turn left to Mundaring Weir Road.
3   At the junction, turn left again and cross Mundaring Weir Road. About 20 m on the right, look for the sign for the next section of the trail.
4   The trail now runs along part of the old horse tramway. To the right is the Kalgoorlie pipeline. The native flora on both sides of the track is predominantly balgas (blackboys).
5   Here, the trail opens out and crosses Hall Road to Mundaring Weir Hotel.
6   The trail continues left of the hotel along Weir Village Road and around a locked gate. On the left is part of the weir gardens with a picnic area and BBQs. To the right there are views across the valley.
7   Mundaring Weir comes into view. Steps on the left lead to the gardens and picnic areas. The trail continues right and down to the O'Connor Museum.
8   The O'Connor Museum, named after the engineer who designed and built the dam, tells the story of the Western Australian Goldfields and the mammoth task of putting in the water supply pipeline to Kalgoorlie. From here, retrace your steps to Fred Jacoby Park.

June Ellis

Where is it?: *Fred Jacoby Park, 37 km from Perth in The Hills Forest*
Travelling time: *45 minutes via Mundaring Weir Road*
Facilities: *Picnic area, carpark, BBQs, toilets*
On-site information: *Information shelters, some signs along the route*
Best season: *Autumn to spring*

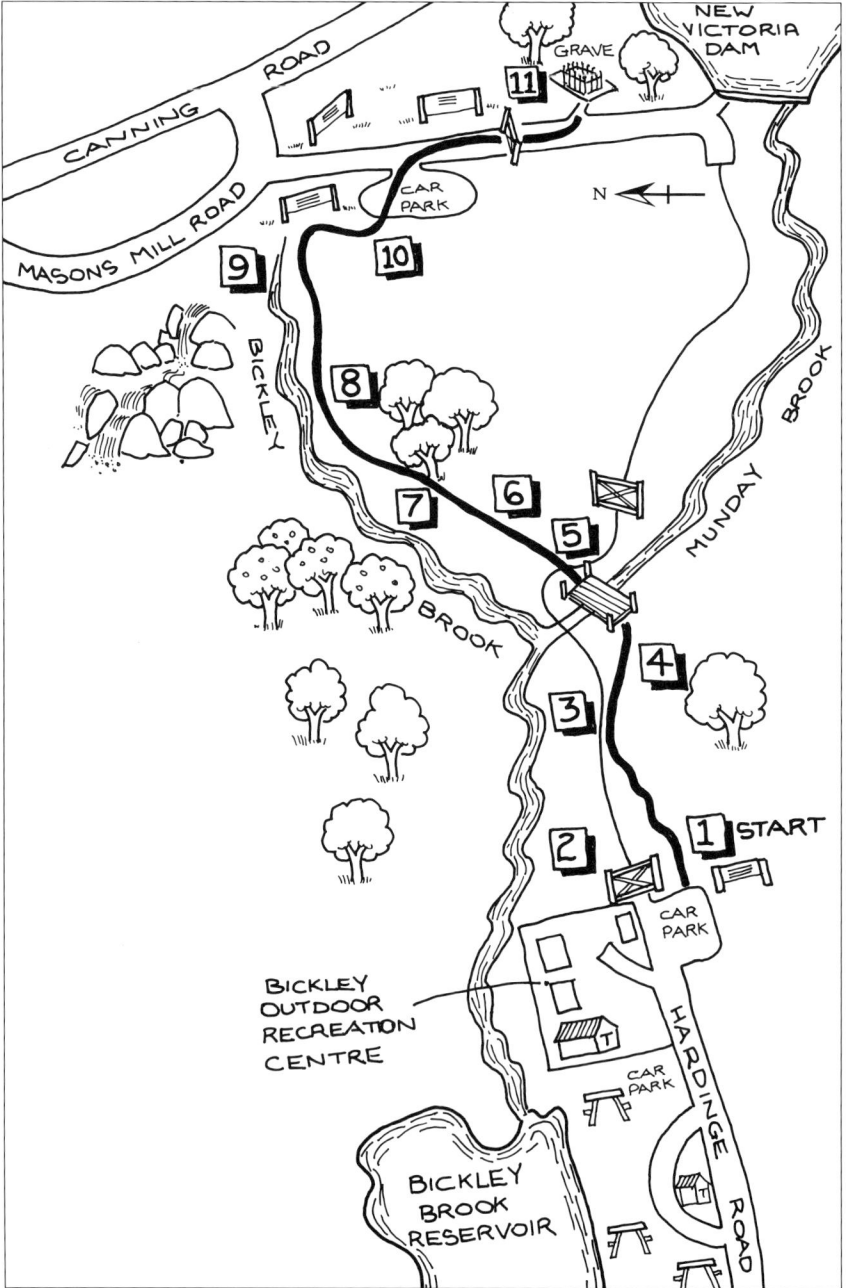

Mason & Bird Heritage Trail 4

Bickley Reservoir

Length: *8 kilometres return*
Grade: *3 (some uphill sections)*
Walk time: *2 hours 30 minutes*

This trail traces part of the route of the Mason & Bird Timber Company's tramway. The tramway linked the company's mill in Kalamunda with Mason's Landing on the Canning River (featured in Woodloes Walk om page 115).

1 From the Bickley Outdoor Recreation Centre, the trail runs up an easy slope.
2 The site of the old Boy Scout Association camp. The trail now levels off and is well graded. There are views of tree lined-slopes.
3 Site of the Boys Brigade camp (nothing remains to be seen).
4 Restored wooden bridge over Monday Brook. The original bridge was built in 1871 and, although the jarrah decking has been replaced, the piles below are thought to be the original wandoo. Cross the brook and walk up a steep stony section. Great views and lots of mixed jarrah-wandoo woodland.
5 The trail continues to rise. A track on the right leads to Victoria Dam.
6 'Devils Pinch': the scene of an horrific horse team accident.
7 On the left are the remains of fruit and vegetable gardens, grown for mill workers. The trail continues to rise steadily past a granite outcrop on the left. Take a break and enjoy surroundings. A series of small waterfalls can be seen here in winter.
8 Kaolin pits are visible to the right of here. Clay was taken from these pits for the Orange Grove brickworks. The trail now levels out.
9 This point marks the site of the old mill town. It is now a rose nursery.
10 Information board and site of Mason's Mill. Turn right towards Victoria Dam.
11 Soon you will come to the grave of two-day-old Francis Weston, on the left. The grave (1876) is worth the extra walk to pay respects to our pioneers.

June Ellis

Where is it?: *19 km south-east of Perth*
Travelling time: *30 minutes via Maddington Road and Hardinge Road*
Facilities: *Picnic area, BBQ, changing rooms, swimming at Bickley, carparks*
On-site information: *Trailhead signs, interpretive plaques along trail*
Best season: *Winter for waterfalls, spring for wildflowers*

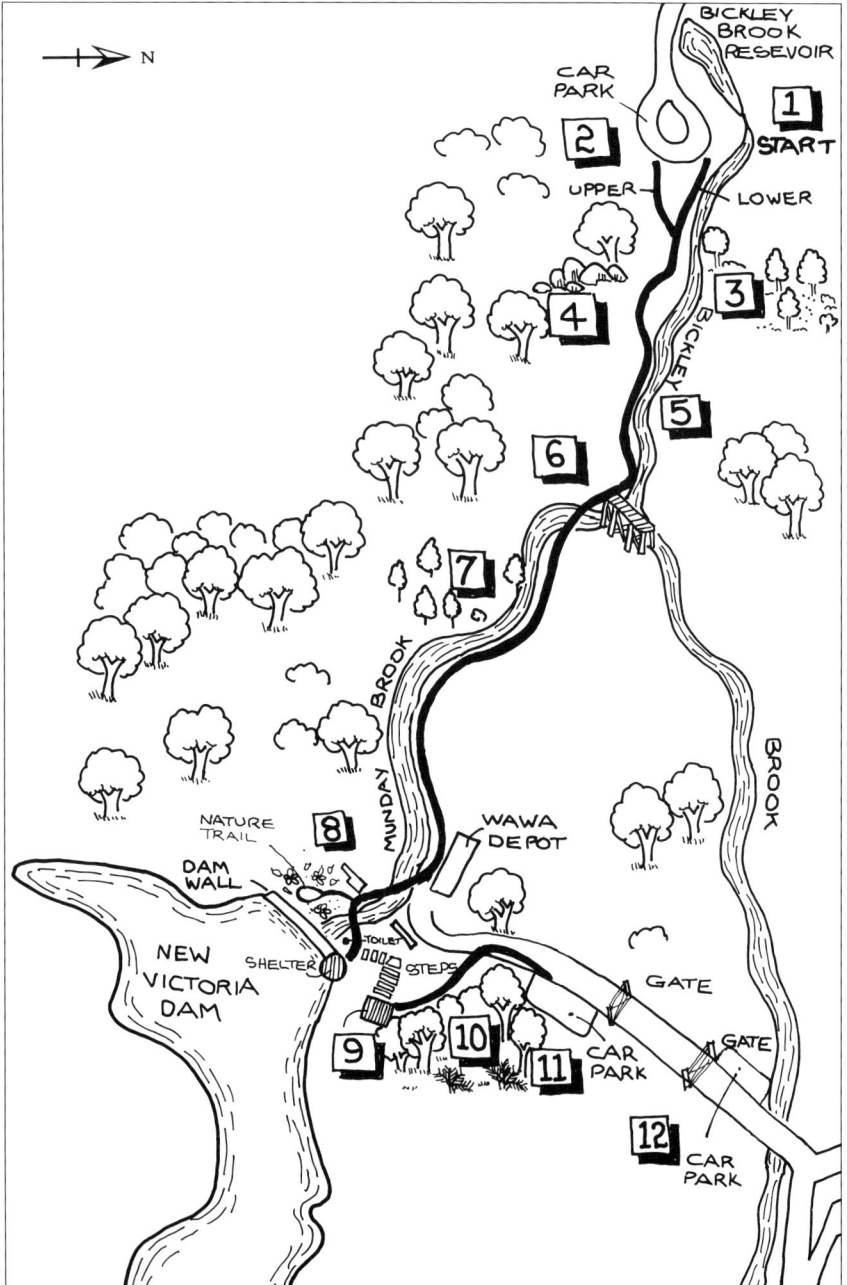

N

BICKLEY BROOK RESEVOIR

CAR PARK

1 START

2

UPPER — LOWER

3

4

5

6

BICKLEY

7

BROOK

MUNDAY BROOK

NATURE TRAIL

8

WAWA DEPOT

DAM WALL

NEW VICTORIA DAM

SHELTER

TOILET

STEPS

GATE

9

10

11 CAR PARK

GATE

12 CAR PARK

New Victoria Dam Walk   5

Bickley Reservoir

Length: *13 kilometres return*
Grade: *3*
Walk time: *4 hours*

The first part of this walk follows the route of the Mason & Bird Heritage Trail. It then branches off towards New Victoria Dam, before turning north to meet the end of the Heritage Trail. Walkers wishing to link the two trails for a circular route can find details of the Mason & Bird Heritage Trail on page 31.

1   Follow the Mason & Bird Heritage Trail to point 5.
2   After crossing the timber bridge over Munday Brook, turn right towards the New Victoria Dam, leaving the Heritage Trail.
3   Munday Brook and its wildlife are of special note. Birds, amphibians and reptiles are commonly heard and seen. The brook is only a few metres from the trail.
4   This WA Water Authority dam area is impressive, with information panels, toilets, walking paths, a pond with a profusion of flowering plants, birds and sitting areas. The old dam wall is partially retained as a special interest feature.
5   Spectacular views can be enjoyed from the timber lookout and the dam wall. A shelter is provided and access to the lookout is via a series of timber steps.
6   This portion of trail is canopied by a fine young jarrah forest with an attractive understorey of balgas (blackboys), zamias and wildflowers.
7   A WAWA carpark provides easy access to the dam, but it may not be open throughout the year. There is an information shelter at the carpark.
8   Walk along the road to the grave site of Francis Weston, who was born and died in 1876. The site is fenced and signed. You have now joined the end of the Mason & Bird Heritage Trail. You can choose to retrace your steps, or walk the reverse route of the Mason & Bird Heritage Trail along Bickley Brook to the recreation camp and the start of this walk.

Richard Hammond

Where is it?: *Bickley Reservoir, 19 km south-east of Perth*
Travelling time: *30 minutes via Maddington Road and Hardinge Road*
Facilities: *Picnic area, BBQ, lookout at dam, carparks at both ends*
On-site information: *Trailhead signs, extensive interpretation at the dam wall*
Best season: *All year, spring for wildflowers*

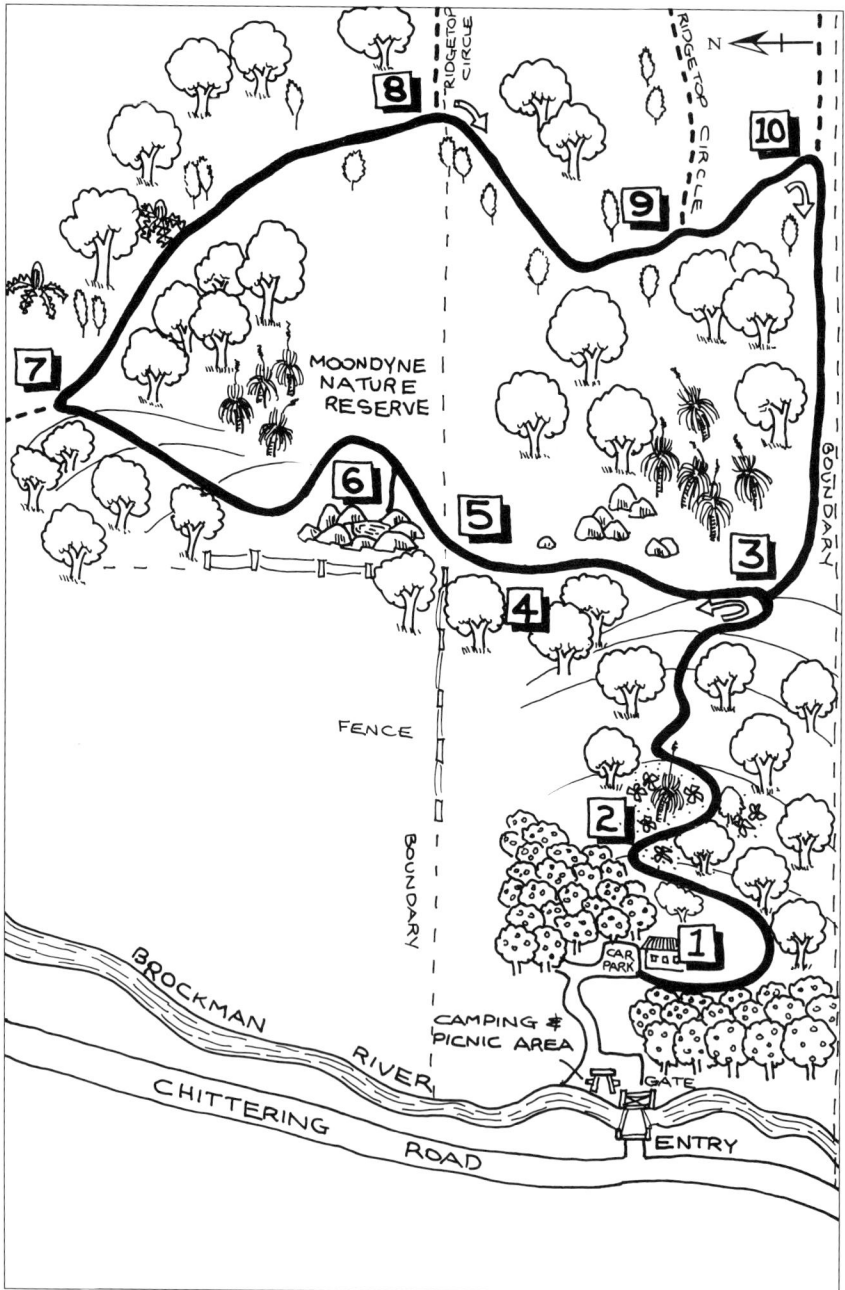

Out & Back Loop Trail **6**
Peace Be Still

Length: *6.5 kilometre loop*
Grade: *3–4 (some steep sections)*
Walk time: *3 hours*

Peace Be Still is a retreat in the tranquil Chittering Valley. The owners are pleased to welcome day visitors who wish to walk any of the eight walktrails on the property. This walk is a combination of the 'Out & Back Trail' and part of the 'Ridgetop Circle Trail'. It has some steep sections, but the views make the effort worthwhile.

1 Leave the guesthouse and follow the same route as the 'Harry Butler Trail' for the first 300 m or so among marri and wandoo trees. Information boards tell about the plants and animals of the area.
2 Continue the zig-zag route, rising steeply up the hill. Some plants to be seen include shrub sheoak, hakea, grevillea, boronia, isopogon and verticordia.
3 At the junction of tracks there is a signpost. Turn left and continue downhill.
4 Just to the left of the track is a rest area—the perfect spot to catch your breath!
5 Here, the track enters the Moondyne Nature Reserve. Shrubs include lemon-scented darwinia and verticordia. Be careful to stay on the track.
6 Here, there is a small rocky pool to the left of the track. The trail continues uphill, providing spectacular views of the valley and orchards.
7 At this junction of tracks, turn right. The walk becomes flatter and easier, and the vegetation changes to dryandra scrub with jarrah and banksia.
8 At the signpost, turn right heading south-west along 'Rigdetop Circle'.
9 The return leg of 'Ridgetop Circle' rejoins from the left. Continue ahead. Occasional WA Christmas trees can be seen in this area.
10 At the unfenced southern boundary, turn right (west) and head along this boundary before descending the hill to the guesthouse. Make sure you take the left-hand trail at the junction of tracks at point 3.

Greg McGauran and Brian Horlock

Where is it?: *57 km north of Perth in the Chittering Valley*
Travelling time: *1 hour 15 minutes via Bullsbrook and Chittering Road*
Facilities: *Wood BBQs, camping ground, tables, toilets, guesthouse*
On-site information: *Leaflet from guesthouse, guided walks available (phone)*
Best season: *All year, except hot summer days*

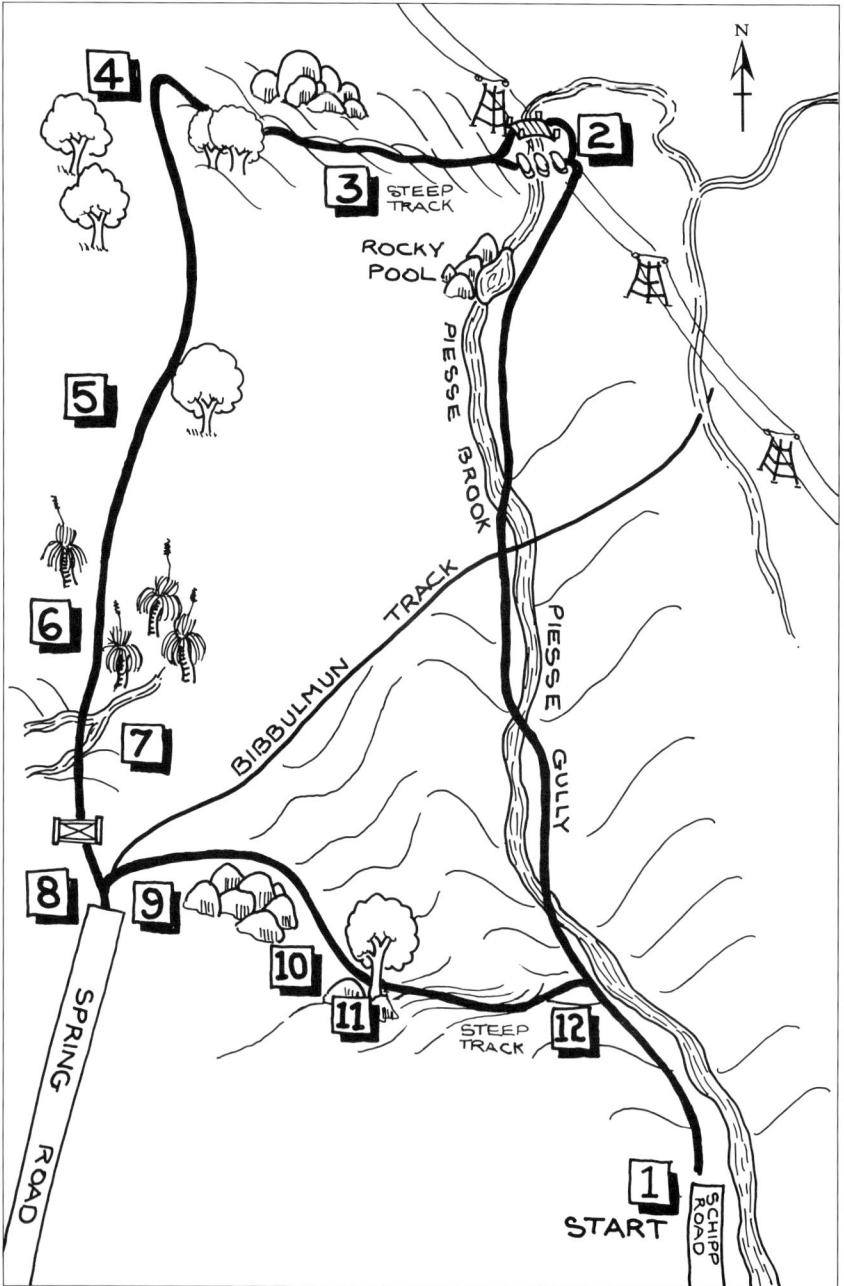

N

4

3 STEEP TRACK

ROCKY POOL

PIESSE BROOK

2

BIBBULMUN TRACK

PIESSE GULLY

5

6

7

8

9

10

11

SPRING ROAD

STEEP TRACK

12

1

START

SCHIPP ROAD

Piesse Gully Loop Trail 7

Kalamunda National Park

Length: *7.5 kilometre loop*
Grade: *5 (some very steep sections)*
Walk time: *3 hours 30 minutes*

This walk is not for the faint-hearted! It has some very steep sections with loose stony tracks. However, the views from the top of the gully are spectacular. The first part follows the easy Rocky Pool Walk (page 41), before continuing to the northern boundary of the national park and up the steep hillside to the west of the gully.

1   Start at the Schipp Road entrance to the national park and follow the Rocky Pool Walk for the next 1.5 km.
2   From the top of the track leading to Rocky Pool, continue north-east and turn left at the junction. Head down, beneath the powerlines, towards the Piesse Brook. There is a track off to the left and here you have two options: turn left down a slight slope to stepping stones (which are passable at low water levels), or continue on the main track and cross a wooden bridge. If you choose the latter, you must double back upstream immediately after crossing the bridge, and walk through a wild thicket path about 100 m to the trail. Head up the steep slope and watch out for loose rocks.
3   About halfway up the hill the trail 'flattens' a little. There is a large group of granite boulders on the right and on the left, about 10 m in and some 50 m further on, are two large WA Christmas trees. Continue the steep climb.
4   The summit offers rewarding views. Look for the sign on the tree and join the track heading southwards along the hilltop. Here, there are couch honeypot and, in season, lots of sundews under the jarrah.
5   Here, a huge wandoo sits on the left of the trail. The views east and north are breathtaking. Here also are spiny granite petrophiles, grevilleas, scrub sheoak and hakea.
6   A little further on, the area opens up with many balgas (blackboys).
7   At this point there are two creeks which cross the trail and an intersection, all within 50 m of each other. In the dry seasons, these creeks may not exist. Don't take the uphill track going west, but continue in a south-easterly direction. Further on, and after a couple of inclines, there is a large WA Christmas tree on the edge of the track. Continue along the track and go through a gate.

8   Where the trail meets Spring Road, note the homes on stilts. Head left, down the Bibbulmun Track for a short distance, until you reach a footpath on the right.
9   Turn right along the foot track. In season there is also a creek here. Head up the hill to a fork in the track, but keep left. You can see the Bibbulmun Track winding below.
10 The trail goes around huge granite outcrops where there are mosses, lichens, herbs, orchids and an array of bonsai-sized shrubs. View from the track as these plant successions are extremely fragile.
11 At this point, a granite outcrop on the right of the track has a marri growing out of the centre. The views along the valley are wonderful.
12 This is the steep hillside track and eventual intersection with point 3 on the Rocky Pool Walk. Watch the loose rocks on the steep decline of the track. Turn right at the bottom and continue back to the carpark.

David Gough and John Hunter

Where is it?: *Schipp Road, 22 km east of Perth*
Travelling time: *40 minutes from Perth via Mundaring Weir Road and Hummerston Road*
Facilities: *None*
On-site information: *None*
Best season: *Winter, spring for wildflowers*

STRIATED PARDALOTE

A very tiny bird of the eucalypt forest and woodland, where, if it was not for its incessant call of 'pick-wick' repeated over and over, it probably would go unnoticed. Although about 10 centimetres long, the short stumpy tail and squarish large head with short thick beak gives an impression of smallness.

The striated pardalote (*Pardalotus striatus*), a common species, is one of many types of pardalote, but some extremely rare. They hop, climb and fly around foliage, branches and trunks of trees, as well as on rock faces and buildings, in search of invertebrates. They have been known to enter houses if the windows are left open, checking the joints of brickwork for spiders.

The upper parts of the bird is coloured olive-grey; crown black, streaked white. The wings are black with a reddish spot near the shoulder and broad white wing stripe. They have broad white eyebrows and are buff underneath.

Breeding usually occurs between August and January, with the nest being cup or dome-shaped, made of grass, bark and rootlets and built in a tunnel in an embankment or a tree hollow.

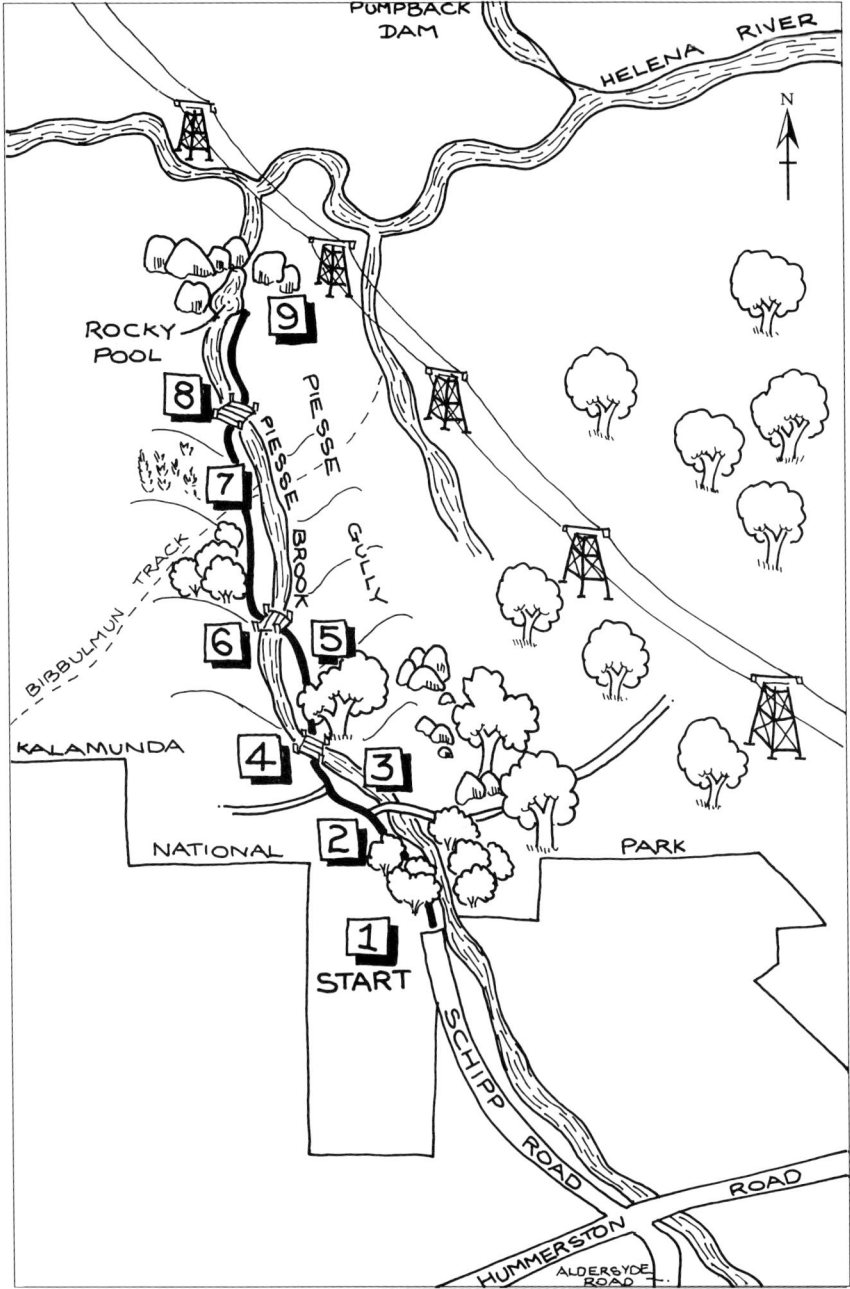

PUMPBACK
DAM

HELENA RIVER

N

ROCKY
POOL

9

8

PIESSE

PIESSE BROOK

7

GULLY

BIBBULMUN TRACK

6

5

KALAMUNDA

4

3

NATIONAL

2

PARK

1
START

SCHIPP ROAD

ROAD

HUMMERSTON

ALDERSYDE
ROAD

Rocky Pool Walk
Kalamunda National Park

Length: *3 kilometres return*
Grade: *2*
Walk time: *1 hour 20 minutes (including time at pool)*

Park in a small carpark at the end of Schipp Road. This walk runs on an easy trail along Piesse Gully to a seasonal waterfall and deep pool. It is a pleasant walk and you should spend at few minutes sitting beside the pool before returning to the carpark.

1   Head north. Alongside Piesse Brook there is a thick understorey of shrubs with mixed jarrah-marri-wandoo woodland and granite outcrops on the hillside.
2   Here, a track goes east on an earth and log bridge over the brook. On the right, just before the junction, is an old and gnarled wandoo. Continue north.
3   Some 150 m further on the left is the return leg of the Piesse Gully Loop Trail. Continuing northwards, the trail undulates through jarrah, marri and many wildflowers in season.
4   Cross the brook on a small concrete bridge. Pardalotes can be heard in the trees overhead. Notice the moss-covered granite immediately on the right, and atop the rise, an old marri leaning low across the track.
5   Further up the rise the trail flattens. Power pylons can be seen in the distance ahead, while across the valley, are outcrops of granite. The trail descends.
6   Cross the brook again. Here, the undergrowth is quite thick. The trail passes through bottlebrush, parrotbush and wattle thicket.
7   The Bibbulmun Track crosses the trail here. A few metres further on, cross a small creek. Here, there are thickets of dryandras.
8   Cross Piesse Brook again. At this point, the valley opens up and is much wider.
9   A little further on a small footpath leads down to Rocky Pool. Here, the brook passes between spectacular, large, granite outcrops, which provide high, sheer drops into deep pools and rapids.

David Gough and John Hunter

Where is it?: *Schipp Road, 22 km east of Perth*
Travelling time: *40 minutes from Perth via Mundaring Weir Road and Hummerston Road*
Facilities: *None*
On-site information: *None*
Best season: *Winter, spring for wildflowers*

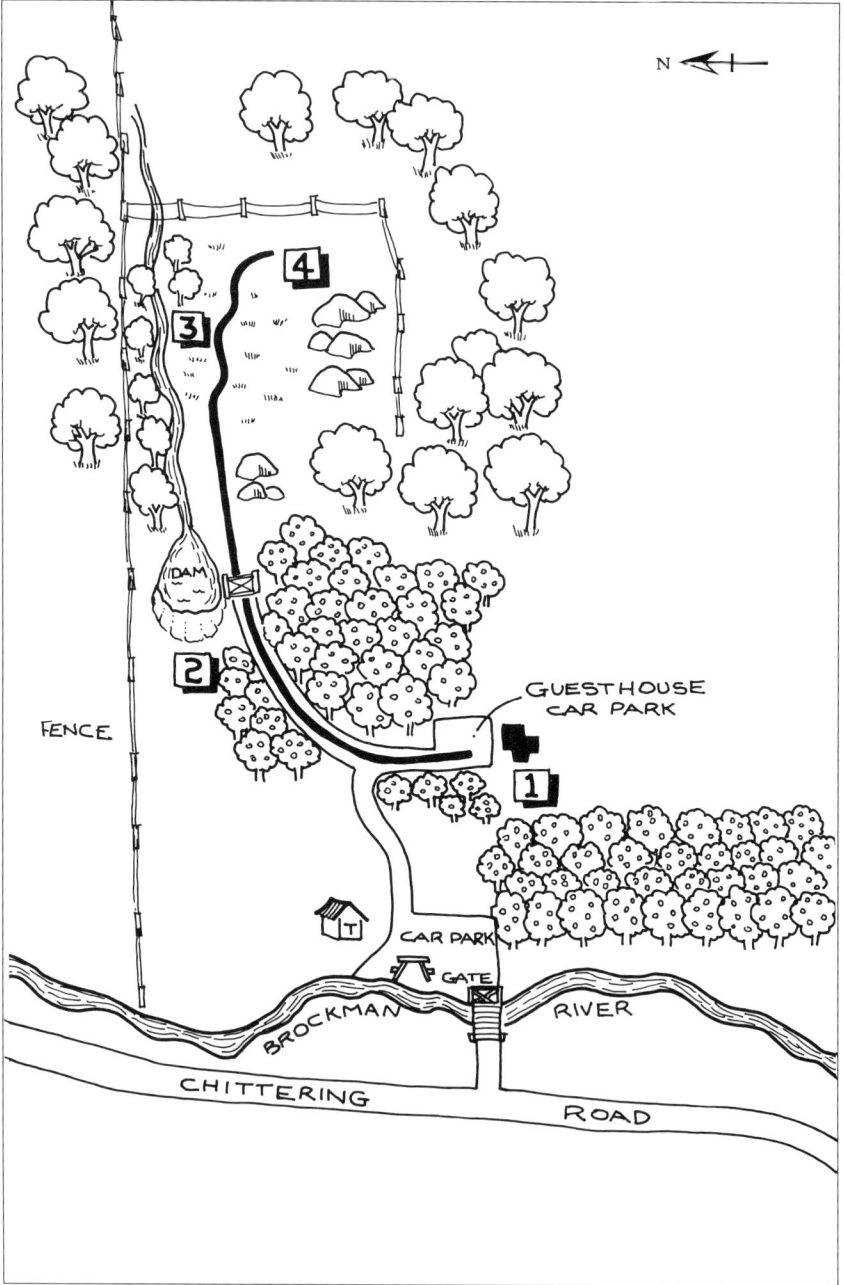

N

4

3

DAM

2

FENCE

GUESTHOUSE
CAR PARK

1

T

CAR PARK

GATE

BROCKMAN   RIVER

CHITTERING   ROAD

Special Valley Walk 9
Peace Be Still

Length: *1 kilometre return*
Grade: *1-3 (uphill section)*
Walk time: *30 minutes*

This is one of the shortest of several walks on the property. It provides access to a pleasant valley surrounded by marri and wandoo. Peace Be Still is a privately owned retreat that adjoins the Moondyne Nature Reserve. The property has sheep, emus and a citrus orchard, and birdlife includes magpies, honeyeaters and wrens. There is a picnic area beside the Brockman River and day visitors are welcome. Overnight camping is available (contact the guesthouse for details).

1   Starting from the guesthouse parking area, head north along a gravel driveway and take the right-hand branch between orchards.
2   Here, alongside the farm dam, the trail goes through a gate. Please close the gate behind you.
3   The trail leads to a cleared grass area alongside the winter creek. Take time to sit and listen to the birdlife in the trees and shrubs alongside the watercourse.
4   Continue uphill from the creek to the rocky outcrops above the valley. Explore the microscopic plantlife that exists on these rocks, but please tread carefully. On warm days, you may see lizards or dragons sunning themselves on the rocks. Retrace your steps to the guesthouse.

Greg McGauran

Where is it?: *57 km north of Perth in the Chittering Valley*
Travelling time: *1 hour 15 minutes via Bullsbrook and Chittering Road*
Facilities: *Wood BBQs, camping ground, tables, toilets, guesthouse*
On-site information: *Leaflet from guesthouse, guided walks available (phone)*
Best season: *All year, except hot summer days*

The North   Walks 10 – 27

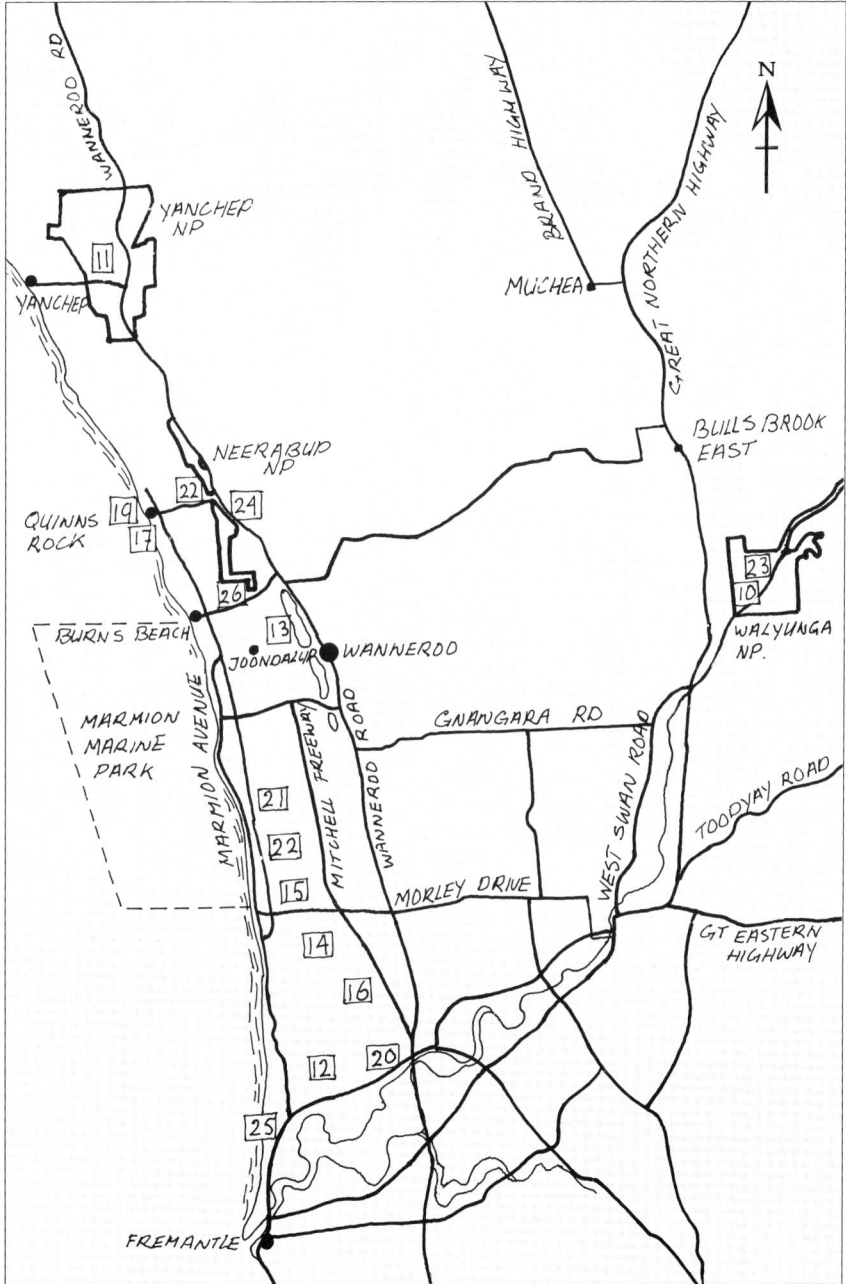

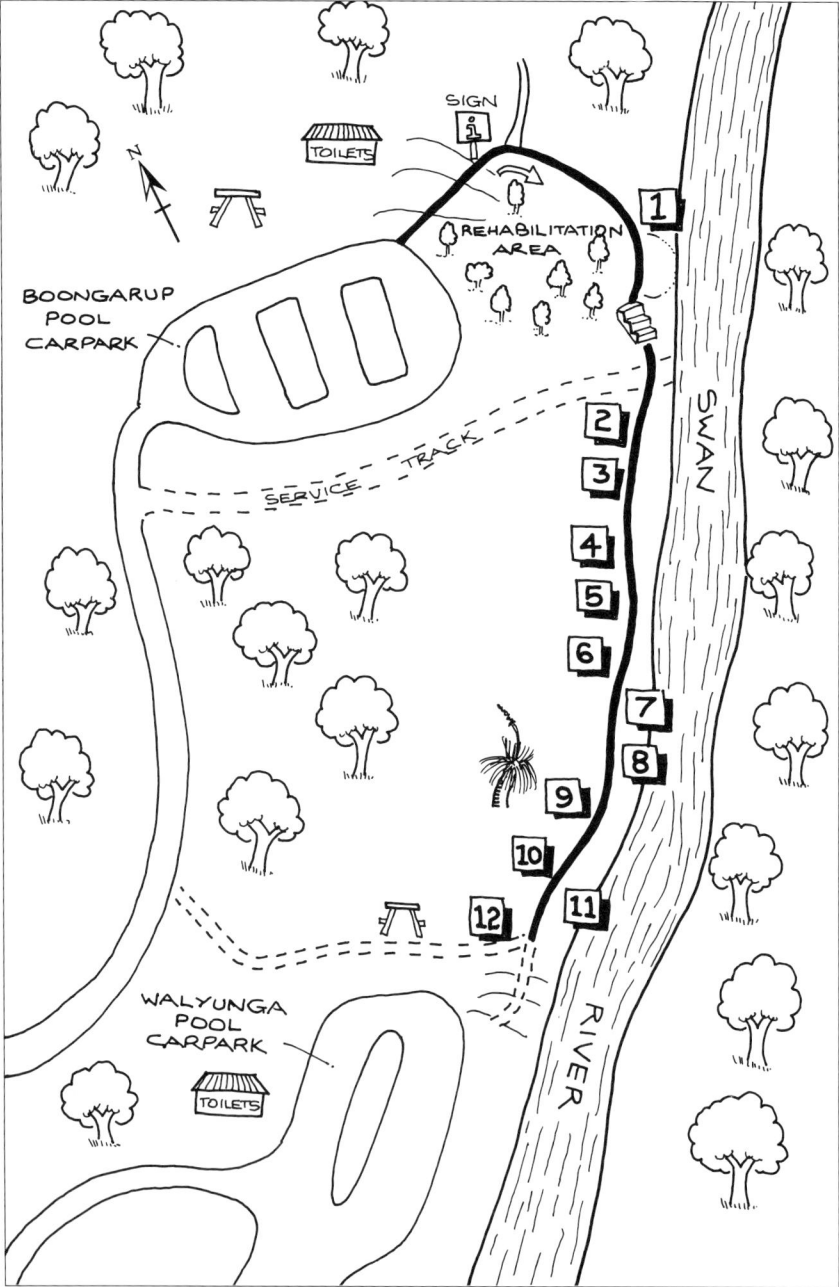

SIGN

TOILETS

N

BOONGARUP POOL CARPARK

REHABILITATION AREA

1

SERVICE TRACK

2

3

4

5

6

7

8

9

10

11

12

SWAN

RIVER

WALYUNGA POOL CARPARK

TOILETS

Aboriginal Heritage Trail
Walyunga National Park ($)

Length: *1.6 kilometres return*
Grade: *1*
Walk time: *45 minutes*

Walyunga National Park sits on the rim of the Darling Scarp and protects nearly 1 800 hectares of bushland and its native plants and animals.

The walk can be started from either end (Boongarup Pool or Walyunga Pool carparks). It is described from Boongarup Pool, but if walked in reverse, it can be linked to the Syd's Rapids Trail (page 79) for an extended walk.

1 Leave Boongarup Pool carpark by a well-constructed path and head down to a junction. Turn right and head downstream to a vantage point overlooking river. There are steps down from here to the riverbank.
2 An interpretation plaque, nearby, marks the start of the Aboriginal Heritage Trail. The plaque explains Nyoongar use of the area.
3 Interpretation sign: Uses of marri.
4 Interpretation sign: *Baio*—about the zamias.
5 Interpretation sign: *Wuanga*—the wattle and how it was used.
6 Interpretation sign: *Yonga*—kangaroos and wallabies. The western grey kangaroo was a main food source for Nyoongar people.
7 This point overlooks a canoe slalom course.
8 Interpretation sign: *Warrdarchi*—the story of an Aboriginal spirit.
9 Interpretation sign: *Balga*—about the balga (blackboy) and its uses.
10 Interpretation sign: Made of stone—the use of stone for axes and other tools. A large, ancient tool-making area is located within Walyunga National Park. There are many stone artefacts at the site.
11 Interpretation sign: *Waugal*—the story of Rainbow Serpent.
12 Walyunga Pool picnic area. Retrace you steps from here or walk up the slope and return to Boongarup Pool carpark along the road.

Terry Hales

Where is it?: *Walyunga National Park, 40 km north-east of Perth*
Travelling time: *1 hour via Great Northern Highway and Walyunga Road*
Facilities: *Picnic areas, BBQs, toilets, carparks, water*
On-site information: *Information shelters, interpretive signs along the trail*
Best season: *Autumn to spring*

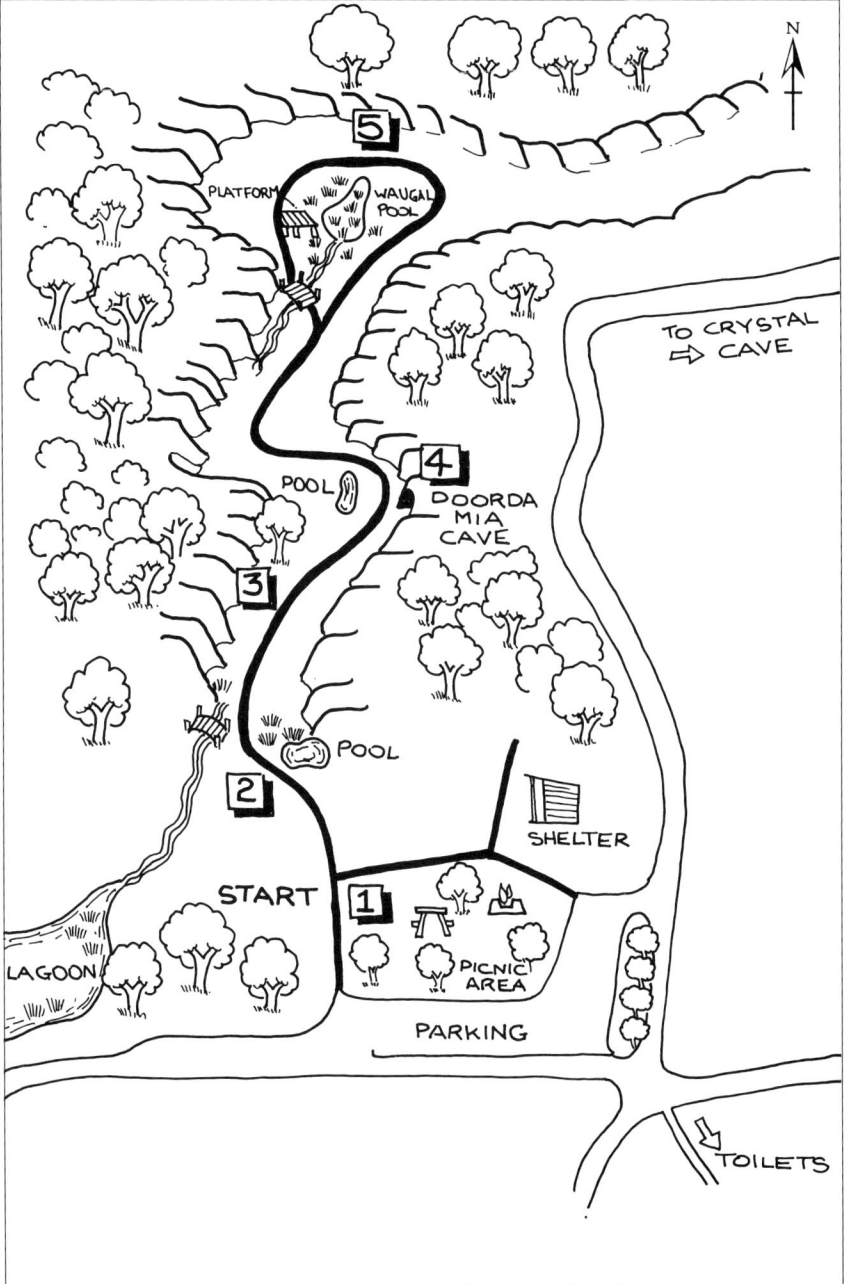

N

5

PLATFORM   WAUGAL
              POOL

TO CRYSTAL
CAVE

POOL

4

DOORDA
MIA
CAVE

3

2

POOL

SHELTER

START

1

LAGOON

PICNIC
AREA

PARKING

TOILETS

Boomerang Gorge Trail 11

Yanchep National Park ($)

Length: *500 metres return*
Grade: *1 (wheelchair accessible)*
Walk time: *30 minutes*

This short, easy walk follows an ancient stream bed through a collapsed cave system. The walls of the gorge are the original cave walls and the trail lies on the now soil-covered ceiling of the collapsed cave.

1   The trail begins near the east side of Gloucester Lodge Museum. Boomerang Gorge was first discovered by Europeans in 1841 when a party, led by explorer John Septimus Roe and Governor Hutt, was taken there by a Nyoongar man named Wowin. Roe's Aboriginal guides were terrified of the caves in the gorge, which they believed were inhabited by evil spirits.
2   At this point, swampy ground surrounds the creek, which flows through a series of pools dotted along the gorge.
3   Tuart trees (*Eucalyptus gomphacephala*) grow throughout the gorge and surrounding area. These trees have been greatly reduced in number on the Swan coastal plain, largely because of land clearing for farming or residential areas.
4   There are several small caves in the walls of the gorge. The largest cave has been found to contain Aboriginal artefacts and was probably used as a shelter. The Aboriginal name for the caves was *doorda mia* (dog's house, approx.), derived from the probable use of the caves as dwelling places for dingoes.
5   Waugal Pool is located at the eastern end of the trail. The pool is almost hidden from sight by large sedge and fern communities.

Geoff Harnett

Where is it?: *Yanchep National Park, 51 km north of Perth on Wanneroo Road*
Travelling time: *1 hour 10 minutes*
Facilities: *Picnic area, toilets, BBQs, water, carpark*
On-site information: *Information board at start*
Best season: *All year*

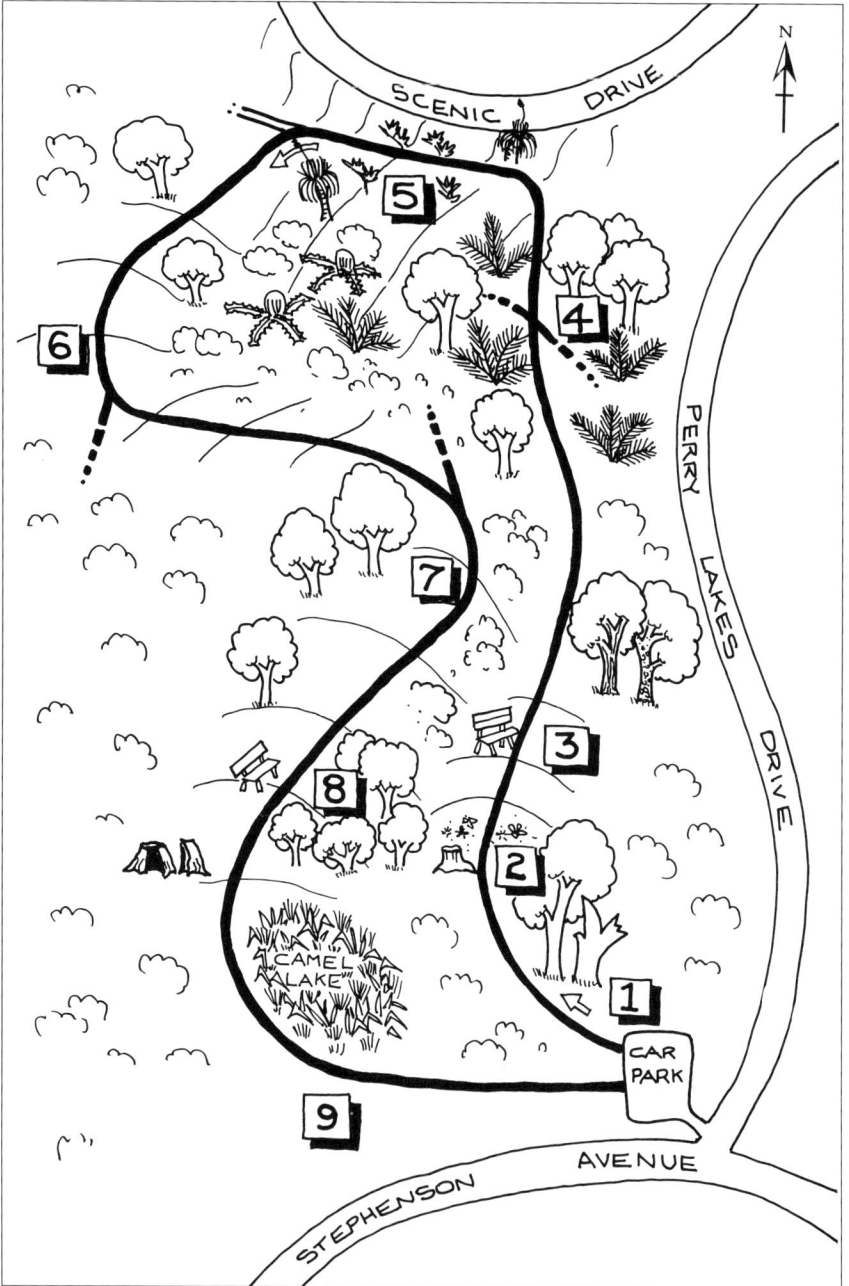

Camel Lake Trail

Bold Park

12

Length: 2.5 kilometre loop
Grade: 1-3 (short steep section)
Walk time: 1 hour

Bold Park is an inner-suburban park of coastal woodlands, wetlands and dune systems, lying between the city and the ocean. Its plant species include tuart, banksias, wattles, zamia, balgas (blackboys) and parrotbush. It features seven eucalypt species, including three—limestone marlock, Fremantle mallee and rock mallee—that are uncommon in the Perth area.

This walk runs parallel to Perry Lakes Drive and uphill towards Reabold Hill ridge. There are good views and varied vegetation around the trail.

1   After walking about 50 m from the carpark, the trail heads north from the information board. Here, there are tuarts on both sides of the track, with banksias, marri, zamias and balgas. On the right and some 20 m in, there are two exceptionally large tuarts; one is dead and leafless and provides nesting sites for quarrelling corellas. Next to the track is an old and very large banksia with moss adorning its massive trunk. There are many dead wattles on the left.

2   Around this point, you will find the moss-covered boles of a very large, old flooded gum and a banksia. There are Guildford grass and lupins here with native wisteria, wild geranium and jacksonia (stinkwood) on both sides of the track. A few pincushion hakeas are also present.

3   Just up the rise, there is a park seat on the left. Have a rest and listen to the birds. A little further on, to the right, is a large jarrah and a marri growing very close together. Study the difference in their barks. Perry Lakes can be seen through the trees to the east.

4   This point is at the intersection of two paths. Here, you are in a small forest of tuart, zamias and weeping peppermint. Around this area there are also hakea and one-sided bottlebrush, both with spectacular red brushes (in season). From here, head north towards Reabold Hill, then turn west.

5   With the Reabold Hill ridge on the right and the valley on your left, you pass through a large clump of parrotbush with many surrounding balgas. Welcome swallows and tree martins whirl about in the lee of the nearby ridge, while magpies strut the path looking for morsels. Look south, down through the valley of zamias and mixed banksia. If you turn around here, the view back to Perth city is exceptional.

6   The views to the three white domes at Floreat Forum and the Perth city skyline are beautiful from here. Note the different light grey soil and low heath under banksia below the path. At the fork in the trail, head east downhill past mixed banksia, small scrub sheoak and parrotbush. Halfway down the hill you will pass large bushes of Geraldton wax and *Grevillea crithmifolia* next to the track.

7   After turning south, you may notice the red brush of hakea and the pink and white Geraldton wax bushes (in season) all surrounded by parrotbush, banksia and low heath.

8   The downhill slope passes another park seat where you can rest awhile to watch and listen to the many bird species. Continue on through a small forest of jarrah and marri, which indicate that the side of this hill is a watershed in winter. Further down the hill, on the left and in about five metres, are the large burnt boles of two very old jarrah trees. The second has almost been completely hollowed out by fire on the uphill side and covered on the other side by a velvety coat of green moss.

9   The last point of interest on this walk is Camel Lake itself. The lake was once a clear swamp about four times its current size. A wall of earth place across the depression some 30 years ago has diminished the surface water in winter to a small pool choked with couch grass. Some rushes exist, with thickets of wattle and surrounding flooded gums.

John Hunter

Where is it?: *Bold Park, 6 km west of Perth near Perry Lakes*
Travelling time: *15 minutes from Perth via Hay Street, Underwood Avenue, Perry Lakes Drive*
Facilities: *Carparks, picnic area and BBQs near Perry Lakes*
On-site information: *Information boards*
Best season: *All year, spring for wildflowers*

AUSTRALIAN MAGPIE

Every spring time, heads turn skywards as humans become targets of nest-protecting magpies, and dive-bombing becomes the order of the day. For those with concern, just give the nest site a wide berth or wear a hat and don't look up. In a few weeks, all will be back to normal, except that there will be one or two extra 'squawkers' in the magpie tribe.

Australian magpies (*Gymnorhina tibicen*) are generally black and white patterned. However, there are two forms of 'maggie': black backed and white backed. Where their ranges overlap, they freely interbreed resulting in some having pure white saddle backs and others having a variety of black and white patching.

Magpies, sometimes called flute birds, have a variety of sounds from harsh aggressive warning squawks to loud territorial carolling and soft chortling at night.

Quite often, the cutting swish of pulsating wings is heard overhead as the dominant male and helpers drive other intruding magpies or birds of prey from a permanent territory which is vigorously defended.

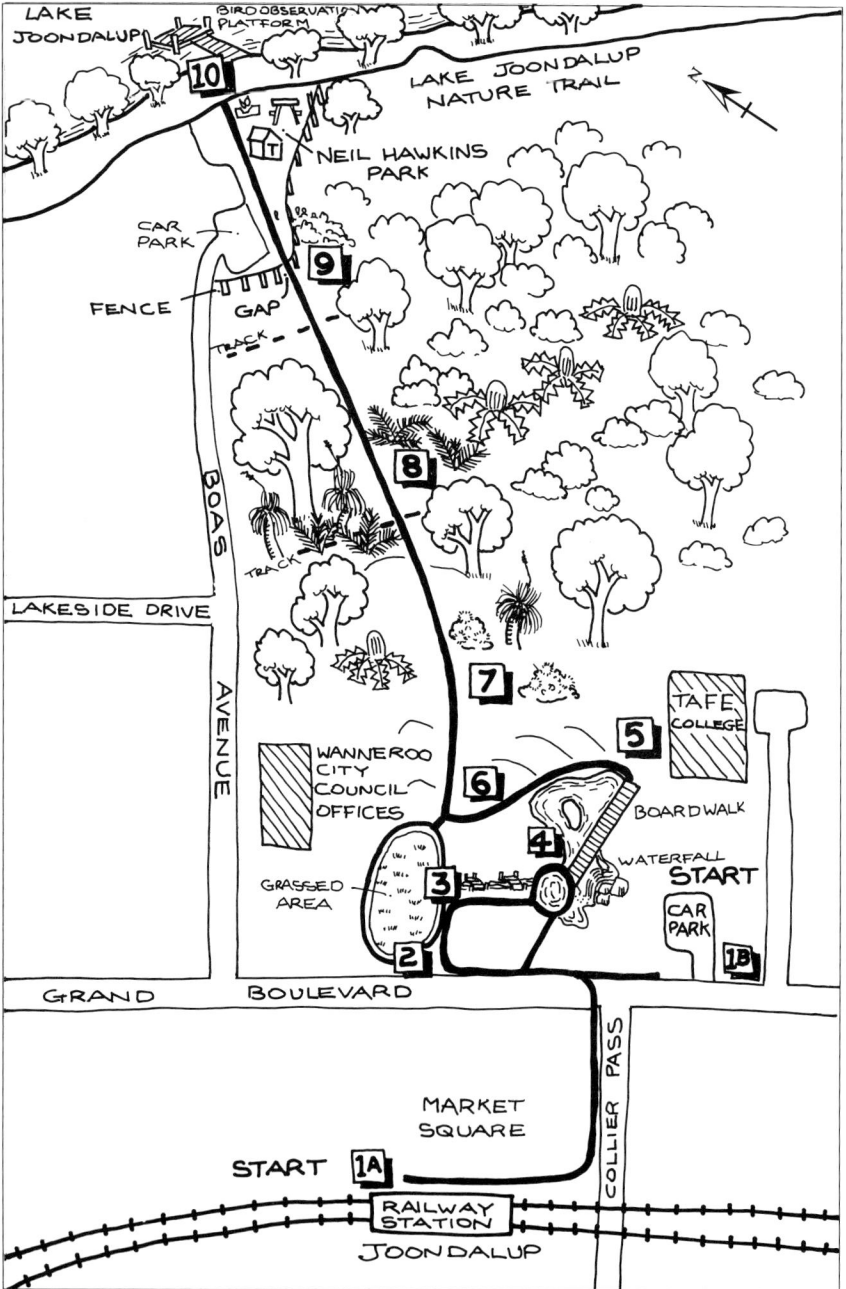

LAKE JOONDALUP

BIRD OBSERVATION PLATFORM

LAKE JOONDALUP NATURE TRAIL

10

T

NEIL HAWKINS PARK

CAR PARK

FENCE

GAP

TRACK

9

8

TRACK

LAKESIDE DRIVE

BOAS AVENUE

7

TAFE COLLEGE

5

WANNEROO CITY COUNCIL OFFICES

6

BOARDWALK

4

WATERFALL

START

3

GRASSED AREA

CAR PARK

2

1B

GRAND   BOULEVARD

COLLIER PASS

MARKET SQUARE

START   1A

RAILWAY STATION

JOONDALUP

Central Park Trail

13

Joondalup

Length: *3 kilometres return*
Grade: *1*
Walk time: *1 hour 30 minutes*

The trail features a mix of artificial and natural lakes and waterways, landscaped areas and undisturbed bushland. The bushland section runs down to Neil Hawkins Park on the shore of Lake Joondalup and is a good example of the way the area would have looked to the local Nyoongar tribespeople who camped by the lake during summer months.

You can begin the trail either from the carpark on Grand Boulevard or, if you come by train, from the rail station on Collier Pass. Barbecues, tables, toilets and children's playground are available at Neil Hawkins Park, where you can also hand-feed 'twenty-eight' parrots and galahs.

1a Get off the train at Joondalup Station and head east along Collier Pass. Cross Grand Boulevard and turn left.
1b Starting from the carpark opposite Collier Pass, head north along Grand Boulevard.
2 Enter Central Park by the large grassed oval.
3 Turn right about halfway along the southern side of the oval. This are has been landscaped around an artificial waterway that winds downhill. Small bridges cross at various points, and children enjoy 'stick racing' down the fast-flowing water.
4 At the end of the waterway is a circular pool. Walk around this and turn left along a boardwalk beside the large artificial lake. This lake has rapidly been adopted by local waterbirds, including several species of duck. On the right of the boardwalk is an artificial waterfall.
5 At the south-east corner of the lake, turn left and walk along the lake's eastern edge. From here you get a good view of the island and the planted areas on the northern shore. Continue uphill.
6 Turn right at the top of the rise and follow the limestone track eastwards towards Lake Joondalup.
7 This entire section, along a limestone track to Neil Hawkins Park, passes through mixed banksia woodland, with balgas (blackboys), parrotbush, prickly moses, acacias an abundance of bush honeysuckle [*bindak*, in the local Nyoongar language] and a few old tuarts. This small area of woodland is a virtually

undisturbed example of coastal plain vegetation. As you walk through it and listen to 'twenty-eight' parrots and galahs screeching in the trees, you can imagine what it was like for the Nyoongar people who camped and fished by the lake during warmer months.

8   After crossing a narrow track, the trail runs gently downhill passing some very large balgas and many zamias. There is a very large, old tuart tree on the left before the trail rises a little.

9   Cross another track and walk downhill again to an area thick with smokebush. Skirting around the shrubs, you come to the fence marking the boundary of Neil Hawkins Park. Enter the park through the gap in the fence and head towards the lakeside.

10 Cross the park and proceed to the bird observation platform. Neil Hawkins Park is the starting point of two other trails—the Lake Joondalup Nature Trail and the Yaberoo Budjara Heritage Trail (Stage 1)—which are described in *Family Walks in Perth Outdoors*.

David Gough and family

Where is it?: *Joondalup, 25 km north of Perth*
Travelling time: *40 minutes by car via Mitchell Freeway, Joondalup Drive and Grand Boulevard, or 25 minutes by Transperth Fastrak from Perth City Railway Station*
Facilities: *Carpark at start; BBQs, tables, water, toilets, playground at Neil Hawkins Park (other facilities and/or features will be developed along the route during the next few years)*
On-site information: *None, except 'totem pole' sign at oval*
Best season: *All year*

TUART

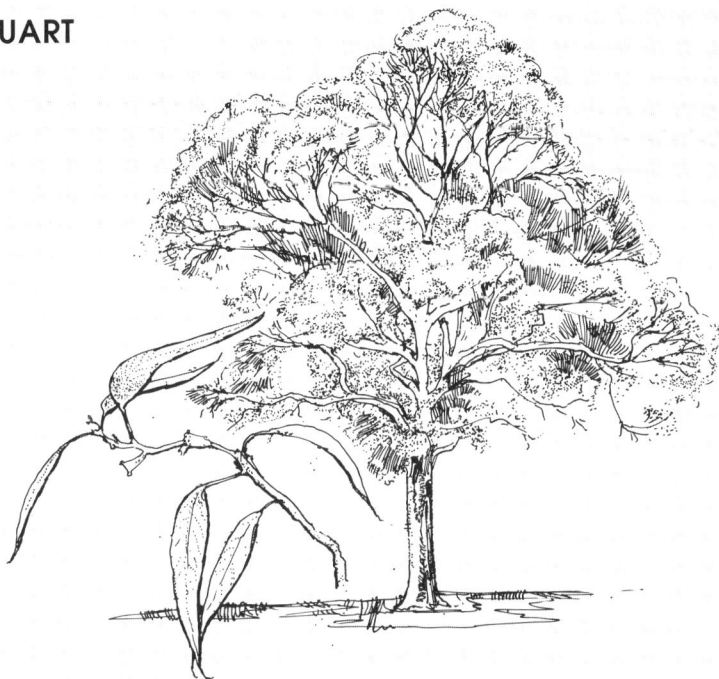

The huge tuarts (*Eucalyptus gomphocephala*) of the Swan Coastal Plain provide residents of the area with a true backyard forest close to the ocean, with an interesting association of fauna.

The early settlers valued the timber for its toughness and it was used where great strength, solidity and durability were needed. The trees are biologically valuable as they are used by bats, possums and many birds and insects for food, nesting and resting. Quite often, the trees look as though they have the disease 'dieback', but the stag heads are, in fact, the result of insect infestation and fungal diseases.

The biggest specimens are found in the Ludlow Forest Reserve near Busselton, where individuals can reach 45 metres in height, with girths exceeding eight metres. The '*tooart*', as first named by Nyoongar Aborigines, occurs from about Jurien Bay to just south of Busselton.

The tuart has pale grey, rough, fibrous bark, which it sheds much more than other eucalypts leaving pale patches of new bark. Unlike other Perth eucalypts, it also has no lignotuber and relies on the shedding of its thick bark to protect it from bushfires. Growing so close to salt-laden sea winds, tuarts do not grow straight and tall, but have a natural tendency to fork and spread, some nearly as wide as they are high.

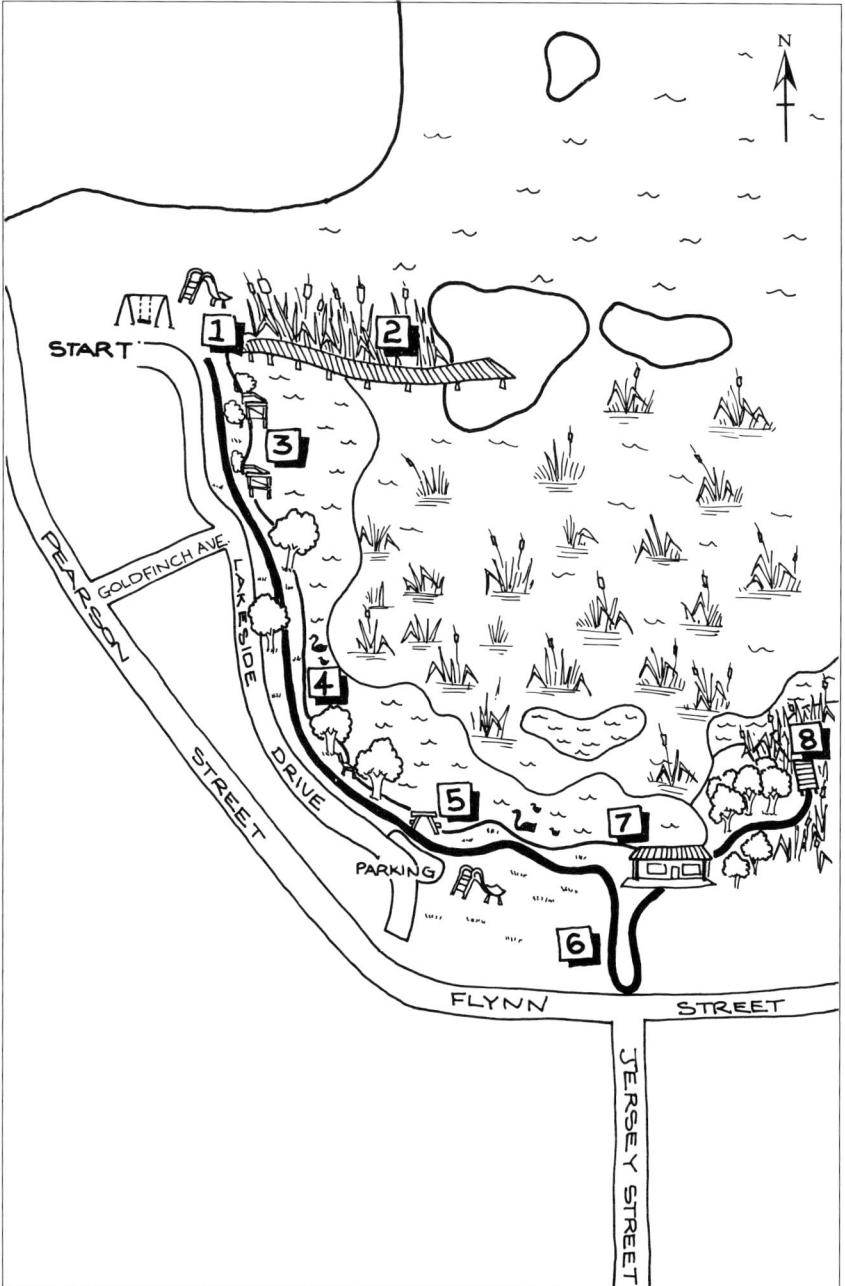

N

START

PEARSON

GOLDFINCH AVE.

STREET

LAKESIDE

DRIVE

PARKING

FLYNN STREET

JERSEY STREET

1
2
3
4
5
6
7
8

Herdsman Lake Walk

14

Maurie Hamer Park

Length: *3 kilometres return*
Grade: *2*
Walk time: *1 hour*

Herdsman Lake is known for its diversity of bird species, particularly waterbirds and birds of prey. Trees and shrubs include flooded gums, coojongs, swishbush and freshwater paperbarks. The walk begins at the carpark and playground at the north end of Lakeside Road. It includes two boadwalk sections that will take you into the lake area and through its dense vegetation.

1   Leave from the north end of Maurie Hamer Park and head lakeside to the start of the boardwalk.
2   This elevated boardwalk takes you through bulrushes into the lake area and onto one of the small islands. Return along the boardwalk to the playground and head south.
3   Along this section are two bird hides from which you can observe the lake's birds.
4   The track follows the edge of Herdsman Lake through a parkland setting of mown grass and trees. Seats are provided for you to sit and enjoy views across the lake and its abundant birdlife.
5   Parking, play equipment, picnic tables and more birds.
6   Follow the track towards Flynn Street then turn back along the access road to the Gould League Headquarters and the Herdsman Lake Wildlife Centre.
7   Herdsman Lake Wildlife Centre offers displays, information and a viewing area over the lake. It is open all day through the week and afternoons only at the weekend. Organised bird-watching walks are available and you should contact the centre for more details.
8   From the Wildlife Centre, follow the track to another boardwalk, which passes through melaleuca thicket and into a denser cover of bulrush. Retrace your steps to the start.

Allan Wicks

Where is it?: *Maurie Hamer Park, 7 km north of Perth*
Travelling time: *15 minutes via Flynn Street and Goldfinch Avenue*
Facilities: *Picnic area, playgrounds, carpark, toilets*
On-site information: *Information shelters*
Best season: *All year*

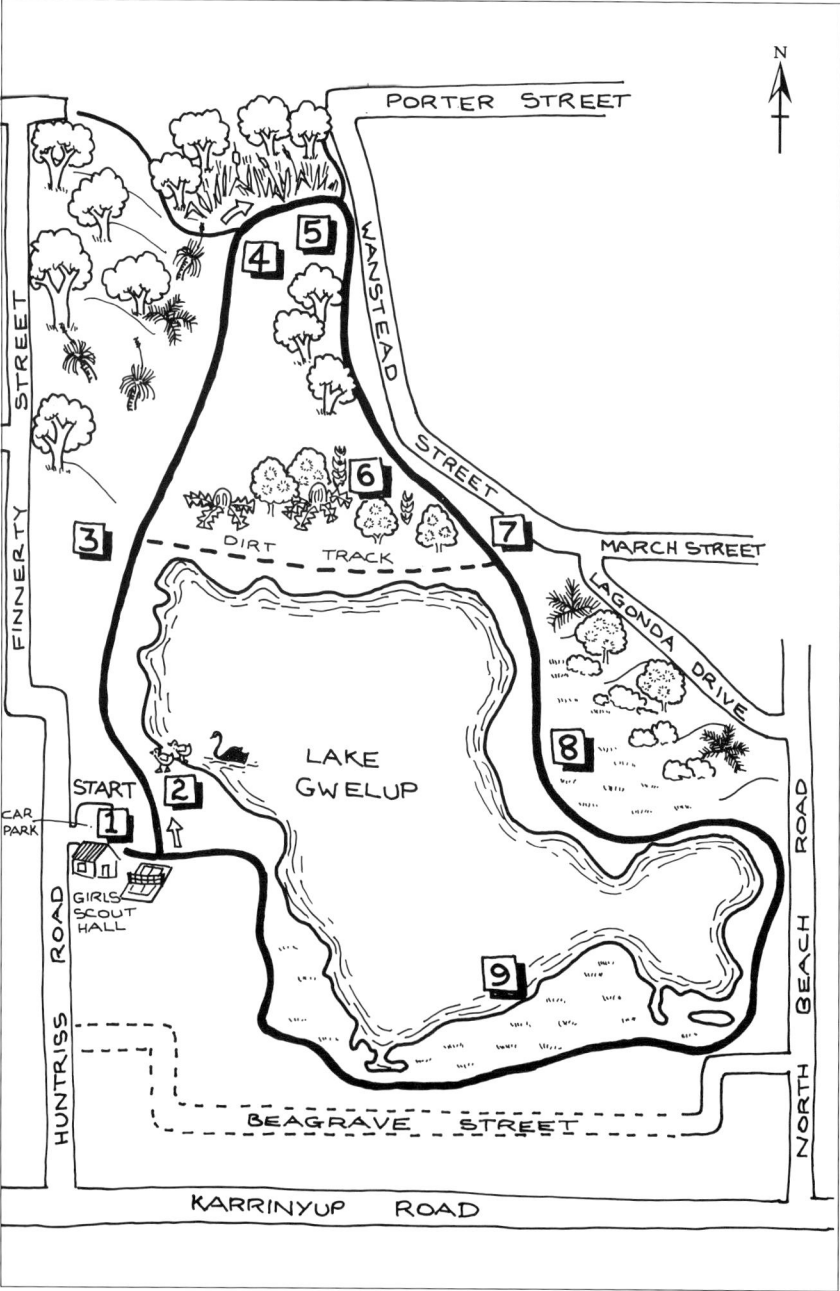

Lake Gwelup Walktrail   **15**
Gwelup

Length: *2 kilometre loop*
Grade: *1*
Walk time: *45 minutes*

Lake Gwelup is, in part, surrounded by woodlands of marri, jarrah, flooded gum, tuart, wattles, banksias and paperbarks, with balgas (blackboys) hakeas, zamias and wetland vegetation. This walk passes through three vegetation types and also takes in the lake's varied birdlife.

1   Start at the Girl Scouts' building carpark off Huntriss Road. Head east past tennis courts to a concrete path, then north heading clockwise around the lake.
2   Along this section, you will see a variety of waterbirds, including coots, ducks and black swans, both on the lake and at its edge. Keep the lake to your right.
3   Leaving the lake, continue north, ignoring paths to the right. On the left is higher ground with tuarts, zamias, balgas and some jarrahs.
4   When you arrive at the 'T' junction, turn right. To the left of the track is a swampy area with rushes, surrounded by eucalypts.
5   Turn right at the fork just before Wanstead Street. Continue south past marris, balgas and shrub vegetation.
6   At this point, there is a pleasant view of lake between the trees. Magpies and kookaburras can be seen and heard here.
7   At the junction of the track opposite the March Street entrance, go straight ahead along a vehicle access dirt track and follow it clockwise around lake.
8   On the left of the track, away from the lake, is an area of wattle heathland and zamias. Closer to the lake is an open grassy area. Follow the track around the south-east corner of the lake and walk along the south side.
9   This section passes through an area of open mowed grassland. Turn north at the south-west corner and head back past the tennis courts to the carpark.

Lotte Lent and Brian Armstrong

Where is it?: *11 km north-west of Perth*
Travelling time: *15 minutes via Karrinyup Road and Huntriss Road*
Facilities: *Tennis courts, manicured lawns*
On-site information: *Sign near March Street entrance*
Best season: *Autumn to spring*

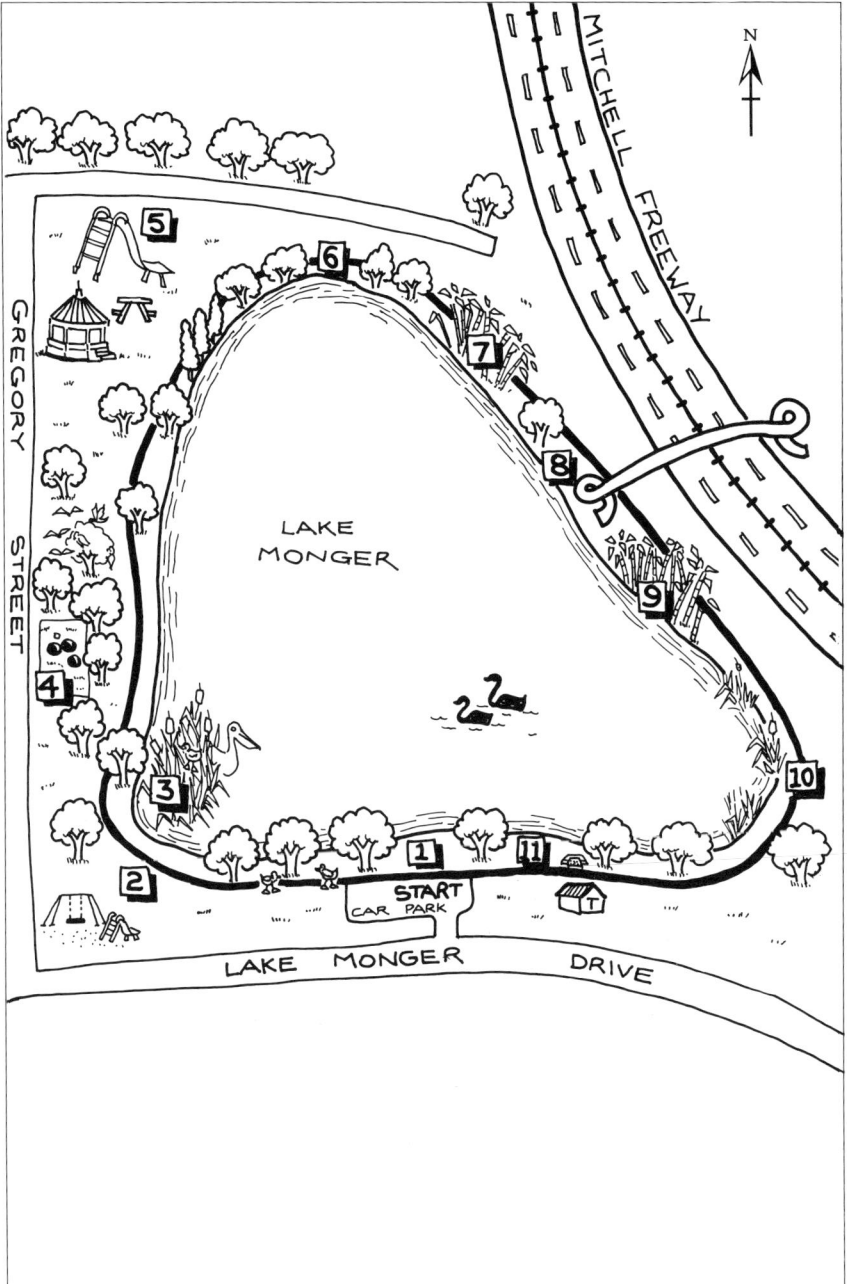

Lake Monger Walk

Leederville

Length: *3.8 kilometre loop*
Grade: *2*
Walk time: *1 hour 15 minutes*

Lake Monger comprises 97 hectares of open water and 49 hectares of recreational parkland. For thousands of years, Nyoongar Aborigines used the lake and its surrounds as an important gathering place. This walk is along a well-maintained, dual-use path. The main features are the lake and its birdlife, including coots, moorhens, musk ducks, grebes, cormorants and swamphens.

1   Start at the carpark off Lake Monger Drive and head clockwise towards the lake's south-west corner.
2   Trees shade the carparks that line this section of the lake shore. This is also a popular feeding spot for waterbirds.
3   There is an artificial island a short distance from the lake shore which was built to provide shelter for the birds that nest there. Next to this spot is a small children's playground. Continue along the western edge of the lake.
4   Here, you pass the Wembley Bowling Club. There are many trees in the area and, at times, a flock of corellas can be seen perched in the branches.
5   At the north end of the lake is a picnic area with a playground and pergola.
6   Many small trees have been planted close to the water's edge along this section.
7   The trail turns south and passes a large clump of bamboo. The pathway is seperated from the Mitchell Freeway by a wire fence.
8   Pass under the footbridge and see the tall buildings of Perth's city centre.
9   Here, a very large clump of bamboo partially obstructs the view of the lake.
10 The bamboo gives way to small patches of reeds, which have become a favourite nesting site for the black swans that abound on the lake.
11 You soon come to a telephone and, at this point, the bitumen path gives way to brick paving, leading you back to your starting point.

Bill Pearson

Where is it?: *3 km north of Perth, beside the Mitchell Freeway*
Travelling time: *5 minutes via Lake Monger Drive*
Facilities: *Picnic areas, BBQs, pergolas, playgrounds, carparks, toilets*
On-site information: *Waterbird identification panels*
Best season: *All year*

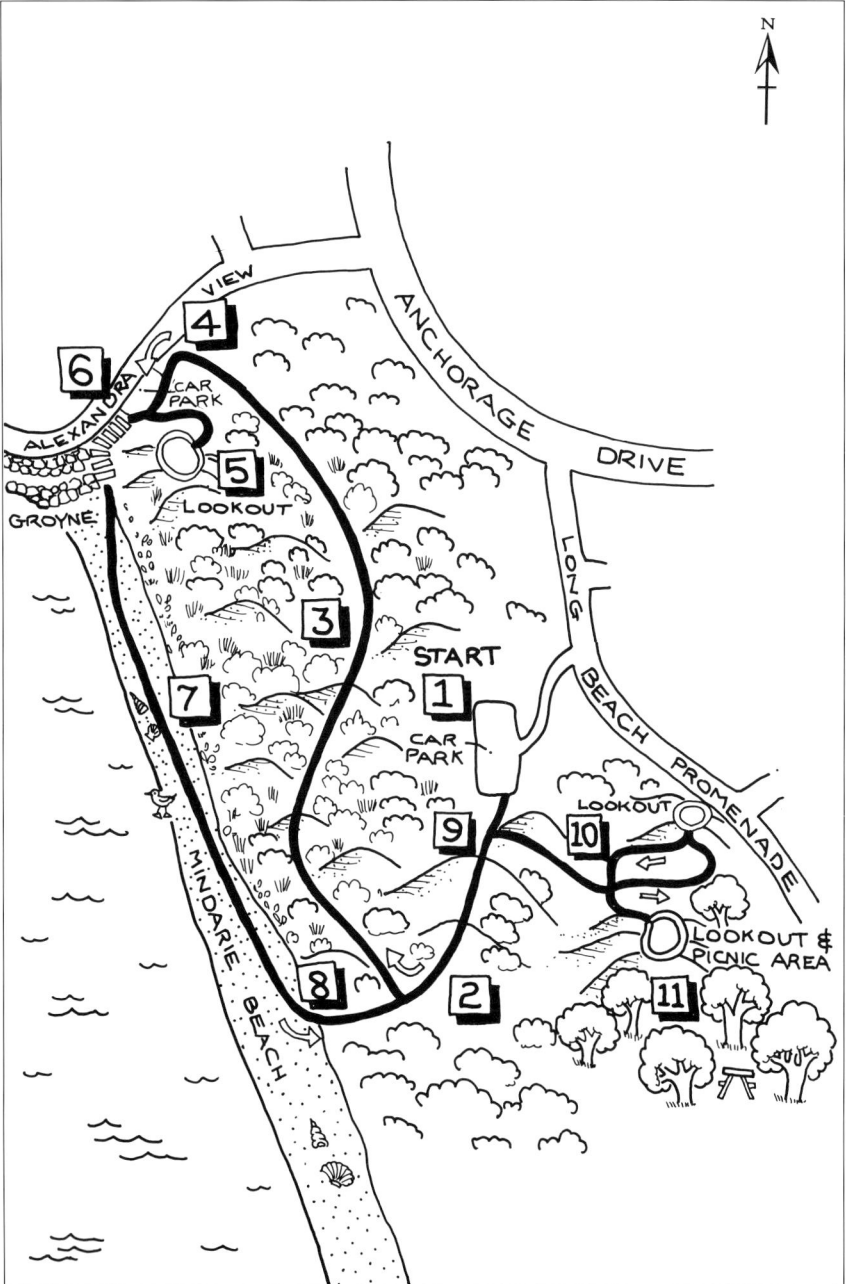

Mindarie Dunes Walktrail   17

Mindarie Beach Foreshore Reserve

Length: *2.5 kilometre loop*
Grade: *2*
Walk time: *1 hour*

The dune system south of Mindarie Keys has been stabilised and developed with minimum disturbance for passive recreation by the Mindarie Keys Harbour Estate. The walk passes through typical dune vegetation, along the beach front and over the dunes to a picnic area in remnant tuart woodland.

1. Leave the carpark and head south-west up a steep rise and over the dune to catch your first glimpse of the ocean.
2. Continue down the wide, surfaced track before turning right and heading northwards through the inner dunes. At this point, take the side track to a vantage point overlooking the beach with fine views north and south.
3. This section passes through typical dune vegetation including spinifex, wattles, dryandra and sedges. There are good views of the ocean.
4. On arriving at the north end of the reserve, turn left and head to the lookout.
5. From the lookout there are 360° views of the ocean, reserve, housing developments and the Mindarie Keys Marina complex.
6. Return to the carpark and continue via wooden steps to the beach.
7. Walking along the beach, you can observe shells, seabirds and foredune vegetation, as well as enjoy the sound of waves and the salty smell of the ocean.
8. About 500 m south of the groyne, turn inland and follow the wide track back towards the carpark.
9. Near the base of the steep dune is a right turn that leads up to another lookout and the picnic area.
10. Skirt around the north side of the tuart grove and walk up to the lookout.
11. Finally, spend some time at the picnic area beneath the tuart trees.

Andrea Carrington-Hughes

Where is it?: *Anchorage Drive, Mindarie Keys, 33 km north of Perth*
Travelling time: *45 minutes via Mitchell Freeway and Marmion Avenue*
Facilities: *Carpark, picnic area, BBQs*
On-site information: *None*
Best season: *All year*

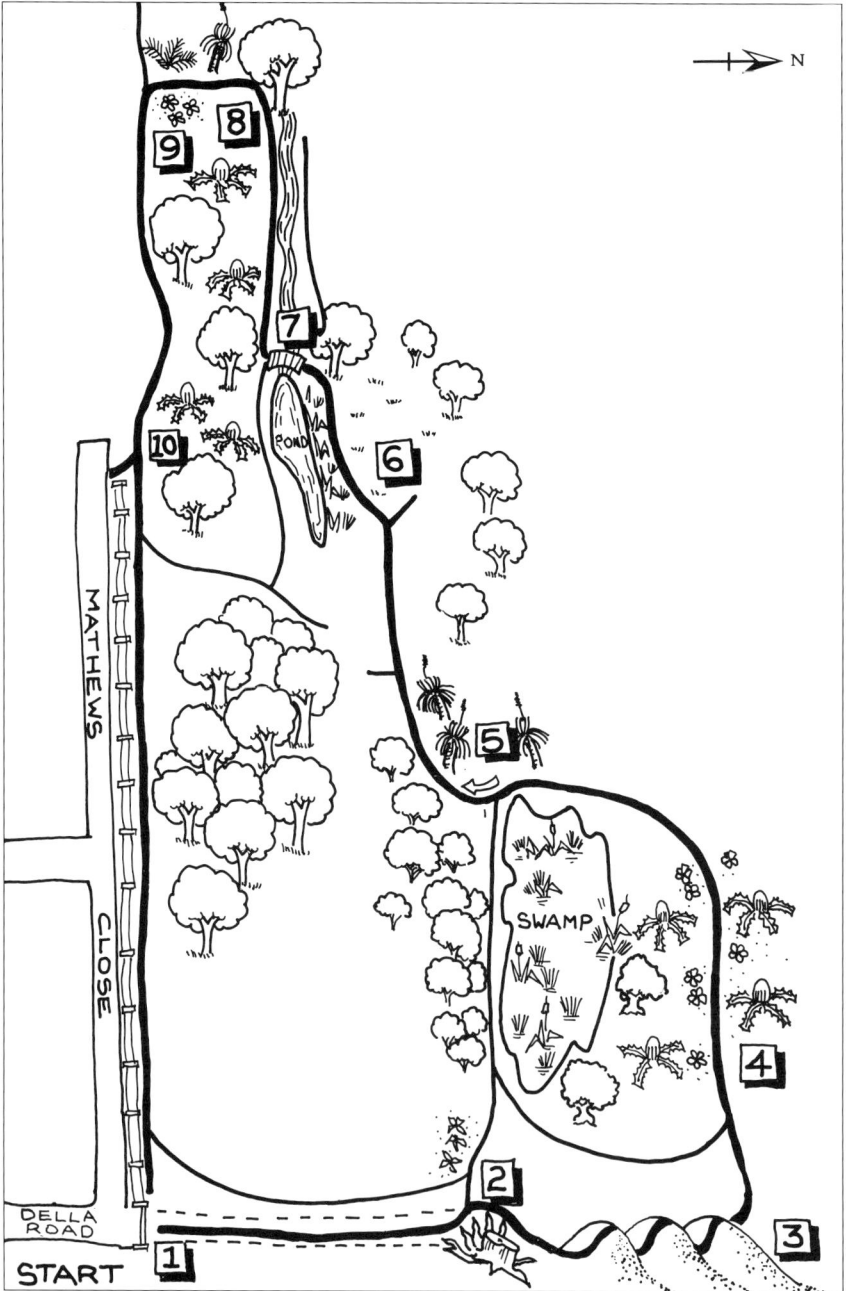

N

9 8
7
10 POND 6
5
SWAMP
4
2
3

MATHEWS CLOSE

DELLA ROAD
START 1

66

Noranda Bushland Walk   18

Noranda

Length: *3.5 kilometre loop*
Grade: *4 (heavy walking on sand)*
Walk time: *2 hours*

This walk passes through an unnamed remnant bushland area in the suburb of Noranda and features wetland areas surrounded by dense bushland. It is largely on sand tracks and would be heavy going in summer and autumn, when the sand is dry. This walk is best done at weekends to avoid traffic noise from Reid Highway.

1   Park at the corner of Della Road and Mathews Close. Go through the barrier and north along an unmade road.
2   Here, the road is blocked by tree roots. Walk around them and continue towards and up a sand dune.
3   From the top of the dune, look back to the Perth city skyline.
4   Follow the sand track to the left (west) and enter banksia woodland with understorey of smokebush, golden hibbertia, kangaroo paws and many other plants. The track curves to the left and the seasonal swamp with frogs, reeds and paperbarks comes into view.
5   Turn right and continue east past balgas (blackboys) on the right and fairly dense bushland on the left. Pass a left turn and continue.
6   Pass a right turn and another pond (on the right).
7   The track crosses a gully and turns right. Continue west until you see a large marri at the junction of tracks. Turn left (south).
8   On the right of the track is open grassed area edged with a line of balgas and zamias. On the left is dense bushland of banksias, with some large eucalypts.
9   Turn left at the boundary fence and follow the fenceline east.
10   Here, an opening in the fence gives you the choice of walking along Mathews Close or continuing along the track to the end of Della Road.

June Ellis and Eric Woodcock

Where is it?: *Della Road, 11 km north-east of Perth*
Travelling time: *15 minutes via Crimea Street and Benara Road*
Facilities: *None*
On-site information: *None*
Best season: *Spring and early summer for wildflowers*

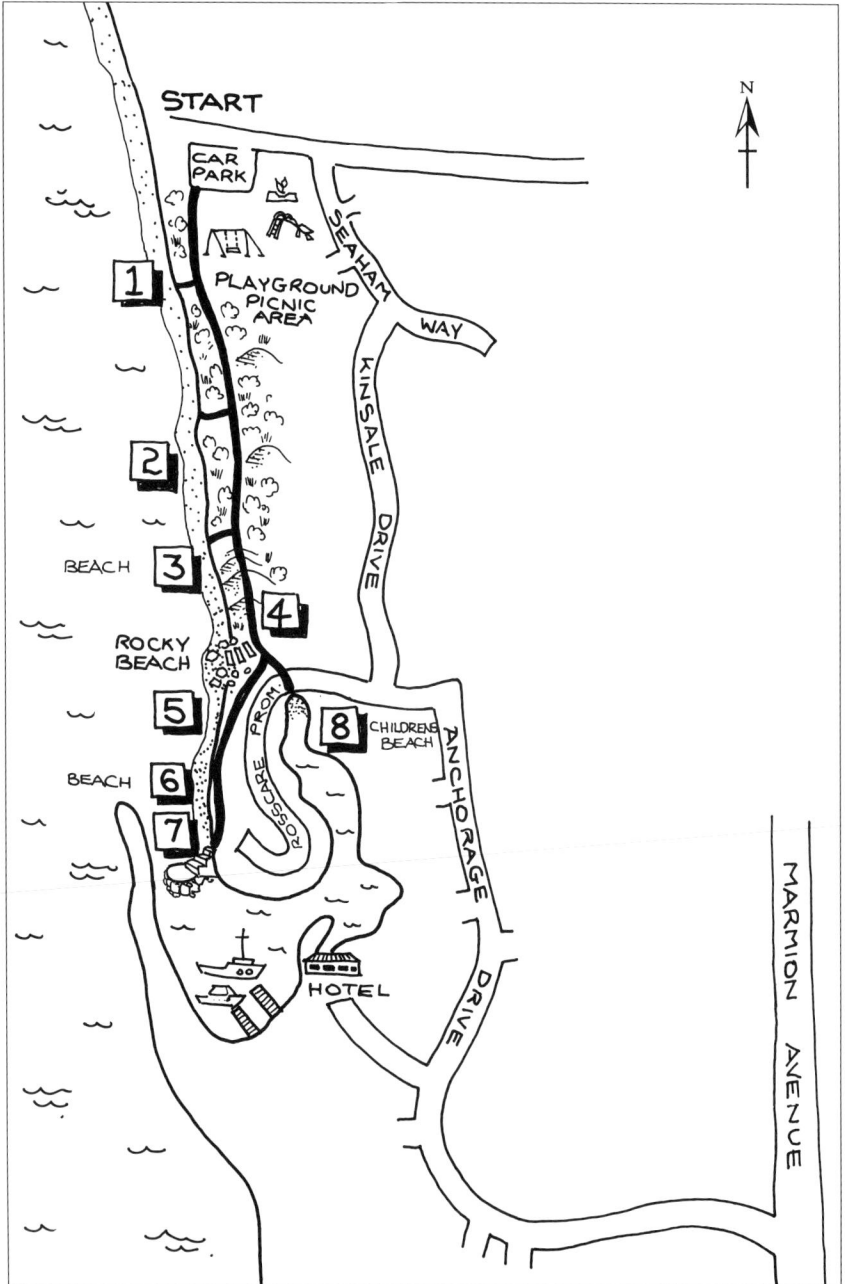

START

CAR PARK

PLAYGROUND PICNIC AREA

SEAHAM WAY

KINSALE DRIVE

1

2

BEACH 3

4

ROCKY BEACH

5

8 CHILDRENS BEACH

BEACH 6

ROSSCARE PROM.

7

ANCHORAGE DRIVE

HOTEL

MARMION AVENUE

N

Quinns-Mindarie Walk   19

Quinns Rocks

Length: *3 kilometres return*
Grade: *1 (wheelchair accessible)*
Walk time: *50 minutes*

This is a pleasant coastal walk through the low dunes between the Quinns Rocks picnic area and Mindarie Keys' north jetty. It follows a fairly level, dual-use, bitumen track and is suitable for wheelchair users. Walkers may wish to do some fishing off the jetty before returning to the picnic site to enjoy barbecued fresh fish.

1 After leaving the carpark, follow the dual-use track south. On the right is a rough track that leads down to the beach. The plants along the walk are typical dune vegetation types—low scrub of wattles, smokebush, prickly moses, some grevilleas and a variety of pea plants.
2 This section provides good lookout spots to the ocean.
3 Access to a small beach.
4 Here, the track is elevated and provides excellent views of the marina and Mindarie Keys beyond. Just past here is a bitumen track and wooden steps that lead to a small, but rocky beach.
5 Take the right fork in the track and head up a slight rise. From here, you can see boats entering and leaving the marina and you may be lucky enough to see a seal.
6 On the right is another rough track providing access to a small swimming beach.
7 At the end of the trail is a boardwalk (steps up and down) that leads to a limestone groyne jutting out across the entrance to the marina. This is a popular fishing spot with good all round views. Bicycle racks are provided.
8 Returning along the same route, take a detour (right at the junction) to a children's beach with grassed area, carpark and paddle-bikes. This area provides a pleasant outlook across to the marina complex.

Andrea Carrington-Hughes

Where is it?: *Ocean Drive, Quinns Rocks, 34 km north of Perth*
Travelling time: *45 minutes via Mitchell Freeway and Marmion Avenue*
Facilities: *Picnic area, BBQ, parking, toilets, kiosk, telephone, caravan park*
On-site information: *None*
Best season: *All year*

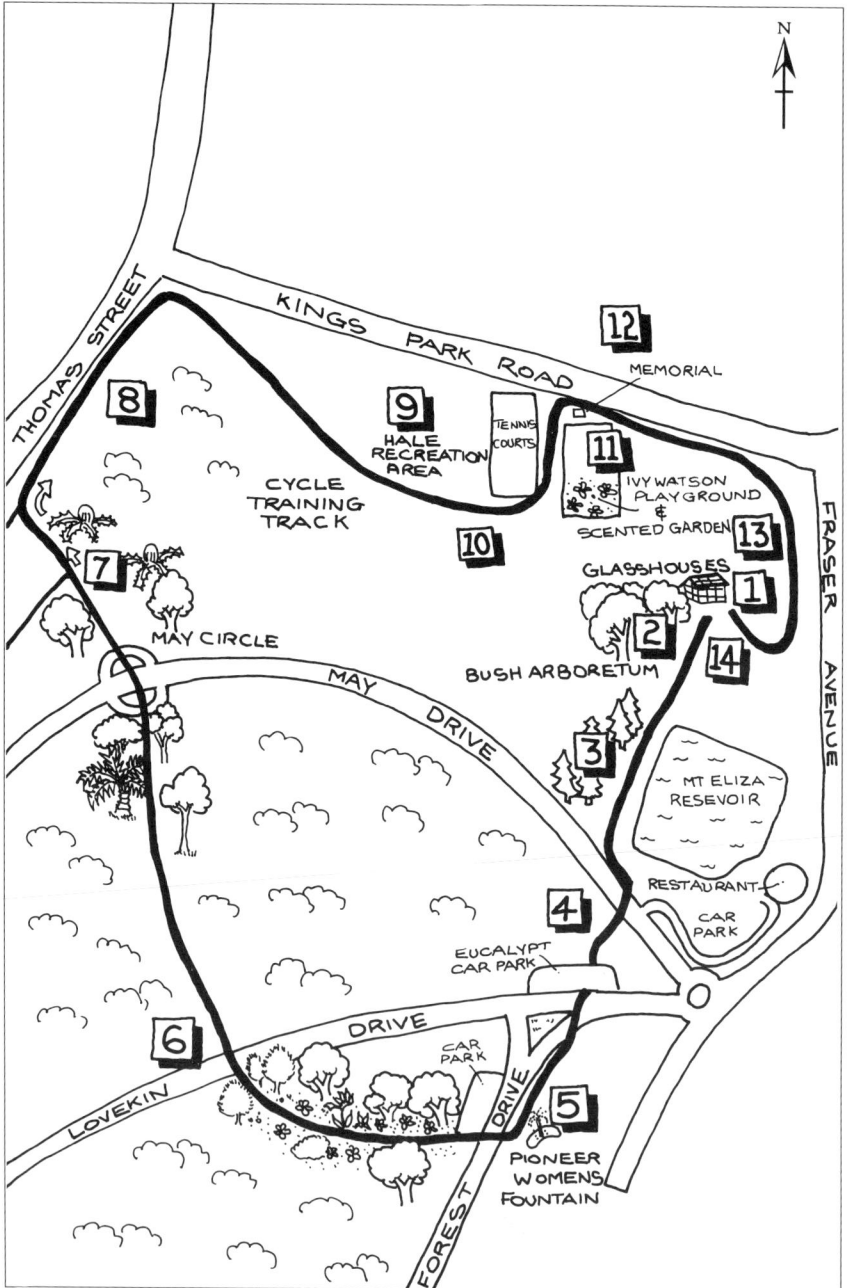

Scented Garden Trail   **20**

Kings Park

Length: *2.2 kilometre loop*
Grade: *3*
Walk time: *2 hours 30 minutes (plus time to visit the glasshouses and garden)*

This walk covers several features in Kings Park and Botanic Garden that are not often known by the public. By beginning at the Display Glasshouses and the Rare and Endangered garden, you can see plants from remote and sometimes inaccessible areas of Western Australia.

On this walk you will pass cultivated areas, bushland, landmarks and areas of historic importance.

1   Start at the carpark by the Display Glasshouses. Enter these from Fraser Avenue, which is entered from Kings Park Road entrance. Time should be taken either now or at the end of the walk to look at the displays in these glasshouses and the adjoining rare and endangered garden. The glasshouses feature plants from the dry, inland Kimberley and Pilbara regions of WA, as well as ferns and carnivorous plants. They are open daily, except Tuesday, from 10 am – 4 pm.

2   Follow the bitumen road through the gates and head south-west. Avoid the bitumen track to the west. At this junction there are several tall tuarts (*Eucalyptus gomphocephala*). They are readily recognised by the buds, which resemble ice-cream cones. To the east is the exhibition ground where the annual Wildflower Festival is held each spring.

3   Avoiding the service road to the east, take the wide dirt path south beside a line of pines. Here, you walk beside the Mt Eliza Reservoir, which was originally constructed in 1891. To the west is the Bush Arboretum where trees and tall shrubs from throughout WA are displayed.

4   Walk along May Drive towards the city until you reach the restaurant carpark entrance. Cross May Drive and follow the formed path to the Eucalyptus Carpark. Here, there are several cultivated eucalypts, which are labelled with descriptive and propagation information to help people wishing to grow them at home.

5   Cross Lovekin Drive at the grassed triangle and follow the brick path south beside the Botanic Garden. Cross Forest Drive at the raised carpark opposite the Pioneer Women's Fountain. Follow the slab path near the southern end of the carpark, where you will pass through mixed marri-jarrah-banksia-sheoak woodland. During the spring, the bushland is spectacular with shrubs and annuals in flower. At the end of the path, note the stone pines (*Pinus pinea*). The pine nuts available

in shops are harvested from this pine. If you do the walk after the black cockatoos have been in the park, you will marvel at the power of their beaks in breaking open these cones to eat the seeds inside.

6   Cross Lovekin Drive and continue through the bushland to May Circle. This area is planted with eastern Australian eucalypts, such as lemon-scented gums (*Eucalyptus citriodora*), palms and a few peppermints (*Agonis flexuosa*).

7   Follow the formed path, NOT the dirt one, and note the sugar gums (*Eucalyptus cladocalyx*). Cross over the next path and continue to the formed path which runs parallel to Thomas Street. At the end of this path there are several acorn banksias (*Banksia prionotes*), a species of limited distribution in Kings Park with a peak flowering period from March to May.

8   Turn north-east and continue along the path. There are several orange-flowered *Eremaea pauciflora* shrubs along this path that add an unusual colour to the flowers of the bushland during September to December.

9   After walking uphill slightly you will pass the Hale Recreational Area, where there is a cycle practice track complete with road signs. To the east of the lawned area is the Metropolitan Bed, where plants readily available in nurseries are grown. This area was used as playing fields by Hale School before the school relocated to Wembley Downs.

10 Next, you pass in front of the Kings Park Tennis Club, where the State tennis tournaments are held each year.

11 Next to the Tennis Club is the Ivey Watson Playground for young children. This is a fenced area that includes a magnificent pergola and the Scented Garden. Time should be spent looking in here.

12 As you leave the playground, there is a statue to commemorate Arnold Cook and his dog. Read the inscription for details. Now you are into tall trees and shrubs, many of which were planted early this century.

13 Cross the service road and continue on the path. This area is referred to as the Fraser Avenue lawns. It is planted with many exotic tree species, most of which are labelled. The fence on the west side protects and hides the nursery complex where all the plants grown in Kings Park are propagated. Public access to this area is not permitted.

14 Follow the path back to the Display Glasshouses and remember to walk through these if you did not do so at the start of the walk.

Eleanor Bennett

Where is it?: *3 km from city centre via St Georges Terrace*
Travelling time: *5 minutes*
Facilities: *BBQs, restaurant, kiosk, toilets, playgrounds, carparks at various locations throughout the park*
On-site information: *Information Centre within the park*
Best season: *All year, except hot summer days*

KANGAROO PAWS AND CATSPAWS

The red and green kangaroo paw (*Anigozanthus manglesii*) has been the floral emblem of Western Australia since 1960. Unbeknown to most Australians, the 12 species of kangaroo paw and catspaws are found only in the south-west of WA.

The name kangaroo paw (originally kangaroo foot) was coined in about the 1850s to describe the taller red and green species and other smaller red and green species., Catspaws is used in reference to four other small, short scaped (flowering stem) species with generally orange, reddish-orange and yellow flowers.

There are 11 genera of Anigozanthus and one of Macropidia, the black kangaroo paw (*Macropidia fulingosa*) which has black and green flowers. Cross-pollination occurs sometimes among the Anigozanthus, but has never been known between the two genera.

All kangaroo paw species have tough irregular underground stems, called rhizomes, that are buried two to ten centimetres below the surface. This is a special adaptation to survive hot dry summers and bushfires. In most species, the leaves and flowering scapes die back after each flowering season. With the onset of new autumn rains, the process of growth starts again.

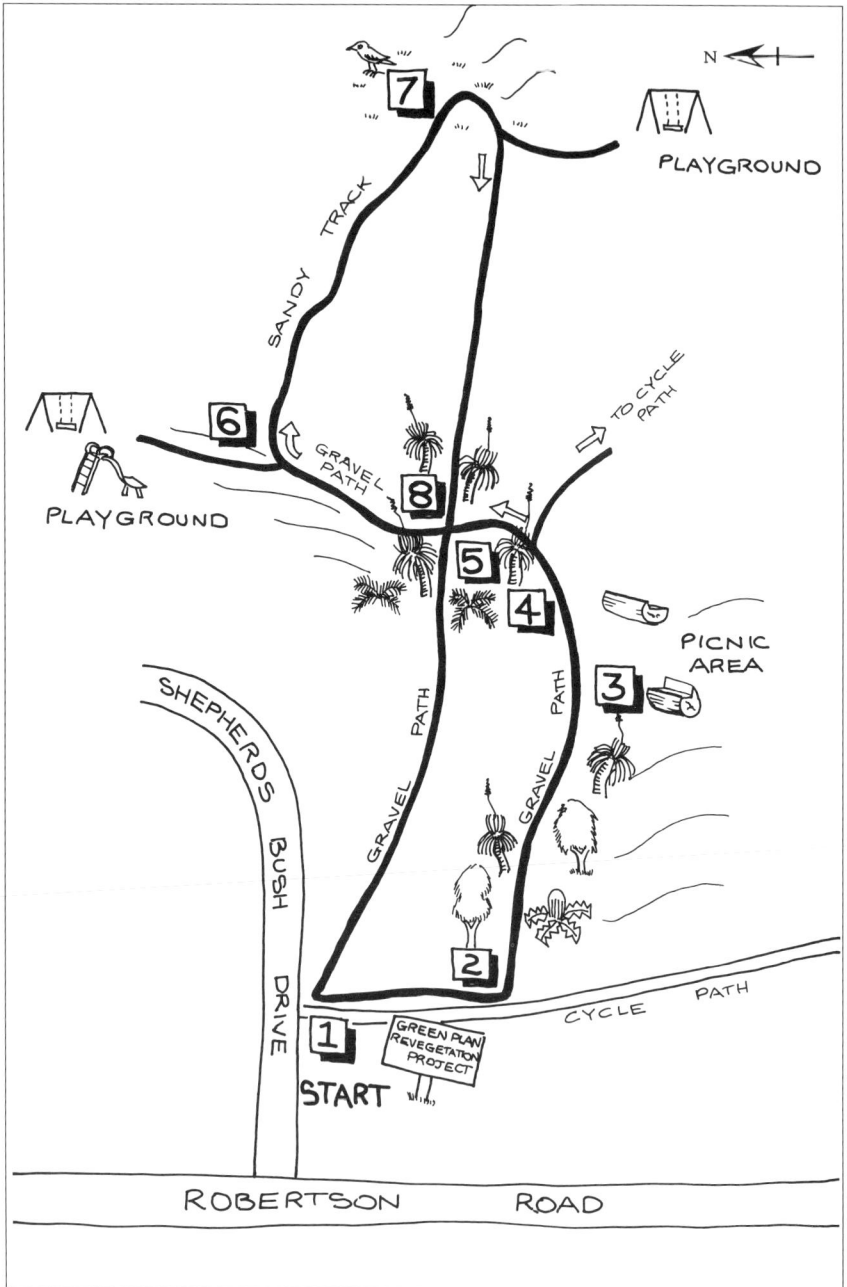

N

7

PLAYGROUND

SANDY TRACK

6

PLAYGROUND

GRAVEL PATH

8

TO CYCLE PATH

5

4

PICNIC AREA

GRAVEL PATH

3

SHEPHERDS BUSH DRIVE

GRAVEL PATH

GRAVEL PATH

2

CYCLE PATH

1

START

GREEN PLAN REVEGETATION PROJECT

ROBERTSON ROAD

Shepherd's Bush Walk   **21**
Kingsley

Length: *1.1 kilometre loop*
Grade: *1*
Walk time: *25 minutes*

This delightful walk is tucked away in the suburb of Kingsley. It features a diversity of plant life, including pigface, wildflowers and some large trees.

1   The walk begins on Shepherd's Bush Drive next to a timber sign that reads 'Green Plan Revegetation Project'. Head south along the dual-use path.
2   After about 50 m, turn left on to a gravel path. Here, you will see sheoaks, balgas (blackboys) and banksias. This section follows a wide path that slopes gently and winds through lush regrowth following a fire in 1983.
3   At this point, the vegetation opens out into a small valley. Natural log seats on the right make this a good spot for picnicking.
4   At a fork in the track, stay left and head for the crosstrack about 100 m beyond the picnic spot.
5   Cross the path and continue to an open area. Here, there are lots of zamias and balgas.
6   Carry on up the gentle slope, then turn right down a sandy track. Alternatively, continue up the slope and spend some time at the children's playground before retracing your steps to the sandy track.
7   Turn right into a manicured clearing at the end of the sand track. Walk around the grassed depression to a gravel track on right. Magpies and 'twenty-eight' parrots can be seen along this part of the walk. There is another children's play area that can be found by continuing around the depression. Backtrack to the gravel track when you are ready to continue the walk.
8   Arrive at the crosstrack you passed earlier and continue along the gravel track up the slope to the starting point.

Lotte Lent and Brian Armstrong

Where is it?: *Shepherd's Bush Drive, Kingsley, 17 km north of Perth*
Travelling time: *20 minutes via Hepburn Avenue and Kingsley Drive*
Facilities: *Playgrounds, parking on verge near 'entrance' to trail*
On site info: *None*
Best season: *Spring for wildflowers, autumn*

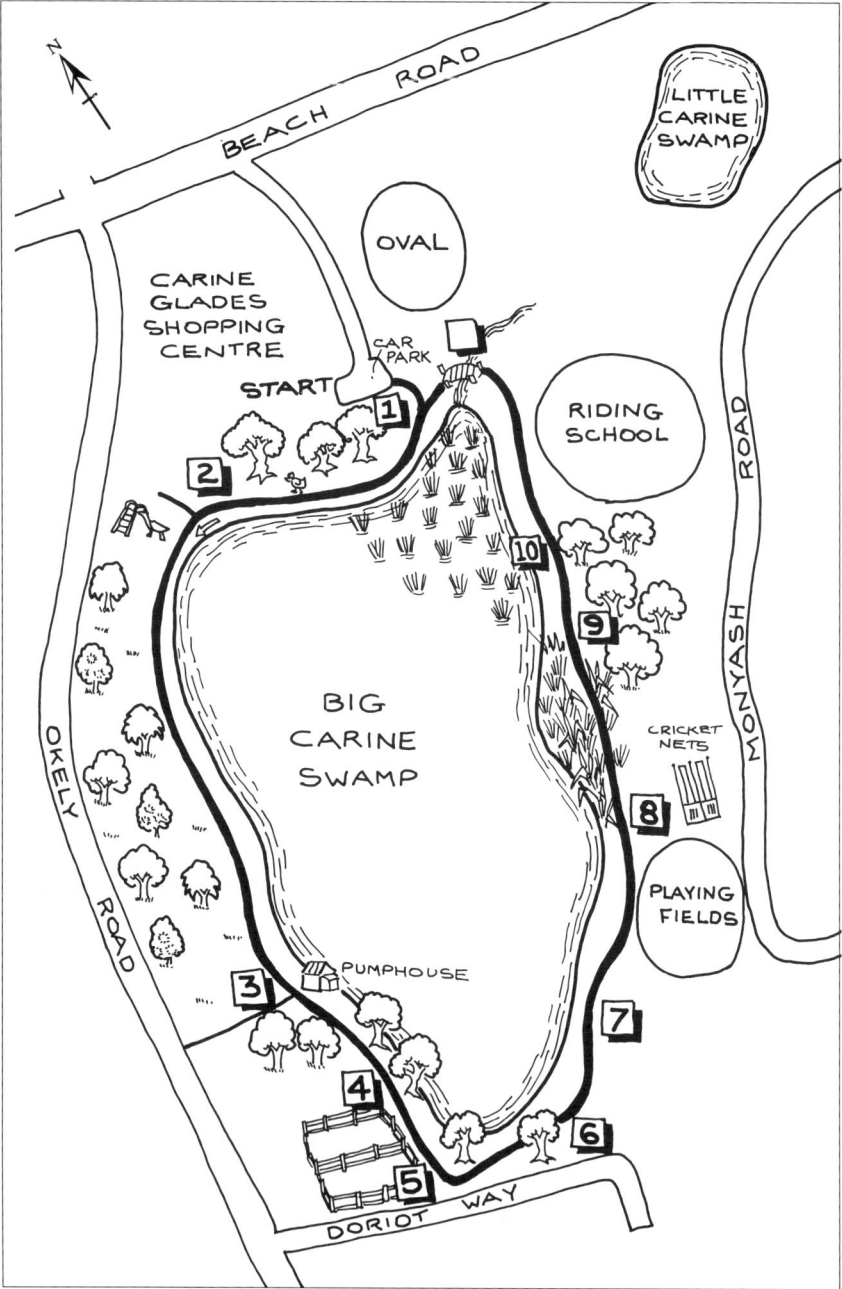

Swamp Trail   **22**
Big Carine Swamp

Length: *2.3 kilometre loop*
Grade: *1*
Walk time: *45 minutes*

The trail begins just south of the oval off Beach Road, Carine. It features manicured lawns, occasional secluded swamp views, and typical coastal wetland vegetation of tuarts, flooded gums, paperbarks and rushes. The extensive areas of open water support assortment of waterfowl.

1   From the south end of the carpark, follow the paved path westwards towards Okely Road. This section passes a waterfowl area fringed with paperbarks. Swamphens, swans and coots can be seen here.
2   Turn left just before the playground and follow the path around the swamp in an anticlockwise direction. This western section features open grassed areas with planted wattles, peppermints and eucalypts.
3   The paved path ends by a pump house, which has a verandah overlooking the swamp. Continue along the grass in a straight line from the path.
4   Keeping the horse paddocks to your right, follow the trail beside the swamp. Here, the water is flanked with flooded gums and paperbarks.
5   After about 60 m, turn left about 10 m before the bitumen road and continue to a wide sandy track beside the paperbarks. Follow the track.
6   Walk up a rise, then keep left on a well-worn single file track close to the swamp.
7   Here, the trail opens out to a playing field with cricket nets on right. Stay close to the swamp. This is a good spot to listen and look for wildlife, particularly water birds. This area may be fairly waterlogged in winter.
8   Low rushes appear on the edges of the swamp, with good views across the water.
9   A well-worn sandy track begins a few metres from where the reeds meet the trees.
10   Keep right, on a wide sand track.
11   With the riding school on the right, cross a small bridge and head to the start.

Lotte Lent and Brian Armstrong

Where is it?: *14 km north of Perth*
Travelling time: *20 minutes*
Facilities: *Picnic areas, BBQs, paved paths, ovals*
On-site information: *None*
Best season: *All year, except hot summer day and after heavy rains*

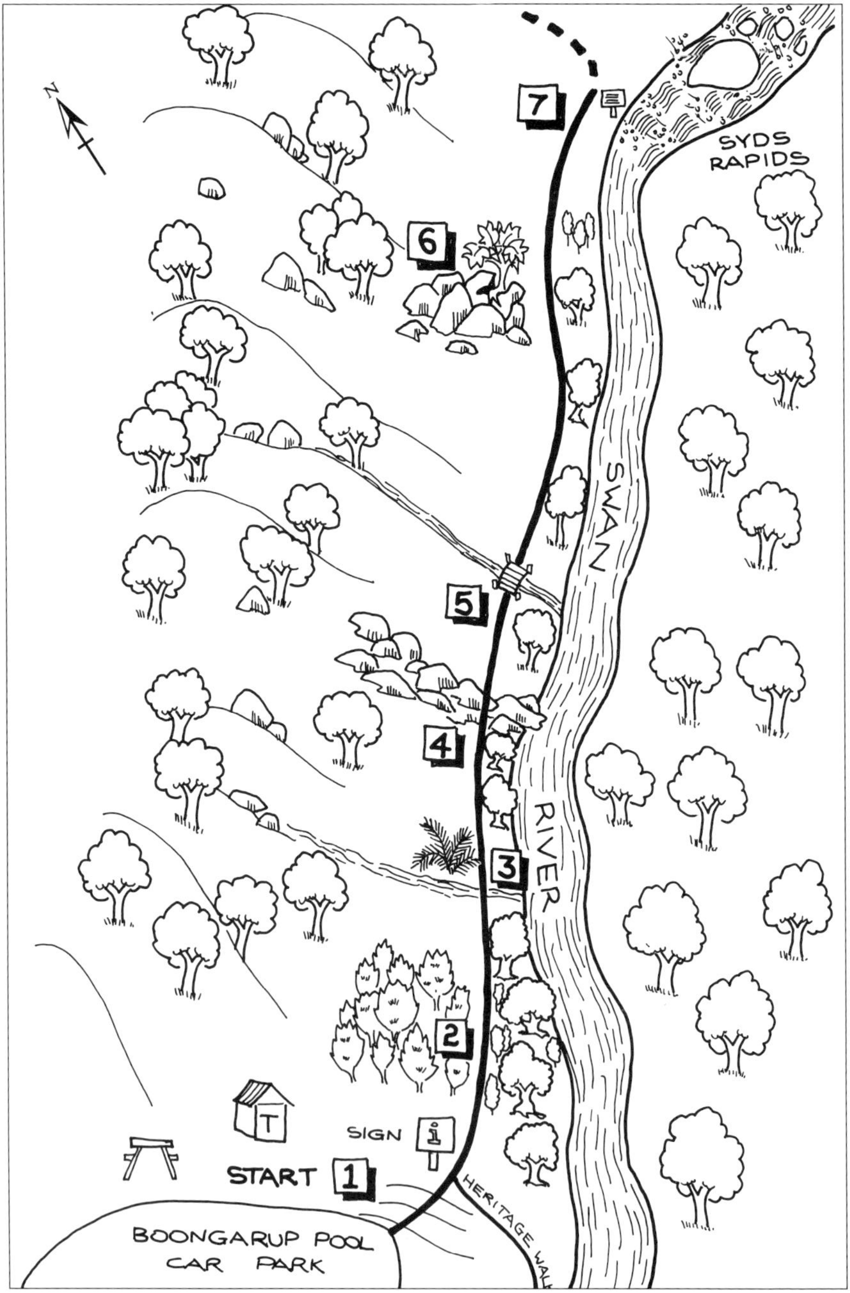

SYDS RAPIDS

7

6

SWAN

5

4

RIVER

3

2

SIGN i

START 1

T

BOONGARUP POOL
CAR PARK

HERITAGE WALK

N

Syd's Rapids Trail   **23**

Walyunga National Park ($)

Length: *3.5 kilometres return*
Grade: *2*
Walk time: *1 hours 45 minutes*

This walk is a gentle stroll along the grassy flood plain of the Swan River. It takes you under shady wandoos and flooded gums as it runs along the river bank that Aborigines walked for thousands of years. If you are quiet, you may see the kangaroos and waterfowl that made the area so attractive to the Nyoongar people.

1   Leave Boongarup Pool carpark by a well-constructed path from the bottom end of carpark. Head down a slope to the junction of two paths. There is an information sign on the left by a creek crossing. Turn left and head upstream.
2   On the left along this section is an area of parrotbush that extends down to the path. The yellow flowers attract honeyeaters in winter and spring. There are paperbarks and teatrees on the river bank.
3   A seasonal creek crosses the path here with an ancient plant form—the zamia— on the left of the path.
4   A granite outcrop ridges down from the hill on the left, crossing the path and continuing into the river, forming a series of rapids. There is a pleasant view of the river from here.
5   Another creek flows down to the river, this time crossed by a simple bridge.
6   The large cluster of granite boulders on the left has a fig tree growing from a large crack in the rock. From here, the sound of Syd's Rapids can be heard.
7   Syd's Rapids. A plaque explains how the rapids got their name. Walk a little further to see the water on both sides of the island. Walkers can either follow the route back to Boongarup Pool carpark, or join the 10.6 km Echidna Trail described in the book *Family Walks in Perth Outdoors*.

Terry Hales

Where is it?: *Walyunga National Park, 40 km north-east of Perth*
Travelling time: *1 hour via Great Northern Highway and Walyunga Road*
Facilities: *Picnic areas, BBQs, toilets, carparks, water*
On-site information: *Information shelters, interpretive signs along the trail*
Best season: *Autumn to spring*

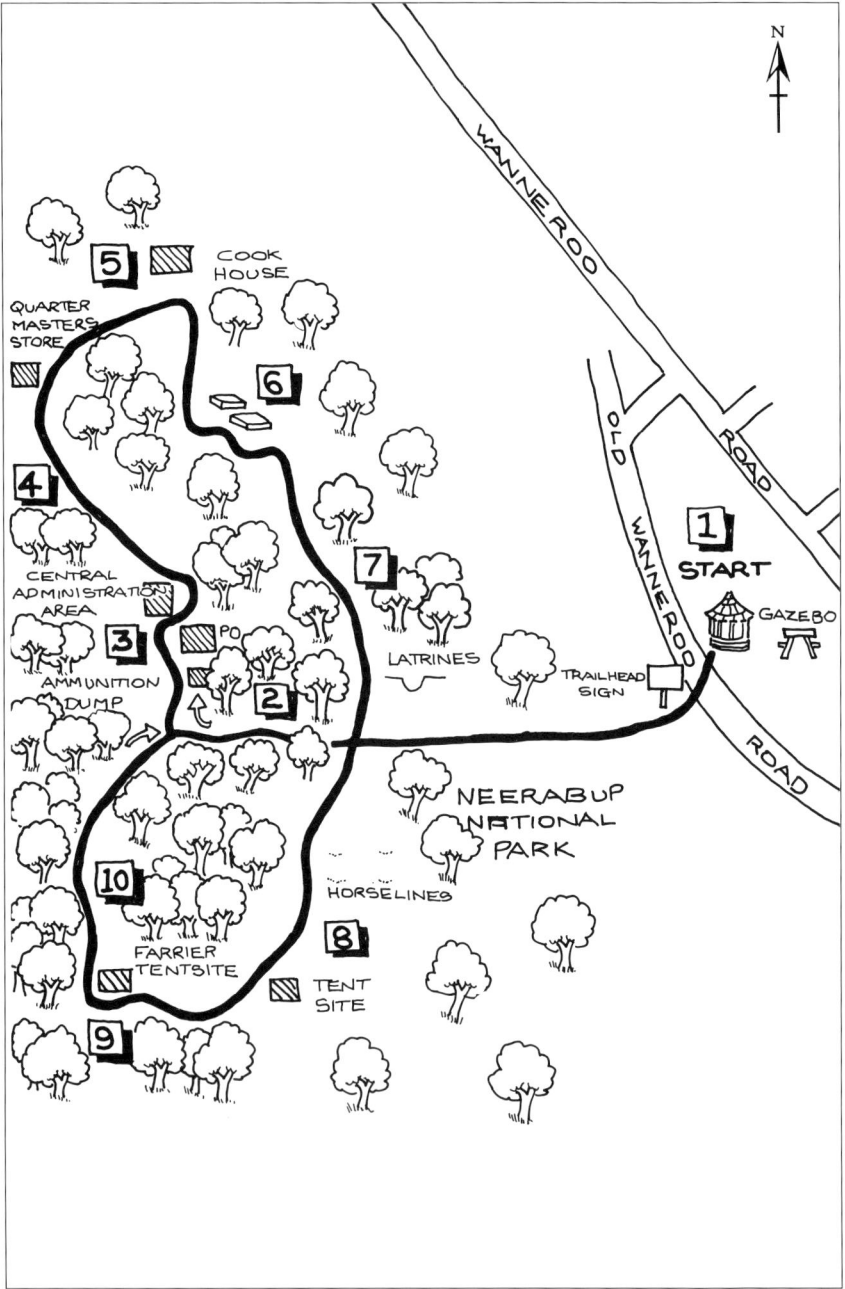

N

WANNEROO ROAD

OLD WANNEROO ROAD

5

COOK
HOUSE

QUARTER
MASTERS
STORE

6

4

7

CENTRAL
ADMINISTRATION
AREA

3

PO

AMMUNITION
DUMP

2

LATRINES

1
START

GAZEBO

TRAILHEAD
SIGN

NEERABUP
NATIONAL
PARK

10

HORSELINES

8

FARRIER
TENTSITE

TENT
SITE

9

10th Light Horse Memorial Trail

****

Neerabup National Park

Length: 1.8 *kilometres*
Grade: 1
Walk time: 45 *minutes*

The trail runs from a roadside picnic area about a kilometre north of Flynn Drive, on Wanneroo Road (Route 60). It is one of only two trails running through Neerabup National Park (the other being the Yaberoo Budjara Heritage Trail). Picnic facilities are available at the start of the trail and interpretational signs point out the activities of the 10th Light Horse Regiment, who camped in the area in the 1940s and were disbanded in 1944.

1 Starting from the gazebo at the picnic area, cross the Old Wanneroo Road (now an access track) to the trailhead sign. From here, follow the limestone track.
2 Cross the eastern leg of the trail and head through tuart-marri woodland to the 'T' junction. Turn right and head north.
3 The trail winds along here past the sites of an amunition dump, the Post Office and the Central Administration Area.
4 The trail rises gently towards the north-west corner before begining to descend past the site of the Quartermaster's Store.
5 The cook house was located at the northern end of the trail.
6 Follow the trail south until you see a couple of large concrete blocks on the left. This is the site where a petrol-driven engine and generator provided power for the campsite and administration areas.
7 The trail winds gently through the tuart woodland. Soon you reach the site of the latrines. These were dug about 1.3 metres (four feet) deep with a 'thunderbox' top and enclosed in hessian to provide some privacy.
8 After crossing the 'entrance' track, continue to the southern end of the trail. Along this section are the horse lines—where the horses were tied, fed and groomed—and the main tent sites.
9 The farrier, who also undertook general blacksmithing duties, was based just beyond the main campsite. It is still possible to find ash and charcoal on the site.
10 Head north along the final leg of the trail towards the 'T' junction at point 2. Turn right and head back towards the picnic site.

David Gough and family

81

Where is it?: *31 km north of Perth along Wanneroo Road*
Travelling time: *55 minutes*
Facilities: *Carpark, gazebo, gas BBQ*
On-site information: *Trailhead sign, interpretation panels along trail*
Best season: *All year*

EMU

Emus (*Dromaius novaehollandiae*) are still to be found in isolated pockets of scrub in the outer areas of suburban Perth, where tracts of bush habitat are linked to national parks, river valleys and open plains. Quite often, land owners have elected to encourage a few birds on farms close to town to enhance aesthetic values.

Found abundantly throughout Australia, the emu is our largest endemic bird, and second largest of the world's surviving flightless birds. It is thought to be an early offshoot of the cassowary that has adapted to more arid regions.

The food of emus consists of native fruits, vegetation and insects taken from the ground. Adult birds grow up to two metres in height and are found usually in pairs or small parties. They are highly nomadic. In the breeding season, they move into areas of recent good rains.

Breeding is usually from March to November, when a sparse nest of grass, bark and sticks is constructed on the ground and between five and eleven dark green eggs are brooded by the male. Black and pale yellow striped chicks are escorted by the male for about 18 months until the large juveniles disperse.

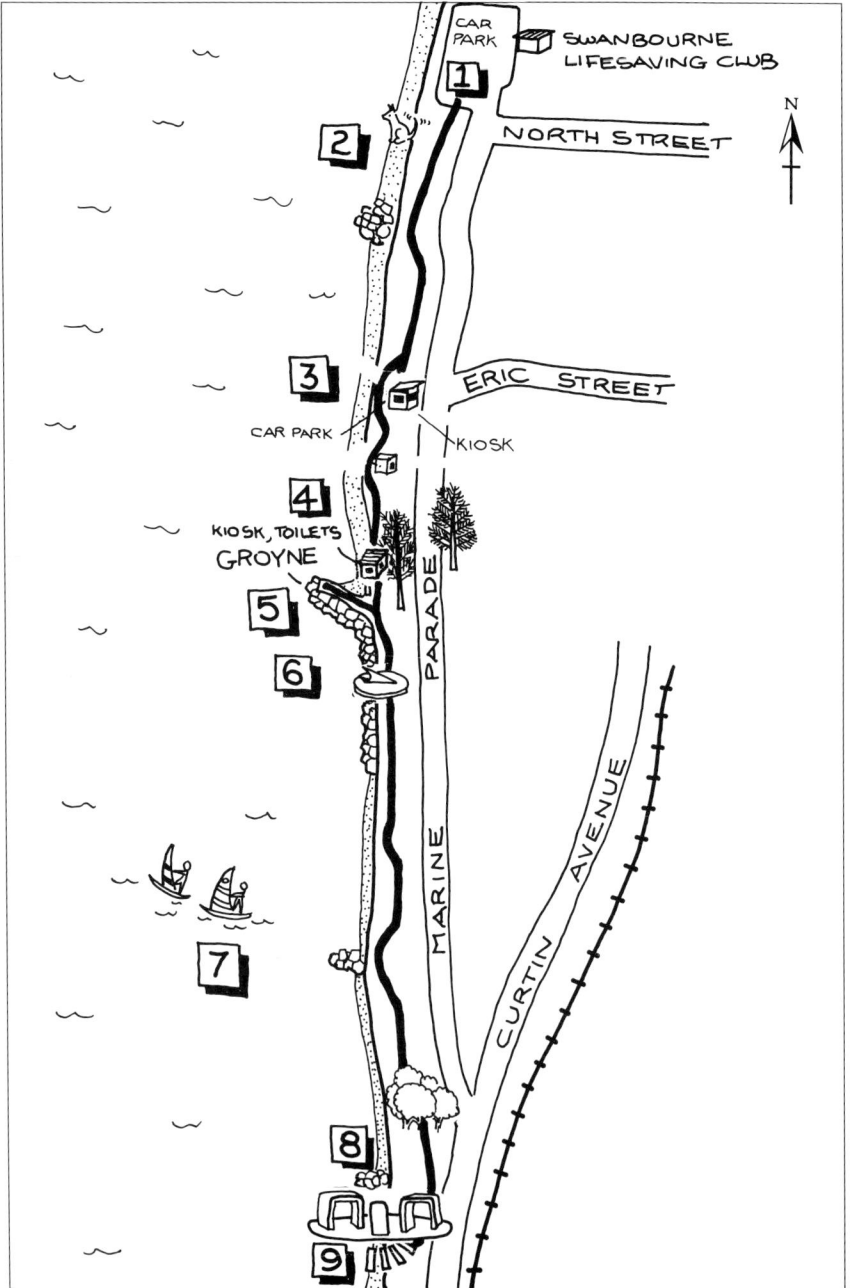

CAR PARK

SWANBOURNE LIFESAVING CLUB

1

2

NORTH STREET

N

3

CAR PARK

KIOSK

ERIC STREET

4

KIOSK, TOILETS
GROYNE

5

6

MARINE PARADE

CURTIN AVENUE

7

8

9

Vlamingh Memorial Walk **25**

Cottesloe

Length: 8.5 *kilometres return*
Grade: 1
Walk time: 2–3 *hours*

The walk is a pavement stroll from Swanbourne southwards to the Vlamingh Memorial, where Marine Parade joins Curtin Avenue. The stretch of sea is Gage Roads, where ships are often visible steaming to or from Fremantle. Rottnest is usually visible on the horizon, as are Garden and Carnac Islands. Hawks are often seen hovering above the grassy dunes in search of a meal.

1 Begin at the carpark near the Swanbourne Lifesaving Club. Just north of where you stand is the Swanbourne nudist beach. At early morning, flocks of pink and grey cockatoos will take to the sky as you approach.
2 Here is a beach where dog owners may take their pets for exercise. Just beyond is a reefy section of beach which offers enjoyable fossicking in small tidal pools.
3 The main shopping and recreation area of Cottesloe begins at the corner of Eric Street. The path forks just before this; follow the right-hand branch down to the beach and rejoin the left branch after 200 m.
4 A fast-food kiosk marks the site of the former Cottesloe Oceanarium.
5 Detour to the groyne downhill, past the cockatoo-filled pines and the terraced grass slope. Retrace your steps to get to the next stage.
6 Check your watch against the huge sundial. It comes complete with instructions.
7 At the groyne, the Vlamingh Memorial appears as a distant small white square.
8 The path dips in a Rottnest-like passage through tea trees, and then the Vlamingh Memorial is in sight. A brass direction-indicator marks the site of explorer Vlamingh's landing, and shows the location of the islands off the coast.
9 Just past the memorial is a flight of slatted steps down to the beach. At the top, a brass OTC plaque marks the site of the cable connection to the Cocos Islands, in use until the 1960s. At the bottom, the cable ends are still visible.

Liz Bailey and Ann Nicholson

Where is it?: North end of Marine Parade, 10 km west of Perth
Travelling time: 20 minutes from Perth city centre
Facilities: Carpark at start, various kiosks along the route
On-site information: None
Best season: All year

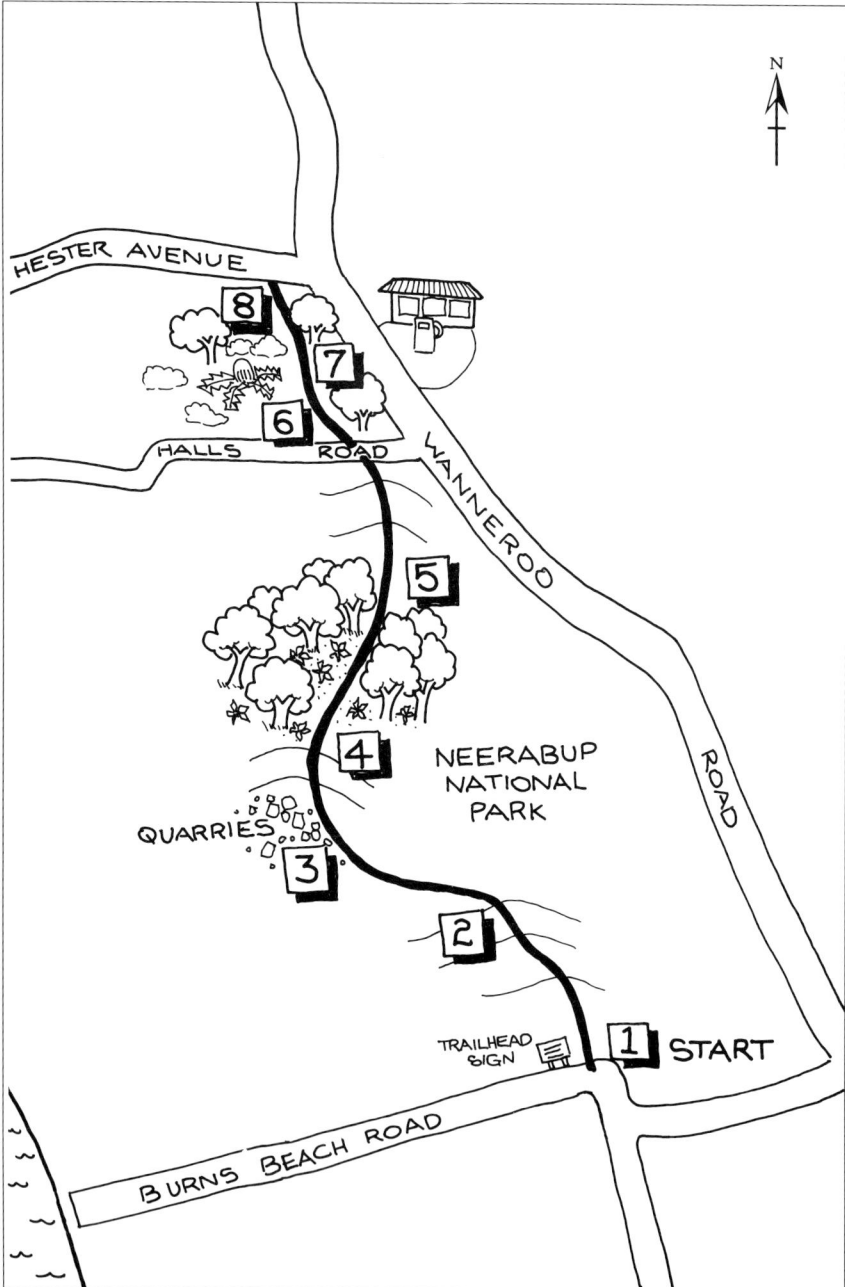

N

HESTER AVENUE

8

7

6

HALLS ROAD

WANNEROO

5

NEERABUP
NATIONAL
PARK

4

QUARRIES

3

ROAD

2

TRAILHEAD
SIGN

1 START

BURNS BEACH ROAD

Yaberoo Budjara Heritage Trail

26

Stage 2 - Neerabup National Park

Length: *15 kilometres return (can be walked one-way)*
Grade: *3-4*
Walk time: *6 hours*

The 28-kilometre Yaberoo Budjara Heritage Trail runs from Lake Joondalup to Yanchep National Park. Sections 1 and 5 are described in *Family Walks in Perth Outdoors* and section 3 is described on the following pages. This section focuses on the plantlife of Neerabup National Park and passes old limestone quarries.

1   Start on Burns Beach Road about 1.5 km west of Wanneroo Road. There are signs on the north side of the road, just below the road level, indicating the park boundary and the start of this section of the heritage trail. Follow the left-hand track, as indicated, uphill towards a limestone ridge.
2   From the top of the ridge you can see Waukolup Hill and the ocean beyond.
3   The abandoned quarries were originally opened to cut limestone blocks, but the poor quality of stone led to them being used to extract road building material.
4   The track turns right, away from the quarries, and runs down a short winding slope to a straight section through mixed woodland of jarrah and marri. This area is particularly pleasant, especially in spring when its varied understorey of wildflowers bursts into flower.
5   As you leave the 'avenue' of jarrahs and marris you pass just west of the last permanent campsite of the 10th Light Horse Regiment. Cross a management track and climb a gentle slope towards Hall Drive.
6   Cross Hall Drive—a private road to properties on the west side of the park.
7   The last section of this stage of the heritage trail takes you through mixed woodland of marri and banksia, and some heathland.
8   As you emerge at Hester Avenue (formerly Quinns Road), you are within a few hundred metres of Wanneroo Road. Retrace your steps or have someone meet you here.

Mark Garnsey and David Gough

Where is it?: *28 km north of Perth on Burns Beach Road*
Travelling time: *45 minutes*
Facilities: *None*
On-site information: *Yellow triangular track markers*
Best season: *All year (except during hot days), spring for wildflowers*

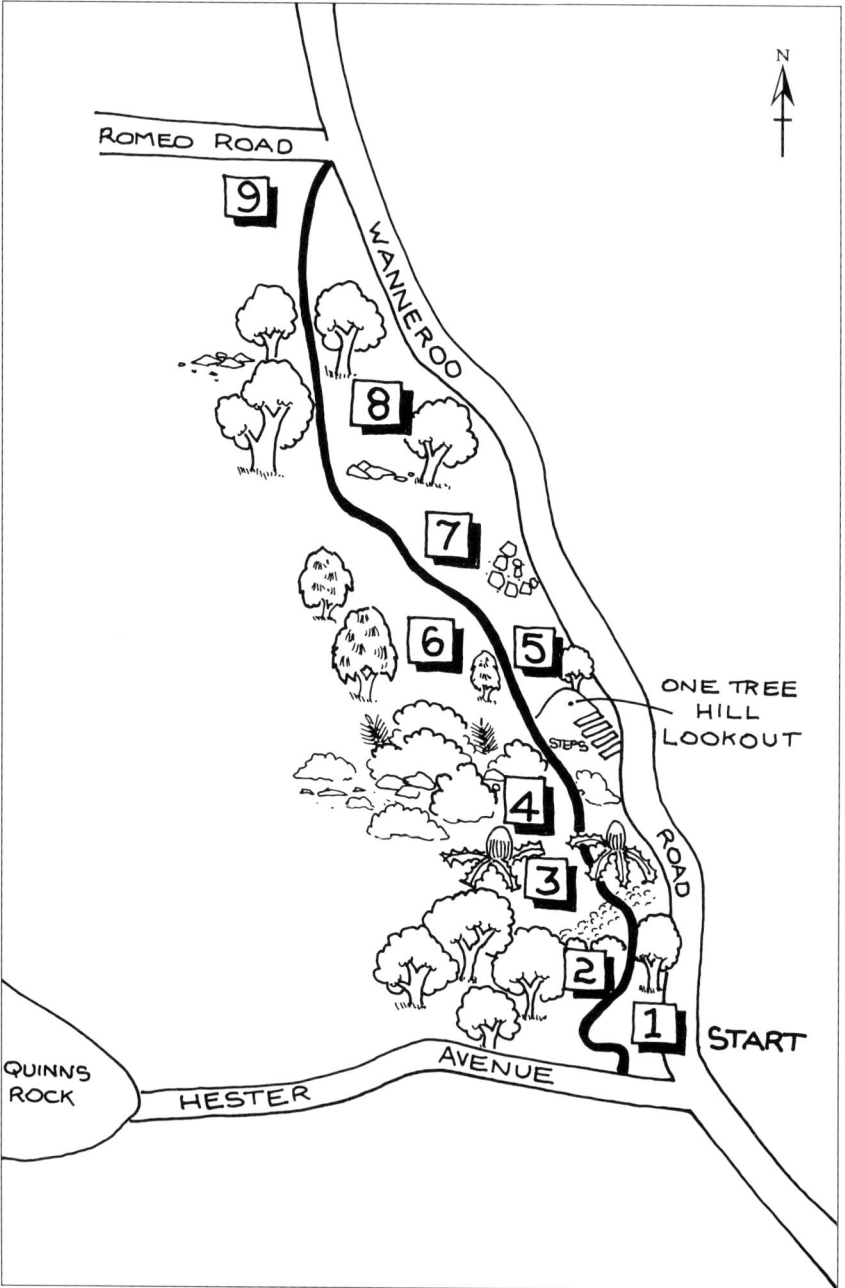

88

Yaberoo Budjara Heritage Trail

27

Stage 3—Neerabup National Park

Length: *13.4 kilometres return (can be walked one-way)*
Grade: *3-4*
Walk time: *5 hours*

The 28-kilometre Yaberoo Budjara Heritage Trail runs from Lake Joondalup to Yanchep National Park. Sections 1 and 5 are described in *Family Walks in Perth Outdoors*. This section passes through jarrah-tuart and banksia woodlands, coastal heaths and areas of limestone caprock.

1   Beginning at Hester Avenue (formerly Quinns Road), the trail runs parallel to the of the road for a short distance before turning into jarrah-tuart woodland. A fire in early 1994 burnt much of the early part of this walk. Invasive weeds such as cape tulip and lovegrass are visible near the track.
2   Grevilleas and jacksonias dominate this section, which is the edge of the jarrah-tuart woodland. Walk down a slight incline. Sundews are common here. Cross the firebreak to open woodland of sheoaks and balgas (blackboys).
3   Banksia woodland (mainly firewood banksia) for the next 500 m.
4   Along this section you will notice a change in vegetation from low banksia to limestone heathland of acacias, bottlebrushes and snakebush. There are also some pricklybarks. Note the limestone caprock.
5   This section passes close to One Tree Hill Lookout, which can be reached up steps from Wanneroo Road. From the top of the limestone ridge there are great views to the coast across the sandplain and woodland-heath.
6   This section of the park suffered a wildfire in 1993. Common and dwarf sheoaks are found though here.
7   About 300 m east of the track is a disused quarry.
8   This section is mainly tuart woodland with limestone caprock.
9   The trail emerges at Romeo Road, there is a roadhouse about 200 m south along Wanneroo Road. Retrace your steps or have someone meet you here.

David Lamont

Where is it?: *34 km north of Perth on Hester Avenue (formerly Quinns Road)*
Travelling time: *55 minutes*
Facilities: *None*
On-site information: *Yellow triangular track markers*
Best season: *All year (except during hot days), spring for wildflowers*

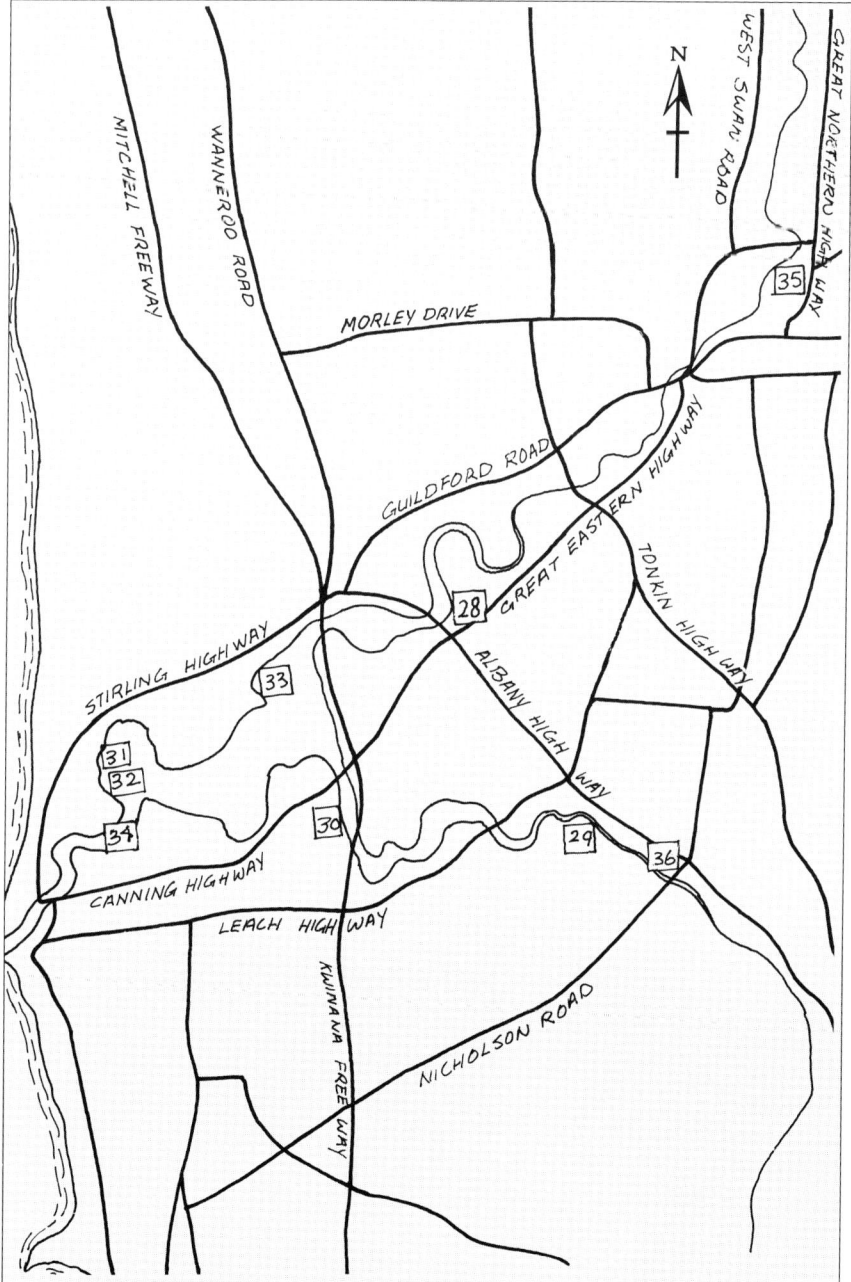

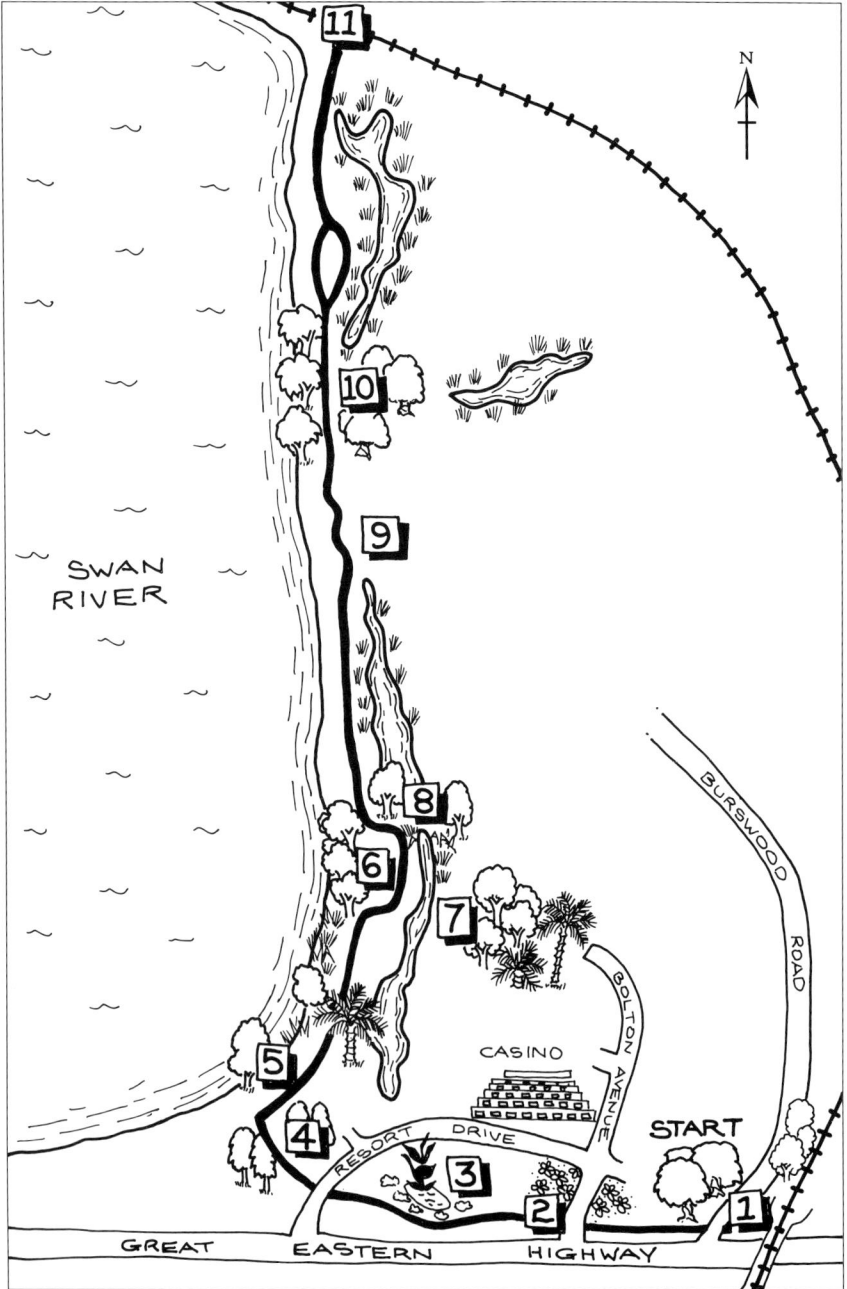

N

11

10

9

SWAN
RIVER

8

6

7

BURSWOOD ROAD

5

CASINO

BOLTON AVENUE

START

4

RESORT DRIVE

3

2

1

GREAT EASTERN HIGHWAY

Burswood Park Walk   **28**

Burswood Resort

Length: *3.4 km return*
Grade: *1 (wheelchair accessible)*
Walk time: *1 hour 45 minutes*

This delightful walk passes through the landscaped parks and gardens of Burswood Park, which surround the Burswood Resort complex, and along the Swan River foreshore beside the public golf course. The park contains many species of waterfowl on its 11 lakes. The surface of the walking path is suitable for wheelchairs and prams.

1   The walk begins at the junction of Burswood Road and Great Eastern Highway. There is a grove of WA peppermint trees on the right and a stand of *Eucalyptus microtheca* on the left.
2   Cross Bolton Avenue, the main entrance to the Casino and Resort. The gardens on either side of the road feature Meideland roses and other annuals, together with four stunning flame trees.
3   The first of the park's lakes is on your right. This is the Citizen of the Year Lake and features the Swan Fountain. Take time to explore the paved heritage trail, which includes bronze sculptures of Henry Camfield and Paddy Hannan, the Swan Shell and a dais on which the names of WA's Citizens of the Year are mounted on brass plaques. The gardens here include grevillias, diosmas, NZ Christmas trees, westringia, leptospermums, melaleucas, pimelias and ericas.
4   Cross over Resort Drive and proceed to the foreshore, passing through a stand of sheoaks (*Casuarina* spp.). The heritage trail continues on your right, and bronze sculptures of a mother and daughter sitting on a bench, with the mother teaching her daughter (the girl is modelled on early photographs of Dame Mary Durack) and children playing hopscotch.
5   Proceed east along the foreshore with its melaleucas, sedges and native reeds along the river's edge. Keep and eye open for a unique triple-headed palm on your right.
6   Native acacias, melalucas and eucalypts have been planted to screen the clubhouse of the Australian Power Boat Club.
7   Across the lake is a stand of red river gums and, near the hotel, several tropical palm trees.
8.   A wetland bird breeding site has been established on the edges of the lake, amid swamp grasses, sedges and melalucas.

9   As you continue along the foreshore you will see large Moreton Bay figs on your left, opposite a stand of WA peppermints.
10 The Burswood Park public golf course. Sedges and reeds have been cultivated around the lakes to help control erosion.
11 The railway bridge over the Swan River marks the end of the walk. Retrace your steps taking in the panoramic views of Perth city and the river foreshore opposite.

Terry Bright

Where is it?: *3 km east of Perth along Great Eastern Highway*
Travelling time: *10 minutes by car, or catch the Perth Tram*
Facilities: *Toilets, playground, picnic areas, carpark*
On-site information: *Burswood Park Board office on Resort Drive*
Best season: *All year*

SLATERS

Slaters (*Porcellio scaber*) are common and prolific dwellers in our urban environment. Most people ignore their presence under and around garden plants, but many are quick to dispose of this harmless creature, which only lives on decomposing organic matter, mainly decaying vegetation.

Woodlice or slaters are terrestrial crustaceans and are relatives of crabs, prawns and lobsters. Humidity and moisture are essential to slaters, as the seven different families found throughout the world breath either through moisture-laden gills or a lung-like cavity.

The animals are a dull pinkish-grey colour and are covered with a segmented armour-like cuticle, which resembles the tail piece of a rock lobster. Like an armadillo, they can roll into a ball which protects them from predators and the loss of body moisture.

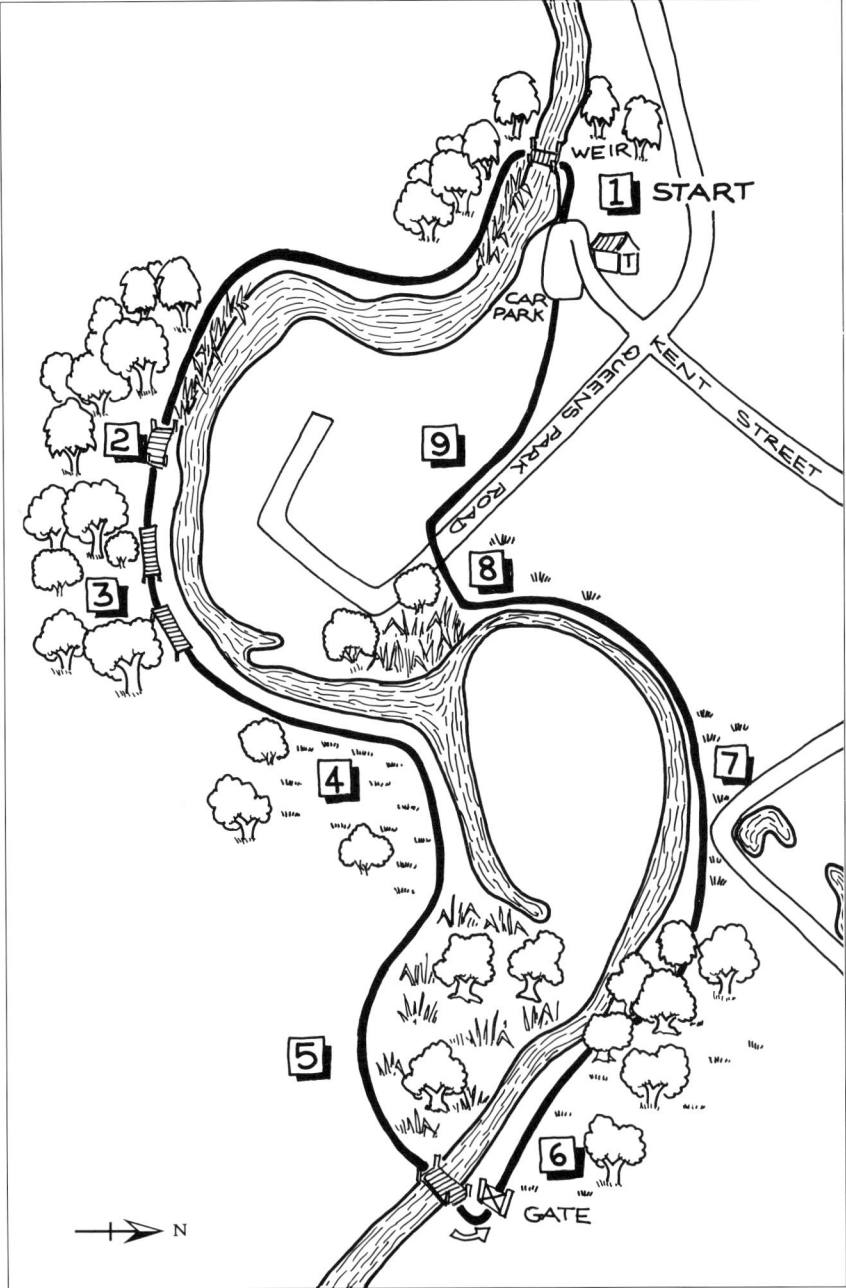

WEIR

1 START

CAR PARK

T

QUEENS PARK ROAD

KENT STREET

9

2

3

8

7

4

5

6

GATE

N

Canning River Trail

29

Canning River Regional Park

Length: *4 kilometre loop*
Grade: *2*
Walk time: *1 hour 45 minutes*

This pleasant riverside walk starts at the car park on the north side of Kent Street Weir. Here, there are lawned park areas, a playground, sheltered seating and toilets.

1   Cross the weir bridge through a thicket of sheoaks, flooded gums and paperbarks. Turn left and follow the path that keeps to the riverbank.
2   Here, the path crosses small bridge and drain. There are rushes and arum lilies on the riverbank and, on the right of the path, a woodland of sheoak and flooded gum. The trail forks to bitumen, so keep left.
3   Pass along raised wooden walkways within a small woodland of flooded gum and wattles, overhanging in places. Rejoin the concrete path and head past housing.
4   The trail swings into grassland and down to the river. Wattles and gums dominate.
5   At the end of the concrete path, follow the road verge. On the left, the wetlands are inundated with rushes and paperbarks. Cross the steel bridge and turn left through a white gate, some 20 m beyond, to a dirt track.
6   This track passes through grassland and eucalypt woodland, with seasonal surface waters on the right and the river on the left. Keep to the riverside track and pass through a close overhanging grove of paperbarks and sheoaks with ground creepers and arum lilies. Continue past the houses.
7   This is the corner of Wharf Street and Fleming Avenue. Over the road are ornamental lakes and council parkland. From the footpath here you look down to the river. Follow the riverbank across the open lawn.
8   Go down a riverside track at the end of the lawned area. There are wattles, rushes and lilies, which harbour small wrens. At the end of this short track is a natural boat ramp. Head out along a fenced property to Queens Park Road.
9   After reaching Queens Park Road head west and back to Kent Street Weir

John Hunter

Where is it?: *Kent Street Weir, 15 km south-east of Perth*
Travelling time: *25 minutes via Albany Highway and Kent Street*
Facilities: *Picnic shelters, carpark, toilets*
On-site information: *None*
Best season: *All year*

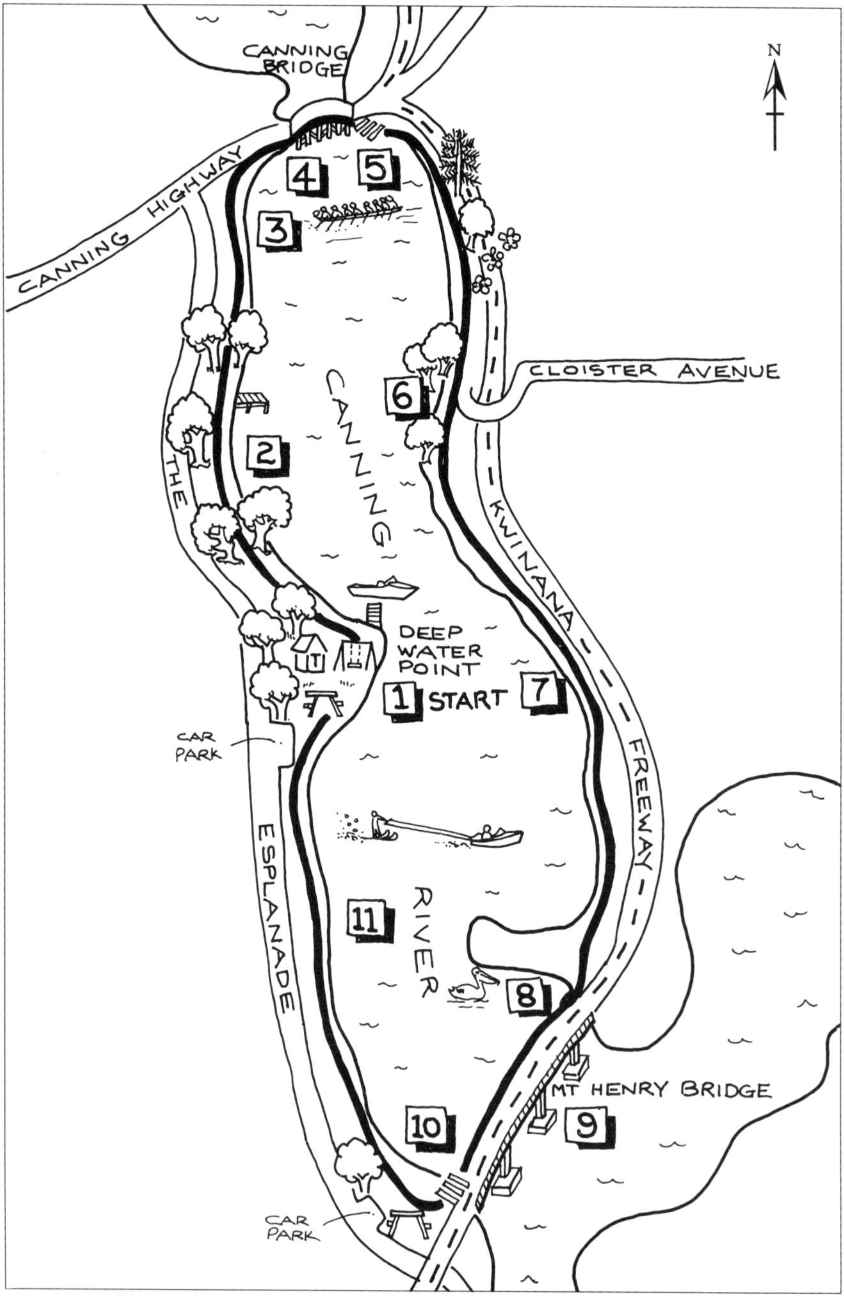

N

CANNING BRIDGE

CANNING HIGHWAY

4 5

3

CANNING

CLOISTER AVENUE

6

THE

2

KWINANA

DEEP WATER POINT

CAR PARK

1 START 7

ESPLANADE

FREEWAY

RIVER

11

8

MT HENRY BRIDGE

10 9

CAR PARK

Deep Water Walk

30

Lower Canning River

Length: 6.5 kilometre loop
Grade: 3 (wheelchair accessible)
Walk time: 2 hours 30 minutes

This near city, circular walk runs along both banks of the lower Canning River between Canning Bridge and Mount Henry Bridge. It provides spectacular outlooks over the river, with the Perth city skyline forming a distant backdrop to tranquil areas of foreshore bushland. The walk follows a dual-use path and is suitable for wheelchairs and prams.

Natural and exotic plants flourish, despite the walk's close proximity to Kwinana Freeway. A fair selection of land and water birds, such as pelicans, coots, large and small cormorants, cuckoo shrikes, magpies and gulls are also present.

There are numerous boating facilities catering for rowing, canoeing, sail boarding and water skiing, and safe swimming and/or paddling areas for children exist along the west banks. A clean grassed area with picnic facilities and nearby kiosk is located at Deep Water Point.

1   Start from the carpark at Deep Water Point. Parking is available free of charge within the signposted areas. This is a popular boat launching area for water skiers, so take the time to read the information signs. This area has toilets, a kiosk, children's playground, ample shade, lawn and picnic tables.

2   Walk north towards Canning Bridge. The pathway winds through grand old paperbarks. Several old tuart trees can be seen almost at the water's edge. Small jetties jut into the river, where a variety of boats are moored in tranquil waters. Seating and rubbish bins are located at strategic intervals.

3   Arriving at Canning Bridge, you are now at the venue of the 7th British Empire Commonwealth Games Rowing Regatta, held in 1962. This is also where the annual Head of the River rowing race finishes. Penrhos College, John XXIII and Murdoch University students can be seen practising early in the mornings.

4   A plaque at the west end of Canning Bridge details the history and construction of the bridge.

5   Cross Canning Bridge and descend the steps, continuing south on the river's east bank. Such is the beauty of this section that the hum of nearby traffic is easily forgotten. A couple of Norfolk Island pines, some large peppermints and numerous Geraldton wax shrubs dot this area.

6   This walk can also be entered or exited via a vehicle overpass from Cloister

Avenue near Mt Henry Hospital. Limited safe parking is available on the river foreshore. The well-preserved section of paperbarks was once the site of an old settlement know as 'The Camps', where up to 21 families lived in appalling conditions during 'The Great Depression'. Their history is well documented on a nearby plaque.

7 Further south, a footbridge links this walk with Edgewater Drive where Aquinas College can be seen to the south-east.

8 The shallow waters of Prawn Bay on your right are the home to pelicans and a variety of bird life. Prawn Bay foreshore is recovering from bush fires, but can be accessed from a series of sand tracks.

9 Crossing Mt Henry Bridge provides spectacular views of Perth city from one side and, from the other, the Darling Ranges in the distance. Heritage plaques describe the bridge's opening, on 9 May 1982, and the Kwinana Freeway's southern extension.

10 Descending at the bridge's southern end, you return to the Canning River's west foreshore. Here, there is another pleasant picnic spot, children's playground and carpark.

11 Proceed north to Deep Water Point. Water-skiers can be seen along this stretch of the walk.

John and James Smith

Where is it?: *8 km south of Perth via Canning Highway and The Esplanade*
Travelling time: *15 minutes*
Facilities: *Carpark, cafe, toilets, picnic area, playground, seats*
On-site information: *Water skiing information*
Best season: *All year, best views during early morning or calm evenings*

BATS

Bats are most prolific in the tropics, as their presence and population numbers are governed by the availability of insects—their food source—which are also in great numbers in warmer climates.

Perth's temperate climate, although cool in winter, still attracts about eight species of bat, which may be infrequently seen or heard on still, hot summer nights.

You are most likely to see bats swirling around a street light or pulling five Gs in an aileron roll as they devastate your local moth and mosquito populations. They are the only major predators of night-flying insects, with one species in the USA eating up to 3 000 in a single night.

The white-striped mastiff bat (*Tadarida australis*) is probably the most widespread species in our city and suburbs, its metallic 'tik-tik-tik' at half second intervals is a characteristic sound as it travels above trees and buildings at great speed.

Most of the bats in the Perth area roost by day in trees. Many will 'snuggle up' in small colonies in hollow limbs while others are solitary beasts living under exfoliating bark or even in dense clusters of leaves.

Bats are the only truly flying mammals and the unquestioned champions of aerobatics. As mammals, they are our own distant relatives and the bones in a bat's wing are essentially the same as those in human arms and hands. Thus the name of the scientific order for bats is Chiroptera, meaning 'hand-wing'.

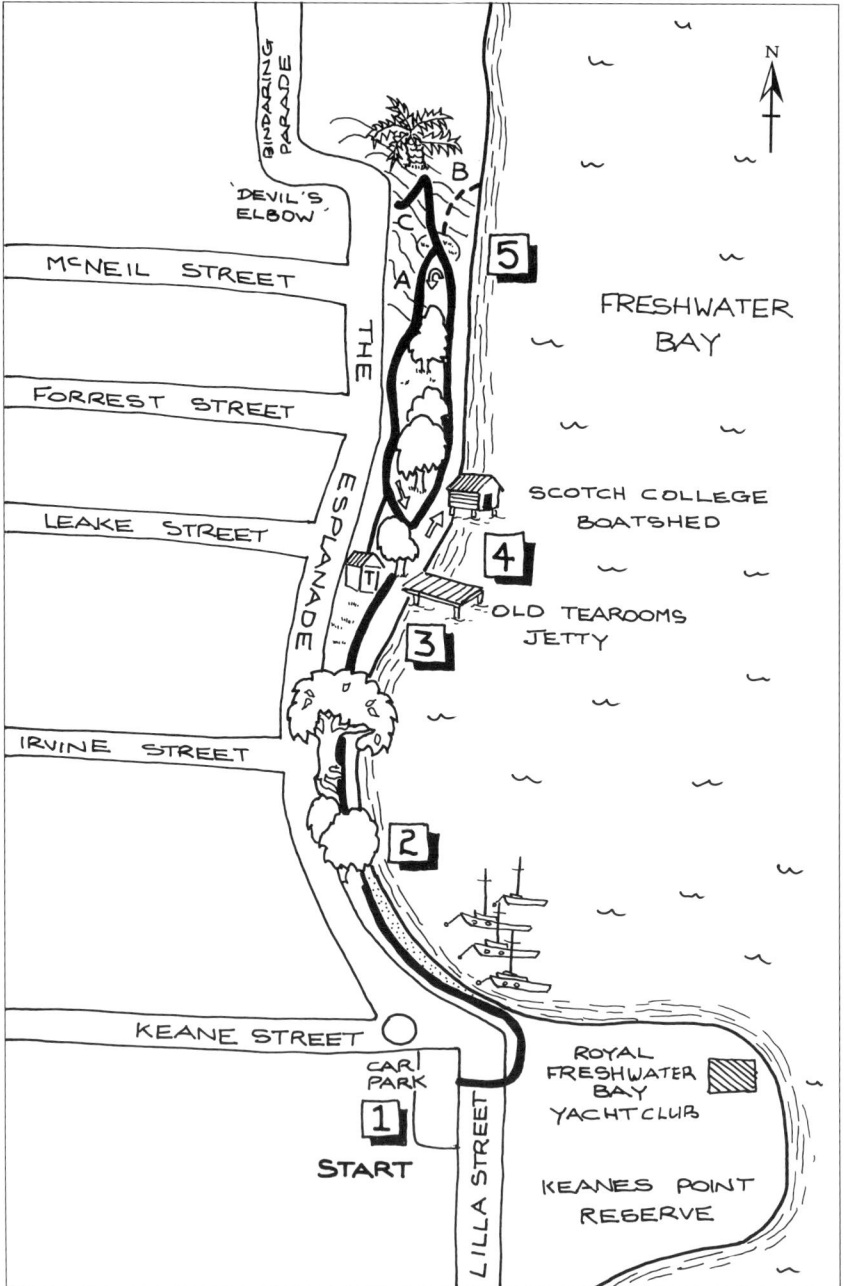

BINDARING PARADE

'DEVIL'S ELBOW'

McNEIL STREET

FORREST STREET

LEAKE STREET

IRVINE STREET

THE ESPLANADE

LILLA STREET

KEANE STREET

CAR PARK

START

B

C

A

5

4

3

2

1

FRESHWATER BAY

SCOTCH COLLEGE BOATSHED

OLD TEAROOMS JETTY

ROYAL FRESHWATER BAY YACHT CLUB

KEANES POINT RESERVE

N

Freshwater Bay Trail 31

Keanes Point

Length: *3 kilometres return*
Grade: *1*
Walk time: *50 minutes*

This riverside walk begins at Keanes Point, Mosman Park, and features excellent views of Freshwater Bay across to the Claremont foreshore and Point Resolution. Compare the Mosman Bay Trail, which also starts at Keanes Point and is featured in this book (page 105).

1   Begin at the Lilla Street car park opposite the Royal Freshwater Bay Yacht Club. Go left (north), joining the foreshore 100 m away.
2   Walk past the moored yachts, with views across the bay. For the first several hundred metres, the walk offers a choice of beach, narrow limestone seawall, or grass. Moreton Bay figs and peppermint trees are plentiful. Near the bottom of Irvine Street, a huge Moreton Bay fig crouches across the foreshore reserve, showing off its enormous roots above the surface.
3   Picnic spots are plentiful until the flat grassy foreshore meets the bottom of the hill along the Esplanade. If you take the path through peppermint trees along the foreshore, you can take the hillside walk for the return.
4   The jetty here is the site of the old tearooms. A path rises from here to join the hillside walk.
5   The walk rises to a picnic clearing at the face of the cliff. Three paths meet here. The right (B) peters out into a rough track down to the shore. The far right (C) is a brick path that winds steeply to The Esplanade, with views of the river.
6   The left path (A) is the return walk. It is a curving brick path that rises to street level and falls again. The path is only 30–40 m above the river, but the views seem quite different. Stay near the road and follow the grass down to the grassed picnic areas and back to Lilla Street.

Liz and Ray Bailey

Where is it?: *11 km south-west of Perth*
Travelling time: *20 minutes via Stirling Highway*
Facilities: *Picnic area, BBQs, tables, kiosk, playground, toilets*
On-site information: *None*
Best season: *All year*

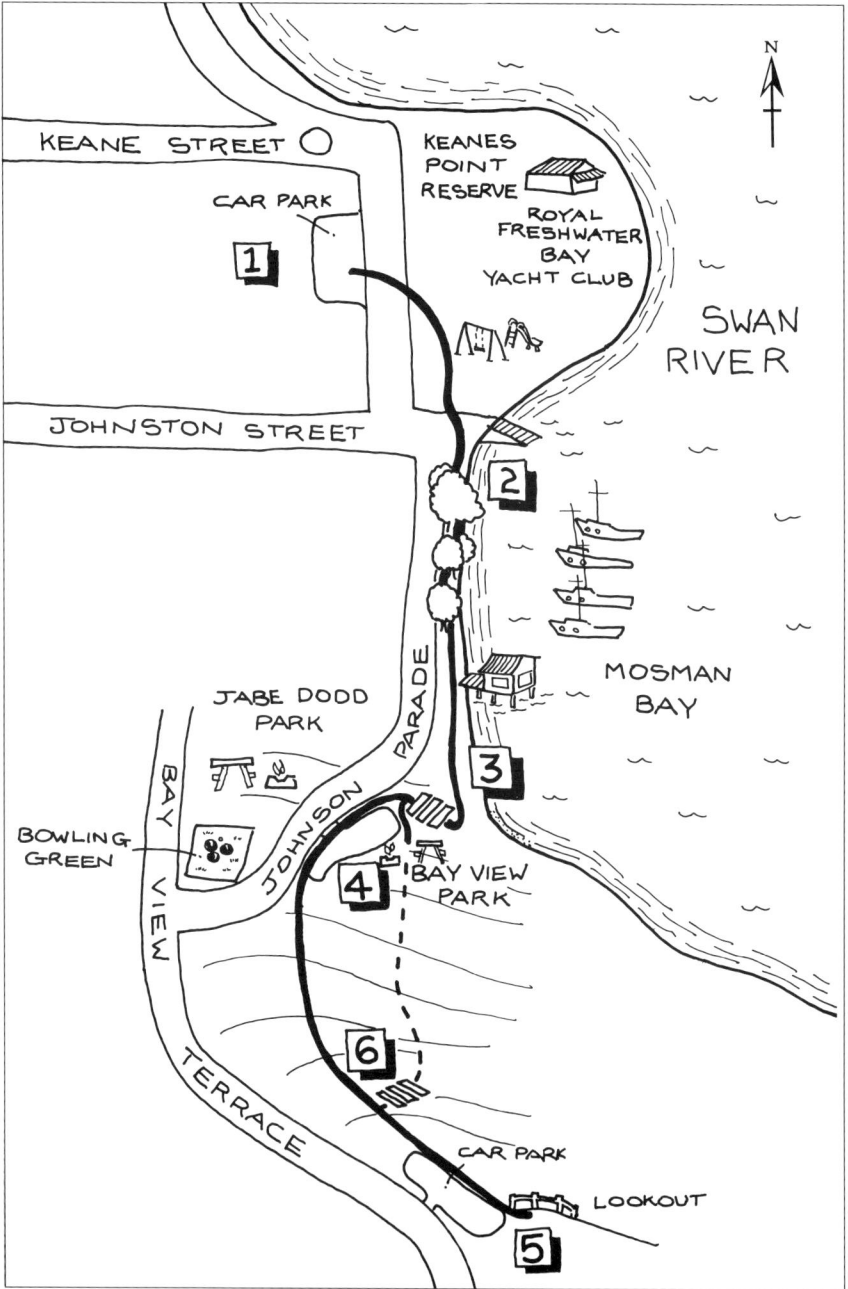

KEANE STREET

KEANES POINT RESERVE

CAR PARK

1

ROYAL FRESHWATER BAY YACHT CLUB

N

JOHNSTON STREET

SWAN RIVER

2

MOSMAN BAY

JABE DODD PARK

3

JOHNSON PARADE

BAY VIEW

BOWLING GREEN

4 BAY VIEW PARK

6

TERRACE

CAR PARK

LOOKOUT

5

Mosman Bay Trail

32

Keanes Point

Length: *3 kilometres return*
Grade: *1*
Walk time: *50 minutes*

The riverside beaches here are safe for children and toddlers and the area is well wooded with grassy picnic spots among shady trees. A variety of waterbirds can be seen along the shores at various times of the year. This is one of two walks from Keanes Point featured in this book (see page 103).

1   Begin at the Lilla Street carpark opposite the entrance to the Royal Freshwater Bay Yacht Club. Go right (south), then left towards the boat ramp at the end of Johnston Street.
2   Go south along Johnson Parade. You can walk along the sand or on the grass, avoiding the low branches of the peppermint trees. At low tide you can see a long sand spit from Point Walter that provides a safe walk at low tide from the other side of the river. (See 'Point Walter Walk' in *Family Walks in Perth Outdoors*.)
3   Go past the waterfront restaurant to the foot of the steps, which lead to a carpark part of the way up the hill.
4   Bay View Park has tables and barbecues, as does Jabe Dodd Park across the road. Walk on the pavement and go up the hill, which is steep for the first 50 m as it winds above the carpark. The view will be increasingly worthwhile.
5   From the top of the hill, follow the path along the plateau's edge to the carpark and lookout next to Chine Street. There are few better views of the river, Point Walter (ahead), Point Resolution (left) and, in the distance, the city of Perth.
6   A small paved area between the path and the cliff edge marks the start of an alternative descent back to Johnson Parade. The path is steep and rough at first, down steps formed partly of old railway sleepers; it is a narrow dirt track, but does lead back to Bay View Park if you remember to bear left and not go straight down to the shoreline.

Liz Bailey and Janet Horne

Where is it?: *11 km south-west of Perth*
Travelling time: *20 minutes via Stirling Highway*
Facilities: *Picnic area, BBQs, tables, kiosk, playground, toilets*
On-site information: *None*
Best season: *All year*

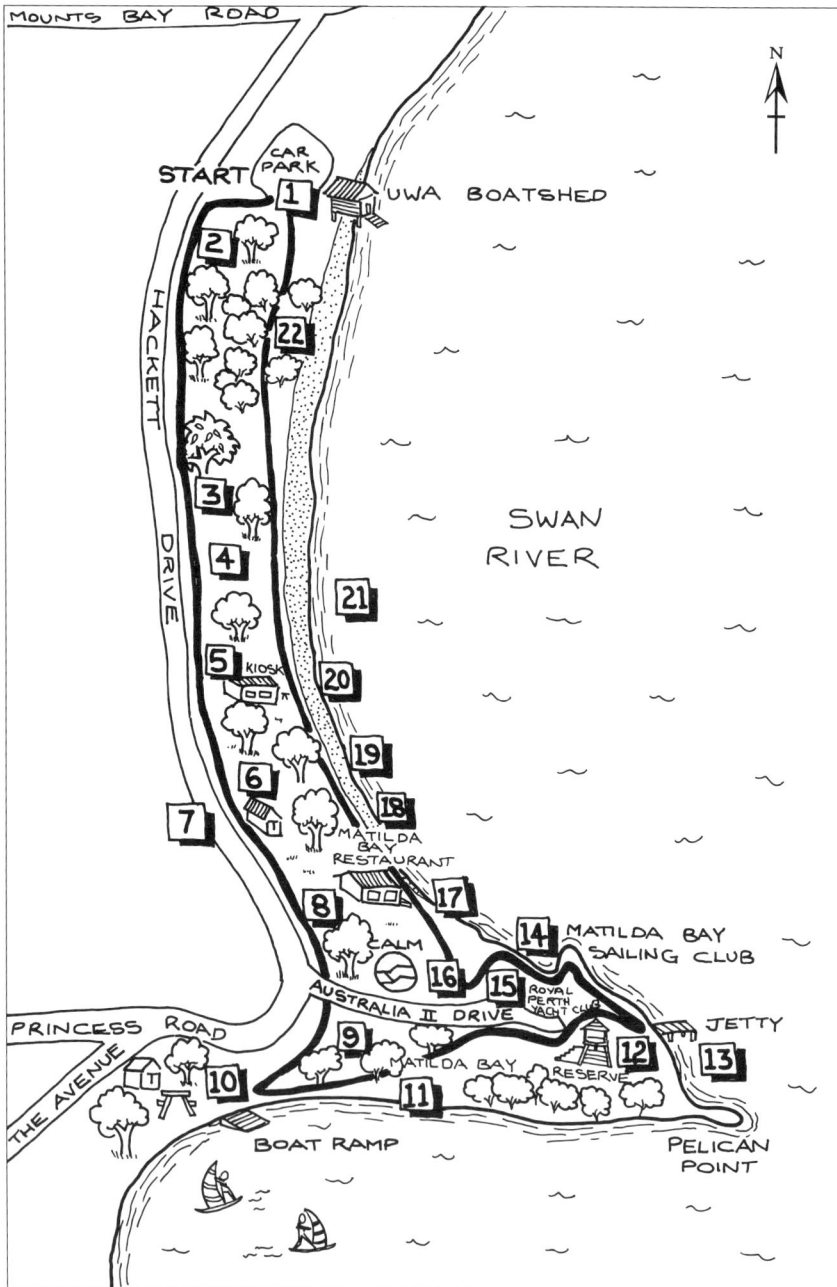

Pelican Point Walk · 33

Matilda Bay

Length: *3 kilometre loop*
Grade: *1*
Walk time: *1 hour 30 minutes*

This pleasant walk begins at the carpark on the corner of Mounts Bay Road and Hackett Drive. It passes through the tree-lined Matilda Bay Reserve to J H Abrahams Reserve, before visiting the Pelican Point Bird Observation tower and skirting along the foreshore on its return leg.

There are plenty of opportunities for picnicking along the route and the varied vistas of the Swan River make this a delightful riverside stroll.

1 Start from the carpark and walk down towards the UWA Guild Boat Shed (one of three boat shed on this stretch of the foreshore). This old wooden building is undergoing long-term renovation. From here, walk up the gentle grassy slope to the dual-use pathway that runs through the reserve.
2 The entrance sign for the reserve is located by the entrance to the carpark. Follow the dual-use path close to Hackett Drive past a variety of planted and native trees. Most trees in the reserve are labelled.
3 At this point there is a splendid Morton Bay fig.
4 The path continues beside a lawned area of shady trees. There are magnificent views of Mt Eliza and the city skyline across the bay. Sit awhile and enjoy the views.
5 Continue close to Hackett Drive and pass behind the Kiosk and Tea Rooms.
6 To the left of the track is an information board about the reserve.
7 Walk back to the roadside and pass behind the toilet and shower block.
8 Another shady lawned area ideal for picnics. Continue behind Matilda Bay Restaurant and cross Australia II Drive.
9 An open grassed area with planted trees and the first views of the south side of the river. Some of the planted trees commemorate Arbor Day and a tuart tree was planted here on 1 September 1989 (World Greenhouse Day) to commemorate the planting of the 13 millionth tree by CALM. Proceed to the boat ramp at J H Abrahams Reserve.
10 The section of river adjoining the J H Abrahams Reserve is popular with windsurfers. The reserve itself has shady picnic areas, BBQs, carpark and toilets.

11 Head back east through the grassy area and on to the end of Australia II Drive. The fenced area to your right is the Pelican Point Reserve—a sanctuary that adjoins part of the Swan Estuary Marine Park.

12 Climb the steps to the top of the Bird Observation Tower. From here, there are clear views across the river and into the reserve and marine park. Bird identification boards help you spot the wide variety of waterbirds found in this area.

13 Walk back down the steps and turn right towards a jetty, then walk north-west along the foreshore.

14 You pass the Matilda Bay Sailing Club and the Royal Perth Yacht Club.

15 Follow the fenceline past yachts and the dry dock to Australia II Drive, then cut back across the carpark on the other side of fence.

16 Pass in front of CALM's Corporate Headquarters. Here you will find a shady lawned area with seating. Stop and enjoy the views.

17 Matilda Bay Restaurant.

18 The lovely long sandy beach with swimming area is backed by open lawns and a small picnic shelter. There are some flame trees here.

19 This plaque commemorates the re-enactment of the voyage of exploration on the Swan River by Captain James Stirling, RN in March 1827. It marks the place where a modern-day 'Captain Stirling' and his party landed and were entertained by the Mayor and Councillors of the City of Subiaco and other guests on 9th March 1979, being the 150th Anniversary year of the European settlement in WA.

20 The Matilda Bay Kiosk has outdoor seating on the river's edge, sheltered by flame trees.

21 Sailboarding area.

22 There is an avenue of tea trees along this part of the reserve, and a paddle-boat hire facility by the shore. Make your way from here along the shoreline to the UWA Guild Boatshed and public carpark beyond.

Maria Duthie and Anastasia Strickland

Where is it?: *5 km south-west of Perth on Hackett Drive, adjacent to the University of Western Australia*
Travelling time: *10 minutes via Mounts Bay Road*
Facilities: *Picnic areas, parking, kiosk/tea rooms, toilets and showers, bird observation platform; BBQs at J H Abrahams Reserve*
On-site information: *Information shelter*
Best season: *All year*

GULLS

The species of gull found in and around the Perth area is the silver gull (*Larus novaehollandiae*). The bird is equally at home in city parks, inland river systems, rubbish dumps and coastal beaches. Most silver gulls in WA are found in the south-west of the State. They breed on about 100 islands around the coastline.

Silver gulls eat almost anything and their diet varies greatly with locality. They feed naturally on dead fish and crustaceans washed up in seaweed. Unfortunately, the great adaptability of silver gulls to human environments, especially open rubbish tips, and the bad habits of people hand-feeding them with food scraps, have seen this bird develop into an urban nuisance.

Seasonally, flocks of silver gulls will venture inland in a feeding frenzy over the suburbs to feast on flying ants. Immature gulls have brown eyes, legs and bills, while mature birds have white eyes with a red eye-ring and scarlet bills and legs.

Gulls are migratory birds and become regular residents of particular places, leaving only to breed and returning year after year.

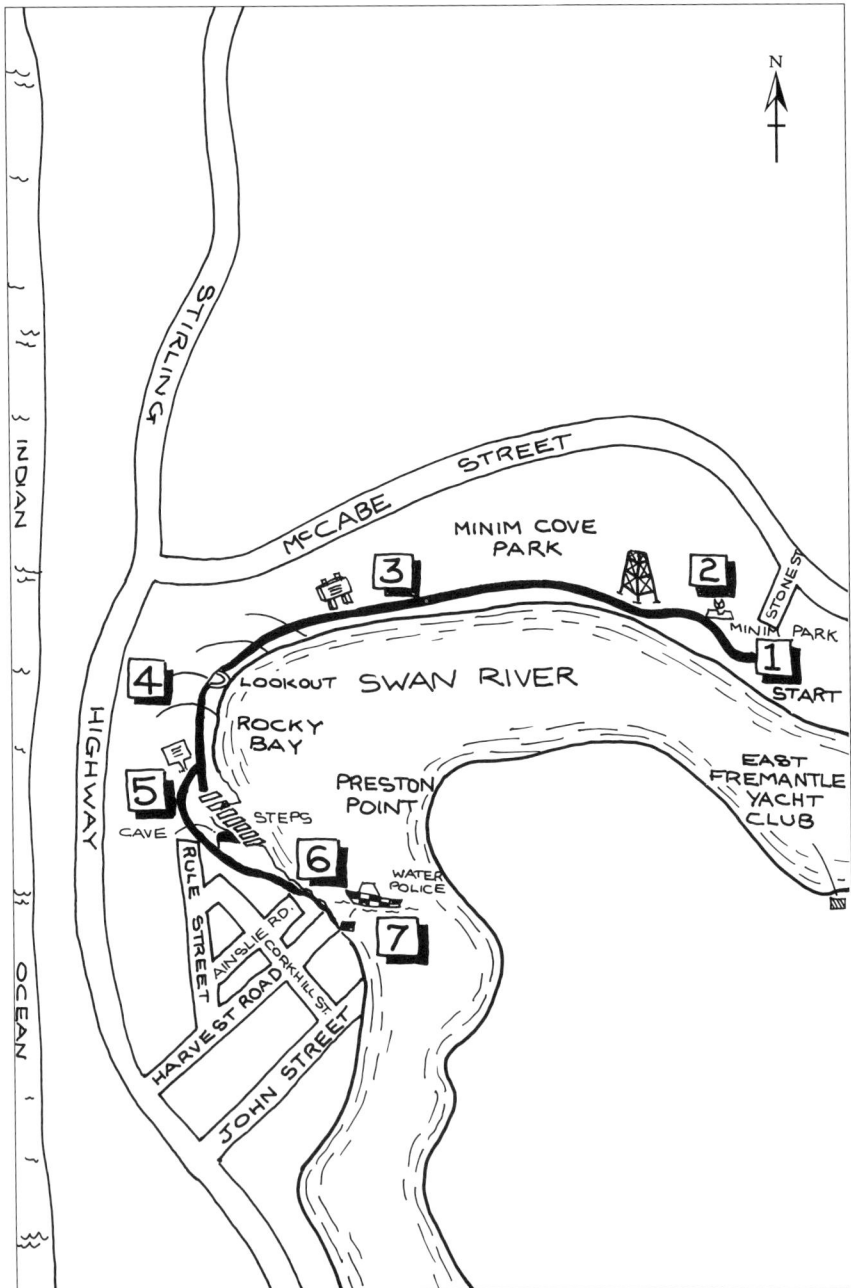

N

STIRLING

INDIAN

McCABE STREET

MINIM COVE
PARK

STONE ST

3

2

MINIM PARK

1
START

LOOKOUT SWAN RIVER

4

ROCKY
BAY

EAST
FREMANTLE
YACHT
CLUB

HIGHWAY

PRESTON
POINT

5

CAVE STEPS

6

WATER
POLICE

RULE STREET

AINSLIE RD.

CORKHILL ST

7

OCEAN

HARVEST ROAD

JOHN STREET

Rocky Bay Walk

34

Minim Park

Length: *6 kilometres return*
Grade: *1 to Rocky Bay Beach, 3 to Cypress Hill*
Walk time: *2 hours*

This walk has views across the Swan River to the East Fremantle Yacht Club. It follows an easy bricked path most of the way, then becomes a rough clifftop walk from Rocky Bay to Cypress Hill. The clifftop leg of the walk is optional.

1   Begin at Minim Park at the bottom of Stone Street, Mosman Park. This section of the walk also forms part of the Mosman Park Heritage Trail. Minim Park was an Aboriginal tool-making site about 10 000 years ago.
2   At the top of the first hill is a gas barbecue next to the brick path. A short way further on, the path forks. Take the left turn down towards the pylon. The path descends quickly at this point and continues for the next two kilometres.
3   A wooden sign (facing west) tells you when you are about to leave Minim Cove Park. The path soon begins to ascend as it follows the line of Rocky Bay.
4   A lookout affords a unique view in opposite directions: over the river and towards the sea. A plaque reveals some of the history of the site.
5   A sign marks the clifftop path down stone steps to Rocky Bay Beach and an Aboriginal cave, from where the *Waugal* is said to have emerged.
6   Cypress Hill provides a good view of the river in two directions. It is reached along a narrow cliff path, which is not clearly visible from the signs at Rocky Bay Beach; you will find it simply by walking along the cliff top. The path is often single-file only, and can be slippery when wet. **Take care if you have small children**.
7   The Water Police HQ is below Cypress Hill, beside a little foreshore area with shelters and drinking-water. The simplest way down to the foreshore is through the car park and down Ainslie, Corkhill and Harvest streets. Alternatively, there is a rough path that gradually descends around the hill to Harvest Street.

Liz and Ray Bailey

Where is it?: *12 km south-west of Perth, adjacent to Mosman Park Tennis Club*
Travelling time: *20 minutes from Perth via McCabe Street and Stone Street*
Facilities: *Wood BBQs, benches, playground*
On-site information: *Some interpretive signs along the route*
Best season: *All year*

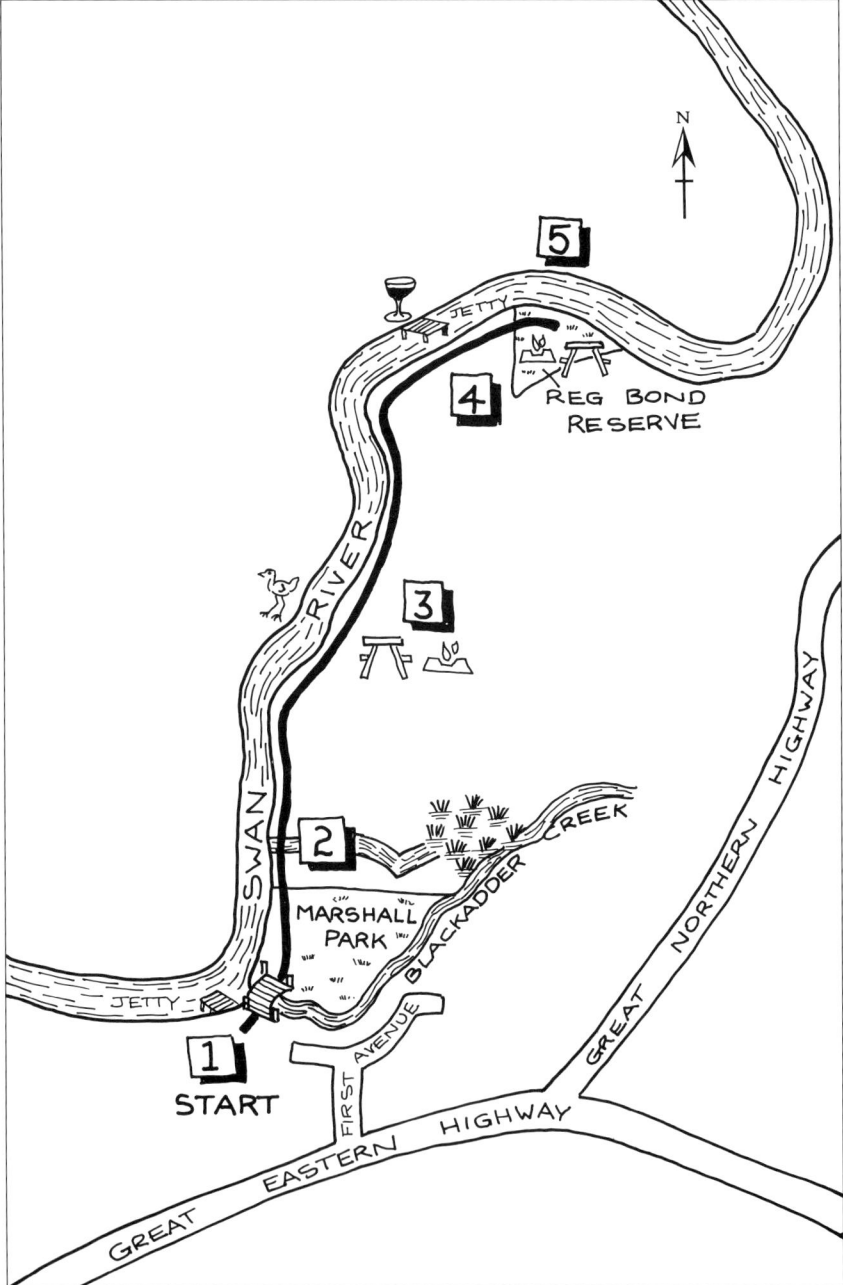

Swan River Heritage Trail 35

Marshall Park

Length: 5 kilometres return
Grade: 1
Walk time: 1 hour 30 minutes

This riverside walk starts at Marshall Park, a large park on the banks of the Swan River between Guildford and Midland. Much of the surrounding area is farmland and the walk runs upstream towards Reg Bond Reserve in Viveash. River cruises from Barrack Street Jetty, in Perth, pass here en route to vineyards and Mulberry Farm.

1   From Marshall Park, which has a fishing jetty and small swimming beach, head due north towards Blackadder Creek.
2   A wooden bridge takes you over the creek.
3   About half-way along the outward leg of the walktrail you will come across a barbecue and picnic table set alongside the river. Here, you can rest awhile and watch waterbirds and boats pass by.
4   Opposite this point, on the other side of the river, is a wooden jetty. Here, pleasure boat passengers alight for Caversham House and Sandalford Wines.
5   Reg Bond Reserve is just around the bend. Here, there are barbecues and picnic tables, but no toilets. After resting here, retrace your steps to Marshall Park.

Barbara Moss

Where is it?: Marshall Park, 15 km east of Perth
Travelling time: 25 minutes via Great Eastern Highway and First Avenue
Facilities: Picnic tables, wood BBQs, jetty, carpark
On-site information: None
Best season: Spring and autumn for greenery and cooler days

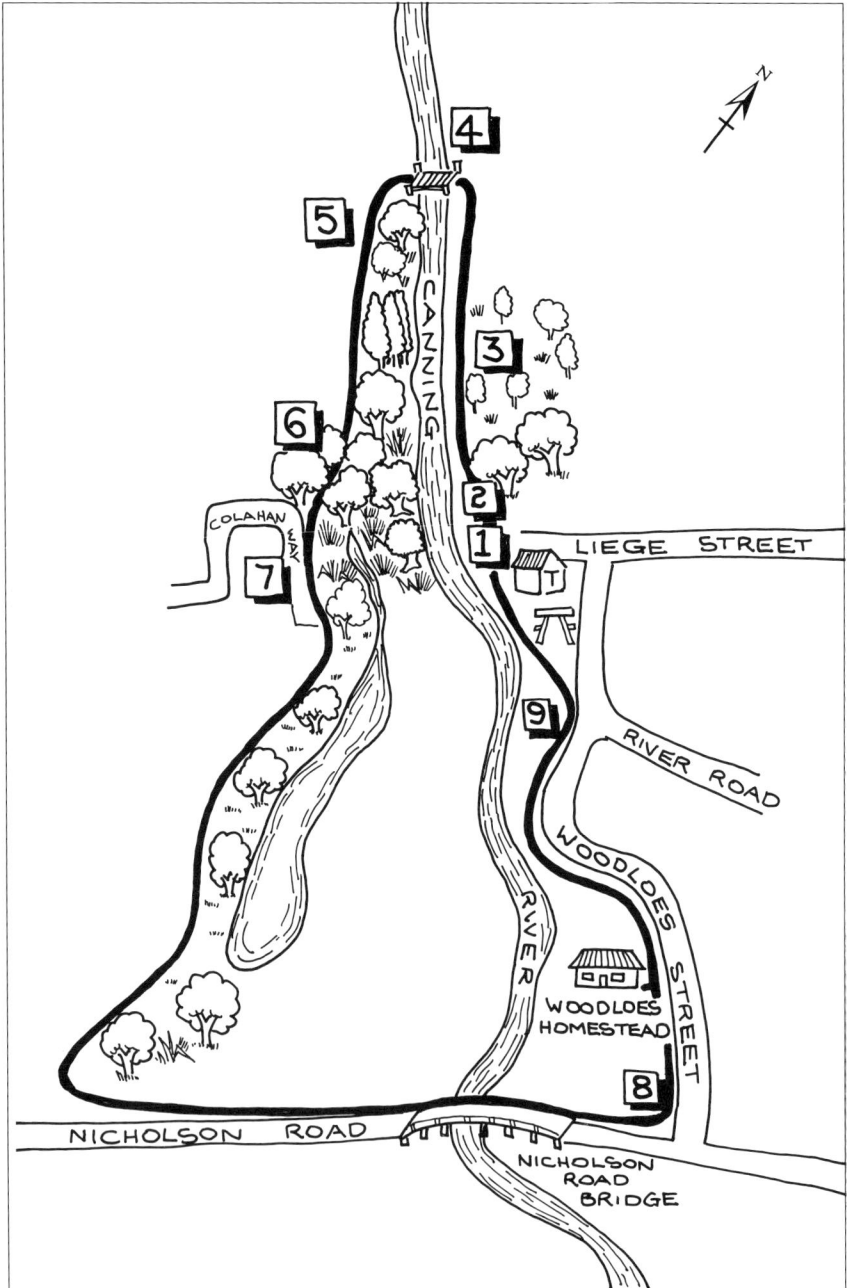

4

5

3

6

CANNING

COLAHAN WAY

2

1

LIEGE STREET

7

9

RIVER ROAD

WOODLOES STREET

RIVER

WOODLOES HOMESTEAD

8

NICHOLSON ROAD

NICHOLSON ROAD BRIDGE

N

Woodloes Walk

36

Canning River Regional Park

Length: *3.5 kilometre loop*
Grade: *2*
Walk time: *1 hour 30 minutes*

This walk begins near Mason's Landing where, in the 1800s, river barges used to take on timber from Mason's Mill (see Mason & Bird Heritage Trail on page 31) and transport it down river. The walk passes along both banks of the Canning River through riverside vegetation and past both old and modern housing. There is an opportunity to visit Woodloes Homestead, which is open on Sundays (check times).

1   Park in the carpark at the end of Liege Street. East of the carpark is Masons Landing, an open grassed area on the picturesque river bank. Flooded gums abound at the water's edge and waterfowl create a sound and spectacle.
2   The carpark is surrounded by flooded gums and some paperbarks. Black ducks, coots, and water hens are seen on the water. Across the river there is a shoreline of paperbarks and rushes with delta flats of grassland behind. At the north-west corner of the carpark is a trotting track, follow this and you will soon see the trail heading west.
3   The path here is on a slight rise through river delta covered in various grasses and weeds. Paperbark and eucalyptus seedlings have been planted at random on either side of the track. In spring, 'twenty-eight' parrots and mudlarks can be seen. Head west to a concrete path and turn left towards the river.
4   The Greenfield Street footbridge was constructed in 1964 when new housing estates were built south of the Canning River.
5   Now on the south bank of the river, the track is a dual-use bitumen path which, at first, passes through open parkland. On the water's edge are rushes, paperbarks and flooded gums. A little further on can be seen three very old and large poplar trees and a large flame tree. The sounds of many birds can be heard here emanating from thickets by the river.
6   The path at this point passes very close to housing, but at the same time, wetland thickets and high water ponds are within a few metres of the path on the riverside. Large flooded gums adorned with creeper overhang a section of the walk here creating a jungle experience. Shafts of sunlight cut through overhead foliage and reflect off pond water, lilies and dense undergrowth, which contains many frogs.

7   The path stops at times, but the 'trail' continues along road verges. At Colahan Way, the view to the river is grassland river flats with flooded gum and rushes, grazing ibis, ducks and swamphens. The waterway here is an offshoot floodway of the Canning River. To the right of the dual-use path is a children's playground. Continue towards the Nicholson Road Bridge past close housing, flooded gums, paperbarks and open grassland. Cross north over the bridge and head along the pathway to the corner of Woodloes Street.

8   Just prior to turning left into Woodloes Street, note the early 19th century housing here. Woodloes Homestead is a short distance along Woodloes Street on the left. On Sundays (when open) you can see through the property, which has been restored into a museum. Note the huge Chinese pepper tree in the front yard and the enormous exotic pine on the right of the building. Continue west along Woodloes Street.

9   At the end of Woodloes Street, turn left into River Road and back to Mason's Landing picnic area and the carpark beyond.

John Hunter

Where is it?: *Mason's Landing, 15 km south-east of Perth*
Travelling time: *25 minutes via Albany Highway and Liege Street*
Facilities: *BBQs, playground, gazebo, canoe launch, toilets*
On-site information: *Plaque about Mason's Landing*
Best season: *All year*

The South   Walks 37 - 52

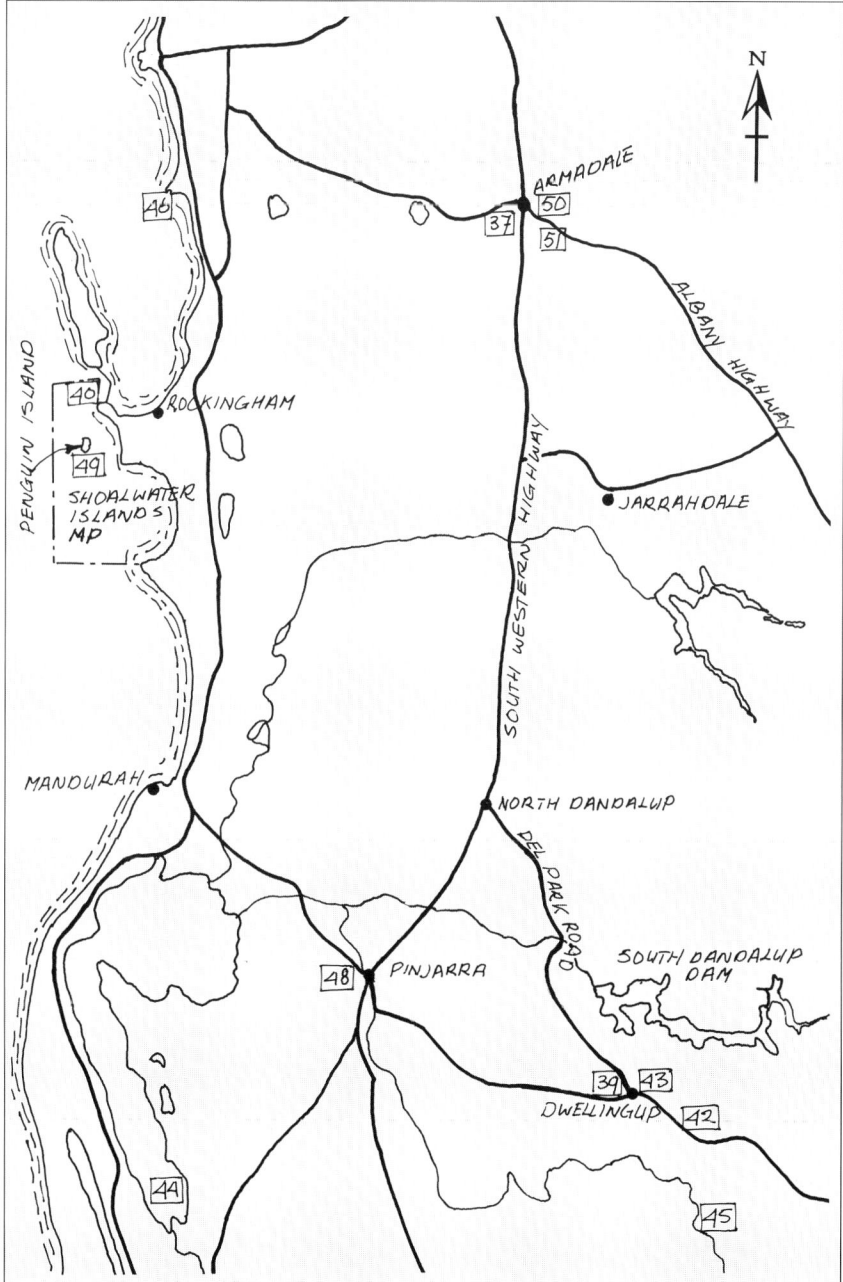

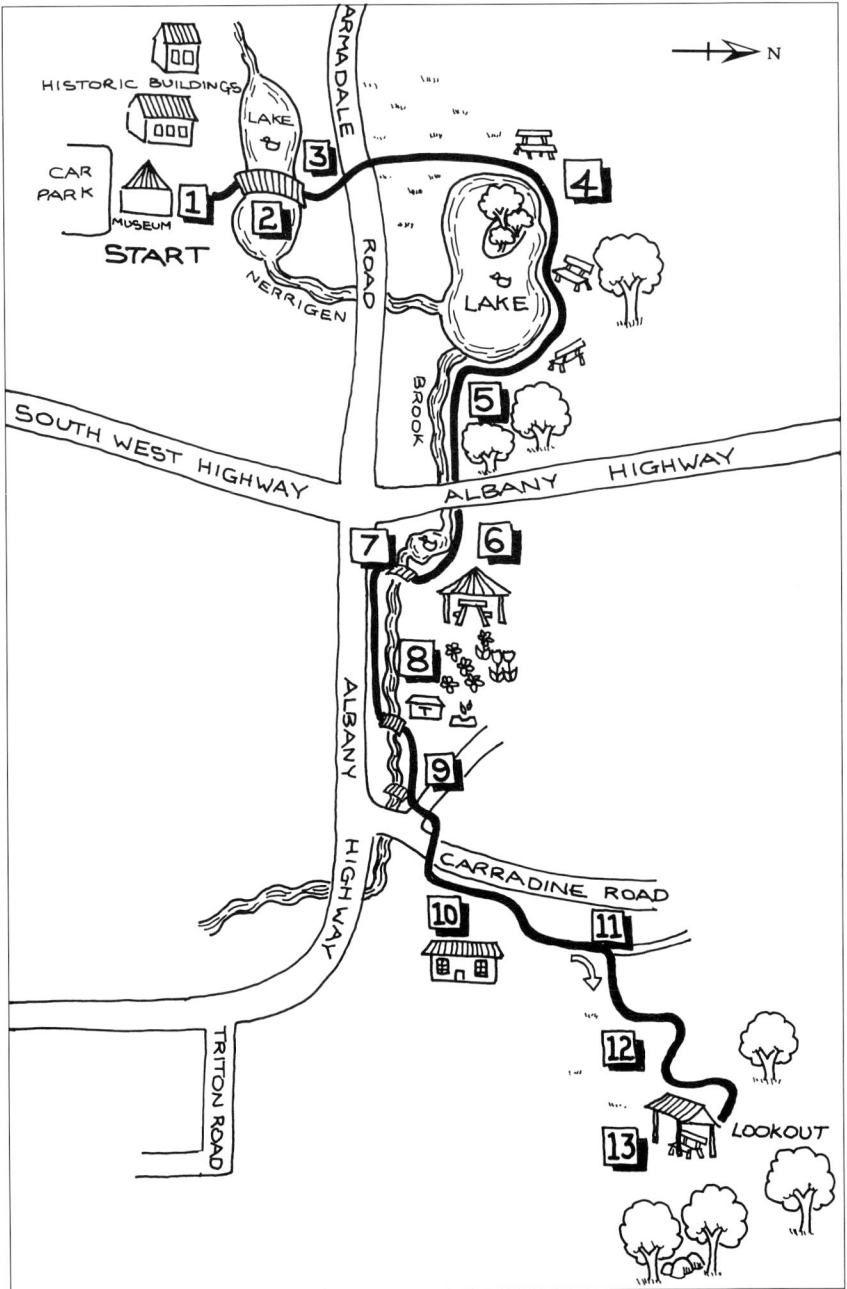

Armadale Tourist Walk   **37**
Minnawara Park

Length: *3 kilometres return*
Grade: *2*
Walk time: *2 hours*

This walk begins at Minnawara Park and the historic buildings of Armadale Museum. Parking is available close by. The first part of the walk follows the Neerigen Brook. It then heads uphill to a lookout above Armadale Primary School.

1   Start from the historic buildings of Armadale townsite and head towards the lake. Take time to visit the museum at the end of your walk.
2   The lake, which is visited by many waterfowl, is set in attractive gardens and fed by Neerigen Brook. Cross the lake using the wooden bridge. Carry straight on towards Armadale Road.
3   Cross the road and make your way across the large grassed area towards the western side of the next lake.
4   Follow the lake edge in a clockwise direction and note the island and the waterbirds found there. There are seats along this section which you may like to use on your return.
5   On the edge of the lake, follow along the north side of Neerigen Brook and pass beneath Albany Highway.
6   Emerging on the opposite side of the road you will see a small pool frequented by local families of ducks. There is also a shaded picnic table and seats. Walk along the edge of the pool.
7   You will soon come to a footbridge. Cross over Neerigen Brook and walk alongside Albany Highway.
8   Part of the way along this section you will see a private property with beautiful gardens on the opposite side of the brook.
9   Cross the brook again at the footbridge opposite the toilets and walk through the picnic area. Cross Carradine Road near the school.
10 Pick up the footpath and walk past the school along the east side of Carradine Road.
11 Within a few minutes you will see a track that branches right and up the hill. Turn right here.
12 From this point on, the path rises steadily in a zig-zag fashion for about 500 m through open grassland.

13 The path ends at a lookout, where sheltered seats allow you to relax awhile and enjoy outstanding views of the surrounding hills and distant coastline. Retrace your steps back to Minnawara Park.

June Ellis

Where is it?: *Minnawara Park, Armadale, 27 km south-east of Perth*
Travelling time: *45 minutes via Albany Highway and Armadale Road*
Facilities: *Carpark, toilets, picnic area halfway along route*
On-site information: *None*
Best season: *All year, except hot summer days*

BUTTERFLIES AND MOTHS

In recent years, many of Western Australia's beautiful and interesting butterflies have dwindled greatly in numbers. Although 116 butterfly species are listed as being found in Western Australia, the one most commonly seen today is the introduced cabbage white (*Pieris rapae*). Fortunately though, some other attractive species are still around, but often we don't take time to notice.

To find these moving jewels of the bush and garden, simply watch out for the preferred decorative and nectar supplying plants such as lantanas and buddleia, and natives such as pimelias, melaleucas and bottlebrushes. Many butterflies prefer plants with blue flowers.

The brilliant blue amaryllis azure, chooses mistletoe foliage on which to lay its eggs. The caterpillars are tended throughout their lives by little black ants, which take honeydew given off by the grubs, which in return are shepherded into the shelter of loose bark, or down to the ant's nest in daytime. At night, the ants escort the caterpillars back to their feeding areas.

Moths, as opposed to butterflies, are often extremely 'downy'—an appearance created by long soft scales. Their generally hairy, feather-like antennae are also often covered in large downy scales, whereas butterflies are characterised by their distinctive clubbed antennae.

There are vastly more species of moths than of butterflies and, unlike butterflies, almost all of them fly at night. When stationary, for example on a stem or leaf, most moths hold their wings flat with the forewing covering the hindwing; butterflies tend to fold their wings upright with the duller underside showing, only occasionally opening them to provide a flash of colour.

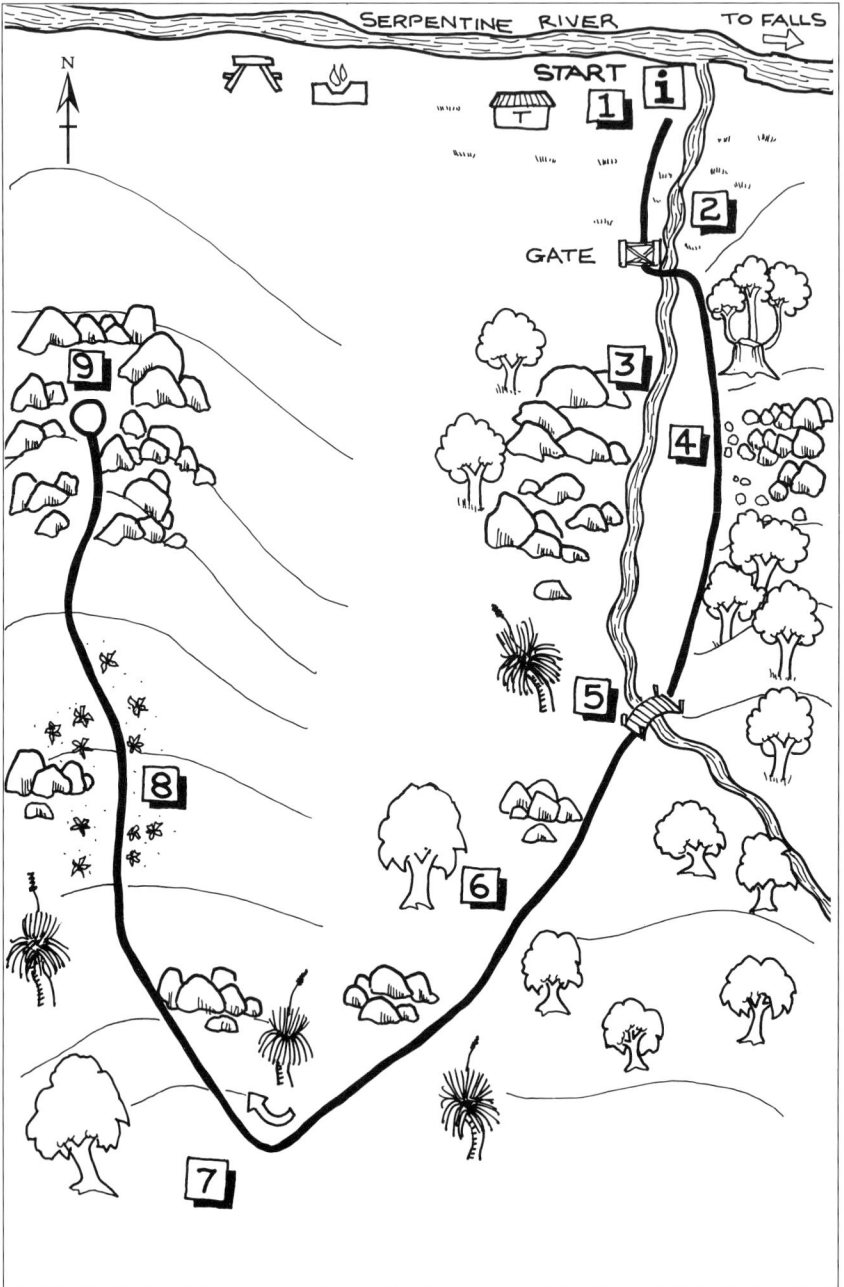

SERPENTINE RIVER   TO FALLS

N

START

GATE

1 i
2
3
4
5
6
7
8
9

Baldwins Bluff Nature Trail **38**

Serpentine National Park ($)

Length: *6 kilometres return*
Grade: *2*
Walk time: *2 hours*

Baldwins Bluff is a large granite outcrop on a north-facing part of the Darling Scarp. At 180 m above sea level, it gives uninterrupted views. During the ascent, you pass through areas of redgum and wandoo forest. The walk features a variety of plant and bird species, scenic views and spectacular granite outcrops.

1   From the information board, walk south behind the public toilets where you will pick up the trail markers.
2   The trail then passes through about 200 m of previously grazed paddock, note the absence of native flora. This land was added to the park in summer 1993.
3   Here, on the left, is an old redgum stump regenerated by coppice shoots. These form when a mature tree is damaged by wind or storm, or when it is cut down.
4   This granite outcrop gives the impression that there has been a landslide. This is not the case.
5   The trail crosses a small stream. Note that the forest trees have changed from redgum to wandoo.
6   Continue up the trail. At this point, take the time to listen for the native birds, especially 'twenty eight' and western king parrots.
7   Turn right here. From this point, the trail meanders along the top of the scarp.
8   Along this part of the trail is an abundant show of wildflowers (in season). There are also several small granite outcrops. If you are quiet, you may see a dragon lizard or two, sunning themselves on the rocks.
9   The summit provides excellent panoramic views of Serpentine Falls and the pastured valleys beyond. Looking west, you can see across the coastal plain to the ocean beyond from Bunbury in the south, to the Perth skyline in the north. After enjoying the views, return to the start along the same route.

Wayne Taylor

Where is it?: *Serpentine National Park, 50 km south-east of Perth*
Travelling time: *1 hour from Perth via South Western Highway*
Facilities: *Carpark, picnic area, toilets, BBQs, water*
On-site information: *Information board, trail markers*
Best Season: *Winter, spring*

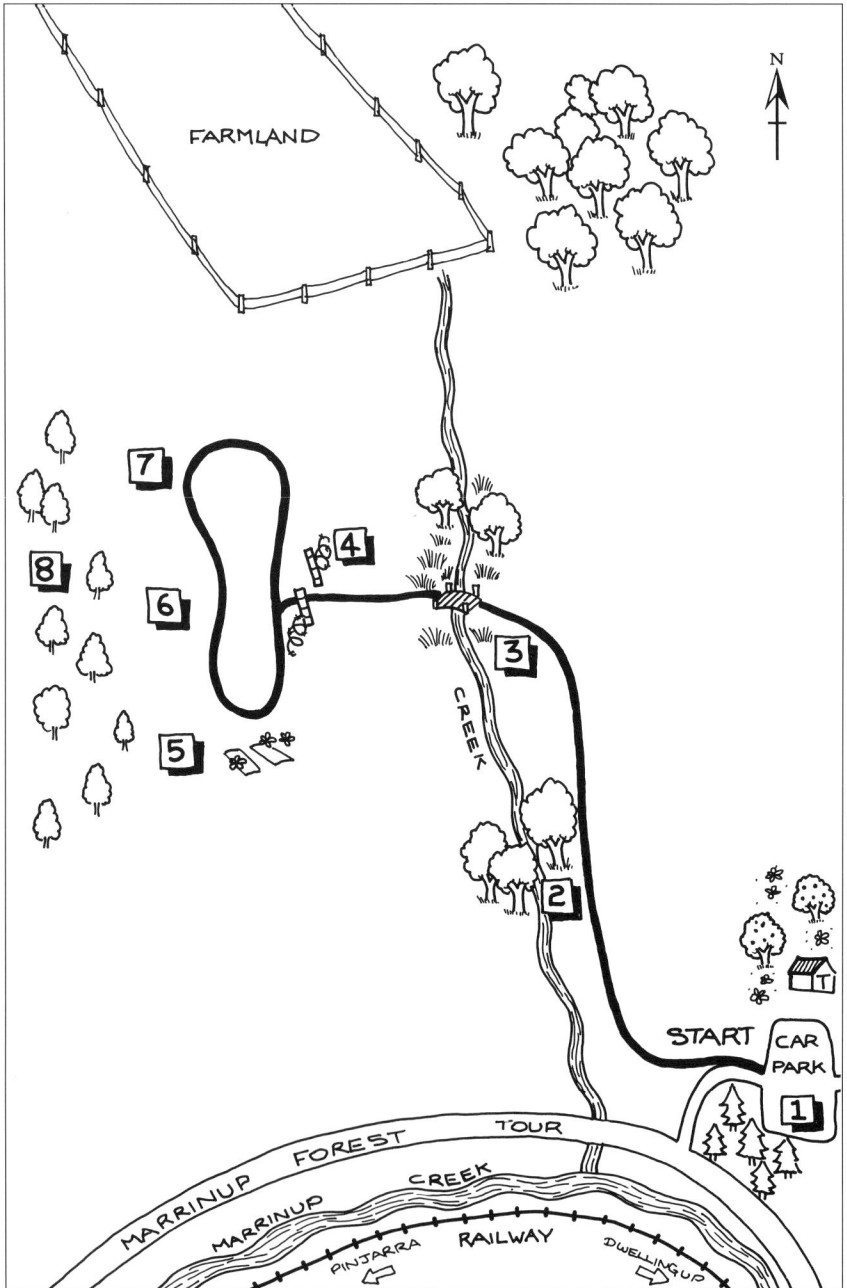

N

FARMLAND

7

4

8   6

3

CREEK

5

2

START   CAR
PARK

T

1

MARRINUP FOREST TOUR

MARRINUP   CREEK

PINJARRA   RAILWAY   DWELLINGUP

124

Cage in the Bush Walktrail 39
Marrinup

Length: *4.5 kilometres return*
Grade: *2*
Walk time: *2 hours*

Between 1943 and 1946, some 200 German and 1 300 Italian POWs were housed or supervised from Marrinup POW camp 16. The walktrail runs from Marrinup Townsite, a few kilometres north-west of Dwellingup, to the site of the POW camp. It passes through forested areas and along an old tramway before arriving at the entrance to the camp.

1 The old Marrinup Townsite was established in the 1880s to harvest jarrah. Timber resource declined and operations moved to Dwellingup. The wildfire of 1961 burnt what remained of the townsite.
2 Large blackbutt trees can be seen growing in the fertile soil of the creek lines.
3 The wooden sleepers of old tramway, built for hauling jarrah logs, can still be seen in place. An old creaky bridge crosses a creek that flows for most of the year.
4 Entrance to the POW camp. Information panels display photographs of camp life in the 1940s.
5 Commanding Officer's area. Here, prisoners were allowed to build and tend flower gardens. Old beds, picked out in gravel stones, are still visible.
6 The German compound area has labelled foundations. German prisoners were used as woodcutters, supplying firewood from the surrounding jarrah forest to Perth. Some 2 500 tonnes per week was shipped.
7 The Italian compound was basically a transit area for workers on their way to farms or rural control centres.
8 The area around the camp and some of the sleeping hut area has been mined for bauxite. These areas have since been landscaped and replanted. All the other forest around the POW camp is the native jarrah and redgum, which is mostly regrowth after the onslaught of the POW firewood cutters.

Tammie Reid

Where is it?: *Marrinup (off Del Park Road), 100 km south of Perth*
Travelling time: *2 hours, follow Marrinup Forest Tour sign near Dwellingup*
Facilities: *Carpark, toilets, picnic area, BBQs*
On-site information: *Trail markers*
Best season: *All year, except hot summer days*

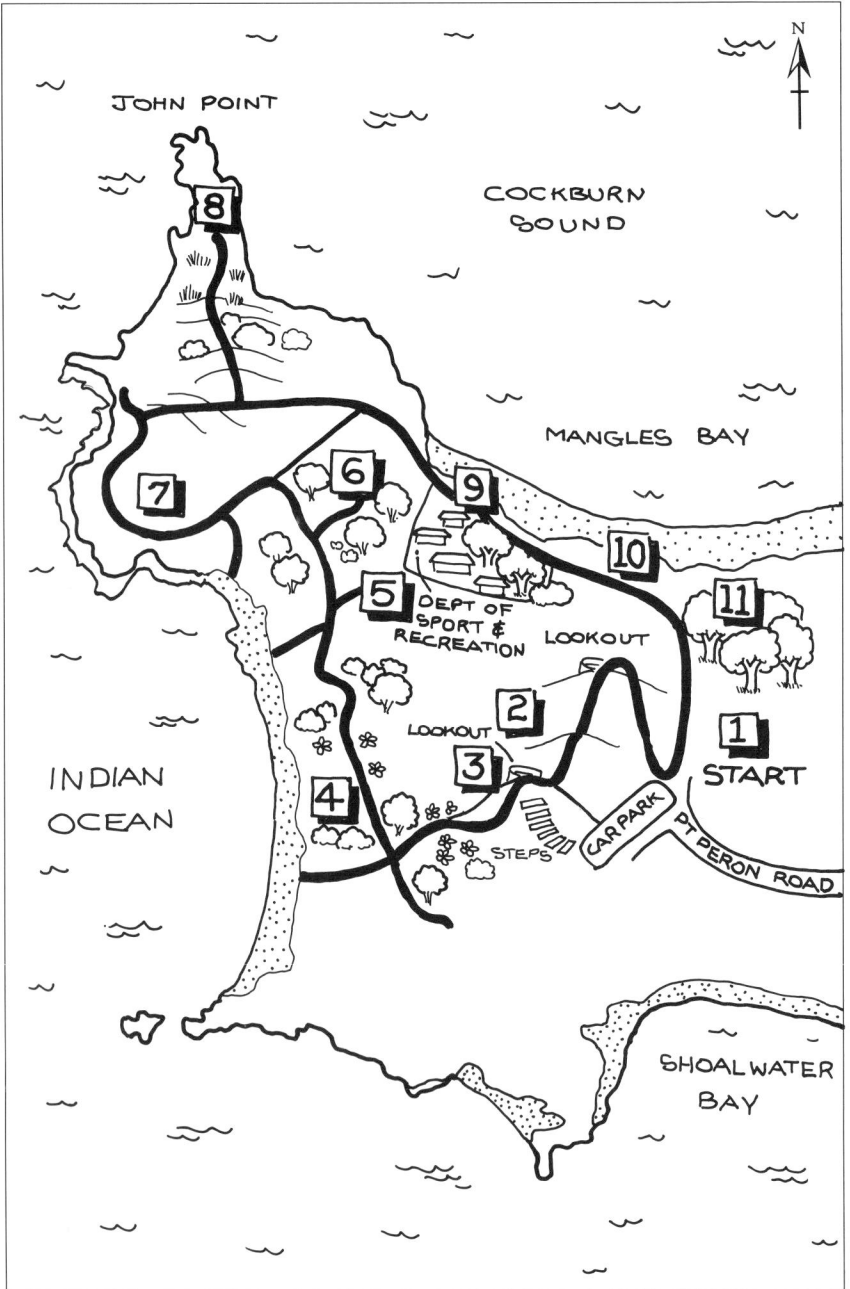

N

JOHN POINT

COCKBURN SOUND

8

MANGLES BAY

7

6

9

10

11

5

DEPT OF SPORT & RECREATION

LOOKOUT

2

1

LOOKOUT

INDIAN OCEAN

3

4

START

STEPS

CAR PARK

PT PERON ROAD

SHOALWATER BAY

Cape Peron Walktrail   **40**

by Shoalwater Islands Marine Park

Length: *2.5 kilometre loop*
Grade: *1 (some steep gradients at start)*
Walk time: *1 hour 20 minutes*

This walk gives spectacular panoramic views of the coastline, a look at the remnant coastal vegetation and the chance to see many sea and land birds. It also gives access to the gun emplacements and associated buildings of one of the World War II coastal batteries set up to defend the approaches to Garden Island and Fremantle. Walkers follow a consolidated limestone pathway which has been fenced in most parts to protect the vegetation.

1   The pathway begins at the northern end of the first car park and climbs quite steeply to the lookout, giving glimpses of the sea on the way.
2   Down the slope to the right is the coastal battery's command post. Once camouflaged by thick vegetation, it is now exposed to view and walkers leaving the track have caused erosion.
3   The two-level lookout, with survey marker on top, was once the field observation post for the battery. It now gives a superb bird's eye view of the Shoalwater Islands Marine Park to the south; Rockingham and the coastal plains, across to the Darling Range in the east; and Garden Island, with its naval base linked to the mainland by a long causeway, to the north. The crest of the Army Engineers unit, which built the battery, can be seen inside. The lookout may also be reached from the car park by a very steep flight of stairs.
4   Leaving the lookout, the track is now fenced to prevent uncontrolled access to the fragile coastal vegetation on the cape's undulating sand dunes. Turn right at the junction and head north. Unfortunately, you will see many introduced plants along the track, including patches of creamy daisies in this area.
5   Tracks to the right lead to gun emplacement No 2, which has been dangerously undermined by erosion and appears to be sliding down the hill.
6   Gun emplacement No 1 is very well-preserved, having been completely covered by sand until recently cleared by the crew of *HMAS Adelaide*. The 155 mm guns moved around in a 270° sweep to cover coastal shipping. The associated buildings are floor shelters for personnel and underground ordnance and storage buildings. The coastal scrub is seen at its best here in sheltered hollows, protected from the strong winter winds. Many of the small trees are wattles, which make attractive patches of colour in spring.

127

7 When back on the main pathway, turn left at the 'T' junction. Side tracks in this area lead down to lovely little bays with rocky limestone cliffs, headlands and fringing reefs. Some also have sandy beaches. Weathering has sculptured the limestone into fantastic shapes in many places. Large numbers of seabirds can often be seen on the offshore islets, or stacks. Walkers and fishermen are advised to keep clear of the cliff edges, which are fragile and liable to collapse.

8 Turn right along the ridge, then left and continue on through low-growing coastal vegetation, grass and sword sedge to John Point at the end of the cape. This rocky headland was flattened during the war to provide the base for a searchlight.

9 Return to the main track and turn left. Walk along the north-east shore of the cape past the Department of Sport and Recreation camp, which was once the barracks for the coastal battery. Taller trees and shrubs are found on the right in areas protected from the wind.

10 From here, you have a good view of Garden Island and its causeway, with the Cockburn Sound industrial area in the background. The causeway has caused sand to bank up and form a wide beach with a large bar at right angles to the shore. Fine stands of spiky-headed spinifex flourish in the dunes.

11 A small number of tuart trees an be seen here. Tuarts are found on sand overlying shallow limestone formations along the coast from Moore River to Busselton. Continue to the carpark and your starting point.

Hillary Merrifield

Where is it?: *51 km south of Perth, at the end of Point Peron Road, Rockingham*
Travelling time: *1 hour from Perth*
Facilities: *None*
On-site information: *Revegetation and warning signs along route*
Best season: *All year*

SOUTHERN BROWN BANDICOOT (QUENDA)

Ever been strolling through an outer suburban bushland or park and zzzip, right before your eyes, a 'rat' dashes across the track from under a patch of scrub? Well, its probably not a rodent, but more likely a southern brown bandicoot or quenda.

Bandicoots prefer habitats of dense low vegetation that is infrequently burnt. The density of vegetation provides some protection from foxes and cats, while the diversity supports abundant insect food.

The southern brown bandicoot is primarily a nocturnal marsupial. When searching for food, it digs shallow conical holes with its powerful fore claws. Although the animals often stay close to cover, residents in the Darling Range near Perth frequently see them feeding on open lawns.

During the day, it usually sleeps in a well-hidden nest, which it builds on the ground in a thicket using grass and plant material mixed with earth.

European settlement, the spread of agriculture and the predation by introduced animals such as foxes and cats have been detrimental to the bandicoots, which now have a patchy distribution over a diminishing range. For this reason they have been declared as threatened.

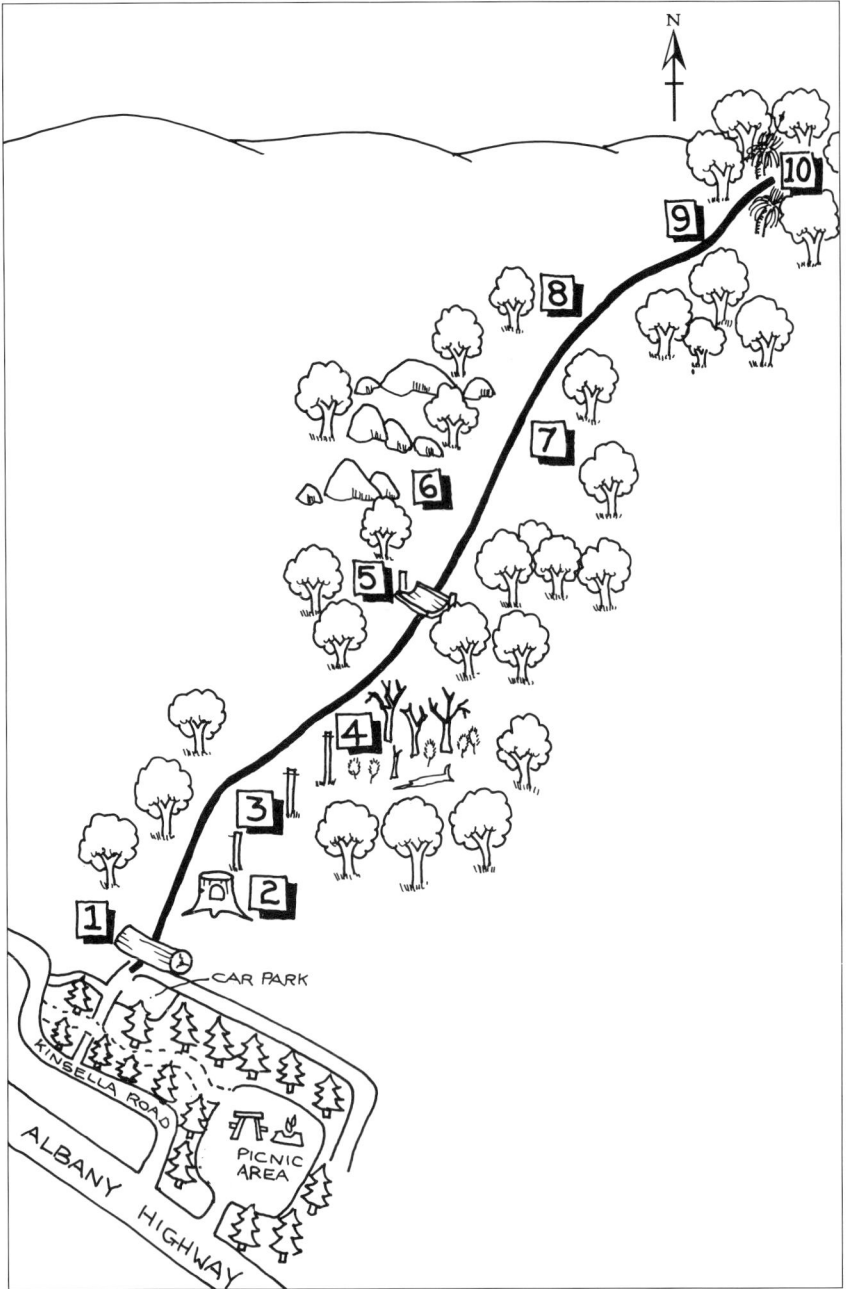

Eagle Hill Trail   **41**

Gleneagle

Length: *3.2 kilometres return*
Grade: *3–4*
Walk time: *2 hours 15 minutes*

Eagle Hill was once a fire tower for the adjacent Gleneagles Pine Plantation and Forestry Settlement. With the closure of the settlement and the advent of fire spotter-planes, the access track was blocked off and the surrounding forests were quarantined to prevent the introduction of dieback. The track is still open to walkers and, although the views from the hilltop are obscured by regrowth, the walk is pleasant and quite easy, apart from the odd fallen tree across the track.

To find where to park, first come about 2.5 km along Kinsella Road from Albany Highway. At a sharp left-hand curve in the road (at the end of the third straight section of road), some large pine trees leaning over the road herald the end and northern tip of Gleneagles Plantation. At this point, there is a small track that starts under these last pines and then turns sharp right. This is the boundary track between Gleneagles Plantation and the Quarantine Forest Monadnocks Conservation Park. Follow this track 1.1 km to a 'T' junction and then turn left. Continue on another 300 m until a sharp right-hand corner, where the old road continues on straight ahead; this is where you will be walking. There is only limited parking at this corner.

1   Climb over the barrier log and head straight uphill through veteran sheoak trees and a few storm victims lying across the track.
2   About 100 m up you may notice an old shield 'marker tree' (BC70) 10 m in on the right. It is now only a stump bearing the footpeg-hole marks of a bygone hand falling era.
3   About 150 m on, the road curves gently to the right. Here, keen observers may spot the old grey bush telegraph poles just off the track—the last remains of the same era of fire tower lookouts, of which Eagle Hill tower was one of many.
4   At about 450 m up the hill, the bush on the right becomes open, following an attack of dieback, and old jarrah skeletons allow us a view of the Gleneagles Plantation below and the hinterland hills of the Monadnocks Conservation Park. The re-coloniser plant parrotbush fills the understorey as the old telegraph cable on its live redgum supporter appear at the track edge.
5   Hints of exposed granite begin to appear on the left as the track crosses another relic from the hand-made era, a wooden box culvert drain complete with guide posts.

6   Boulders, moss and lichen then give us visual images after playing out their dynamics over time with fire, weathering, and the seasons. Road builders of old followed the edge of this rocky theatre in their quest for a practical route to the hilltop lookout.
7   The boulders turn to rocky outcrops on the left of the track, as the forest on the right stands unaffected—perhaps trying to claim back some of its old marginal territory of the track.
8   Still a gentle upward slope, the track begins to straddle the ridge, as a steep gully forms on the right.
9   Thinner vegetation allows a glimpse towards the Wheatbelt for the only vista to the north-east.
10 Lichen grows on the bare exposed clay of the track, as parrotbush, balgas (blackboys) and regrowth marri and jarrah begin to win back their old domain at the summit. Only a few domestic relics remain on the hilltop to hint at the now long-burnt, vigilant fire tower, barely noticeable even to the spotter planes overhead that replaced it.

Andy Darbyshire

Where is it?: *55 km south-east of Perth on the Albany Highway*
Travelling time: *1 hour 20 minutes via Kinsella Road*
Facilities: *BBQs, seats, tables, playground, toilets at Gleneagle*
On-site information: *None*
Best season: *All year, except hot summer days*

WEDGE-TAILED EAGLE

One of the most maligned birds of prey, the wedge-tailed eagle (*Aquila audax*) was persecuted for decades because of the misapprehensions that it was a destroyer of agricultural livestock. It is one of the larger of the world's nine or so 'booted' eagles and now enjoys full protection.

The 'wedgie', nests in a variety of sites depending on the landscape: in a low dead tree in a desert, a prominent tree top on a hillside, on the ground on an island or on a cliff, but always far away from human habitation.

Immature eagles move out of breeders' territories, some moving to the coastal plains where often they are surprised feeding in groups like vultures squabbling over carrion road kills.

There is a great colour variation, many birds being a general blackish-brown to nearly black, while others are a pale brown with creamy-buff highlights.

While most individuals are seen in country areas gliding over paddocks and woodland, scanning the suburban skies with binoculars on any day will enable you to pick up a bird which is otherwise invisible.

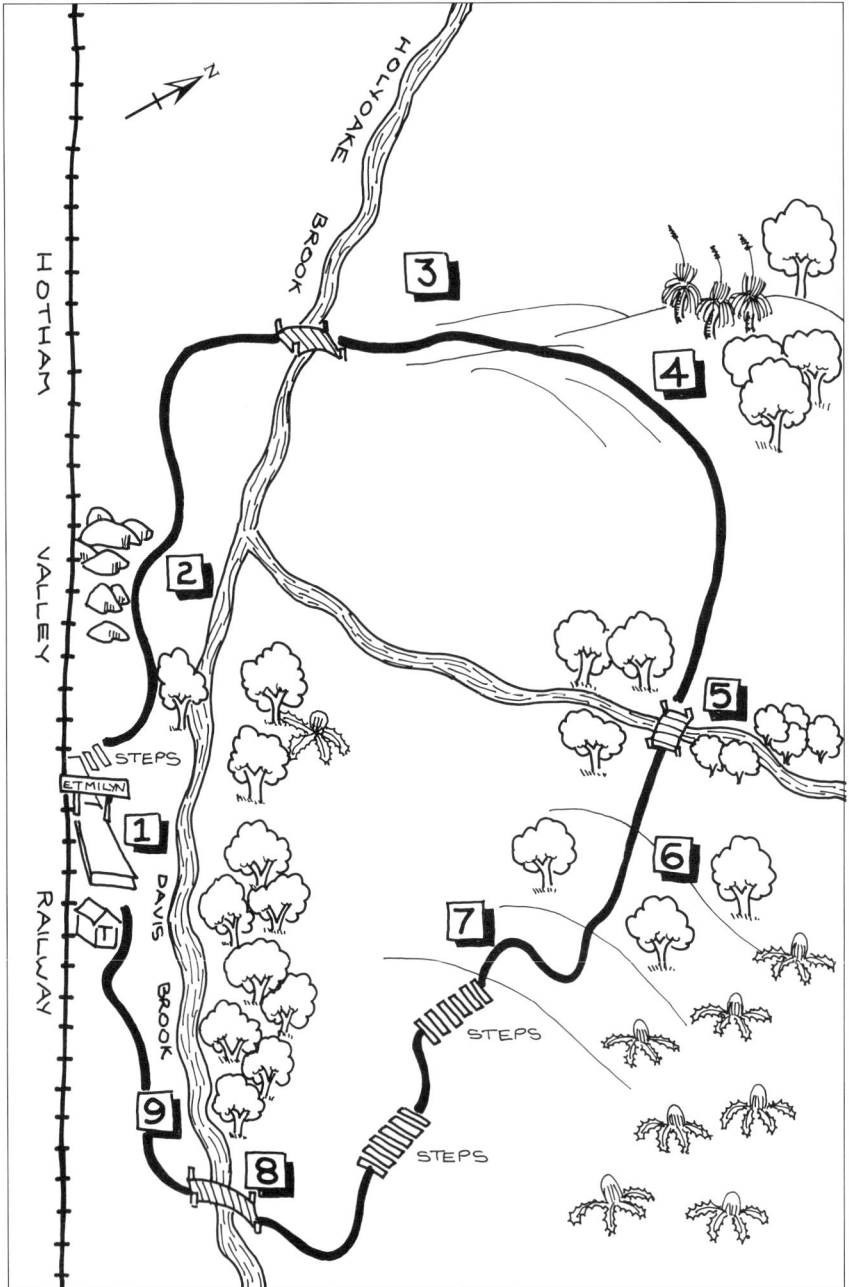

HOLYOAKE BROOK

HOTHAM VALLEY RAILWAY

DAVIS BROOK

N

3

4

2

5

6

7

STEPS

STEPS

STEPS

ETMILYN

1

T

9

8

Etmilyn Forest Trail **42**
Etmilyn Siding near Dwellingup

Length: *1 kilometre loop*
Grade: *3 (some slippery sections and steps)*
Walk time: *30 minutes (plus 1 hour return train journey)*

This loop trail is an integral part of the Etmilyn Forest Heritage Trail, which can be done by taking the train from Dwellingup Station along the Etmilyn Tramway Trail (see next trail) first, then alighting here and walking along the forest trail.

The trail features excellent examples of jarrah, blackbutt, marri, balga (blackboy), banksia and a variety of forest vegetation, some unique to this part of the forest. It climbs the north side of the valley, looping around through jarrah forest growing on the higher drier sites, before descending to the creek and back to the siding. There are good views across the valley without much exertion! It's only a little valley system, but it has a cosy feel to it.

Etmilyn Siding was first established in the early 1920s as a steam locomotive watering point, with water coming from a small dam and gravity fed to an overhead tank at the railway siding.

1   Start at the site of the old water tank (foundations visible) and follow the forest track to the left.
2   Trail winds along the Davis Brook, through blackbutt trees. This species seeks out moist deep valley soils in which to grow. There are also marri and banksias along this stretch. On the left is a granite outcrop, which is a good place to spot for orchids.
3   Cross the brook via the footbridge. There is a large granite outcrop to your left and you can see the flooded gum near the creek. This tree has smooth white upper branches while fibrous on the lower trunk. It is able to withstand 'wet feet', growing on the edges of rivers and creek systems.
4   This uphill section marks the transition from wetter deeper valley soils to drier, rockier, higher ground. The hillside here is dominated by balgas. The forest on this steep slope is old and mature—the tops are dying back not from disease, but from old age. They are probably more than 250 years old.
5   The trail crosses a creek. The blackbutts again dominate the wet, deep soil. Soap bush is found in the creek. This is a two-metre shrub with oak-like leaves that lather up and are useful for washing hands (detergent free and hence, environmentally friendly!). They have a pungent smell when flowering in late winter to early spring.

6   Now the trail works its way higher around the hillside. Lots of coral fungus grows on the lower side of track in winter months. The deep, red, lateritic soil has been exposed by trail cutting. Eucalypt forest has very little soil nutrients—low in nitrogen and phosphate. Plants have adapted by having a huge root system (banksias), root nodules to 'fix' the nitrogen (wattles), or internal input nutrient recycling abilities (jarrah).

7   From this point there are good views across the little valley. You can spot the species distribution as you look into the grey-blue leafy tree tops of the blackbutt in the creek and across to the brighter lighter green of the jarrah on the upper slopes. Continue down a series of steps to the creek below.

8   Many birds inhabit the creek, where there are more insects, dense cover and good nesting perches. There is a termite (white ant) mound on the edge of the footbridge. Termites are important in the jarrah forest as they help to breakdown tough leaves, twigs and wood which are absorbed into the soil and taken up again by the tree roots. While termites do a good job in the forest, they are also good food for echidnas, who claw mounds such as these to get to their favourite food.

9   Follow the track back to the rail siding. Note the jarrah sleepers, which were used extensively in railways around the world, but have since been largely replaced by concrete sleepers.

Tammie Reid

Where is it?: *Etmilyn Forest near Dwellingup, 100 km south of Perth*
Travelling time: *1 hour 30 minutes via South Western Highway and South Dandalup Dam (turn off highway at North Dandalup)*
Facilities: *Toilets at the siding*
On-site information: *Hotham Valley Tourist Railway Guides*
Best season: *All year, except hot summer days*

RACEHORSE GOANNA (BUNGARRA)

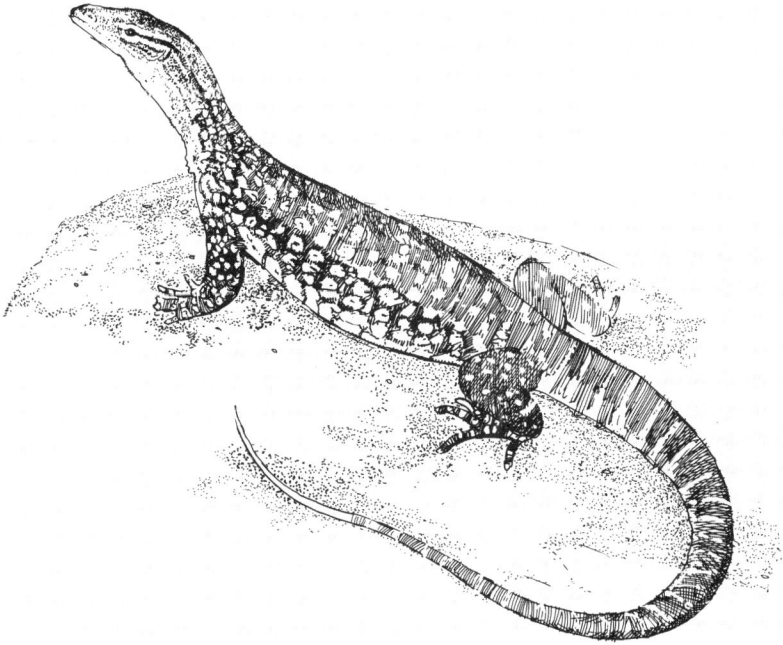

The bungarra or racehorse goanna is probably found in the larger natural park areas of our metro region. It is found throughout the State, with the biggest specimens reaching about two metres in length, but the usual sighting is about one metre.

Bungarras (*Varanus gouldii*) have sharp claws and powerful limbs, which are used in self defence or when helping to dismember prey. If cornered or approached brashly, they may raise and inflate their bodies, sometimes standing on their hind legs. Their colour is generally a dark brown with yellowish splotches in horizontal lines.

The name 'racehorse' was given because their best defence is their great speed in escaping danger.

These widespread lizards are primarily carnivorous, feeding on plants, animals, refuse and carrion. Bungarras are most active during the warmer months of spring and summer, but when it is very hot they shelter in burrows, cracks and crevices. They usually have a specific large home range or territory and use several burrows within that territory at night.

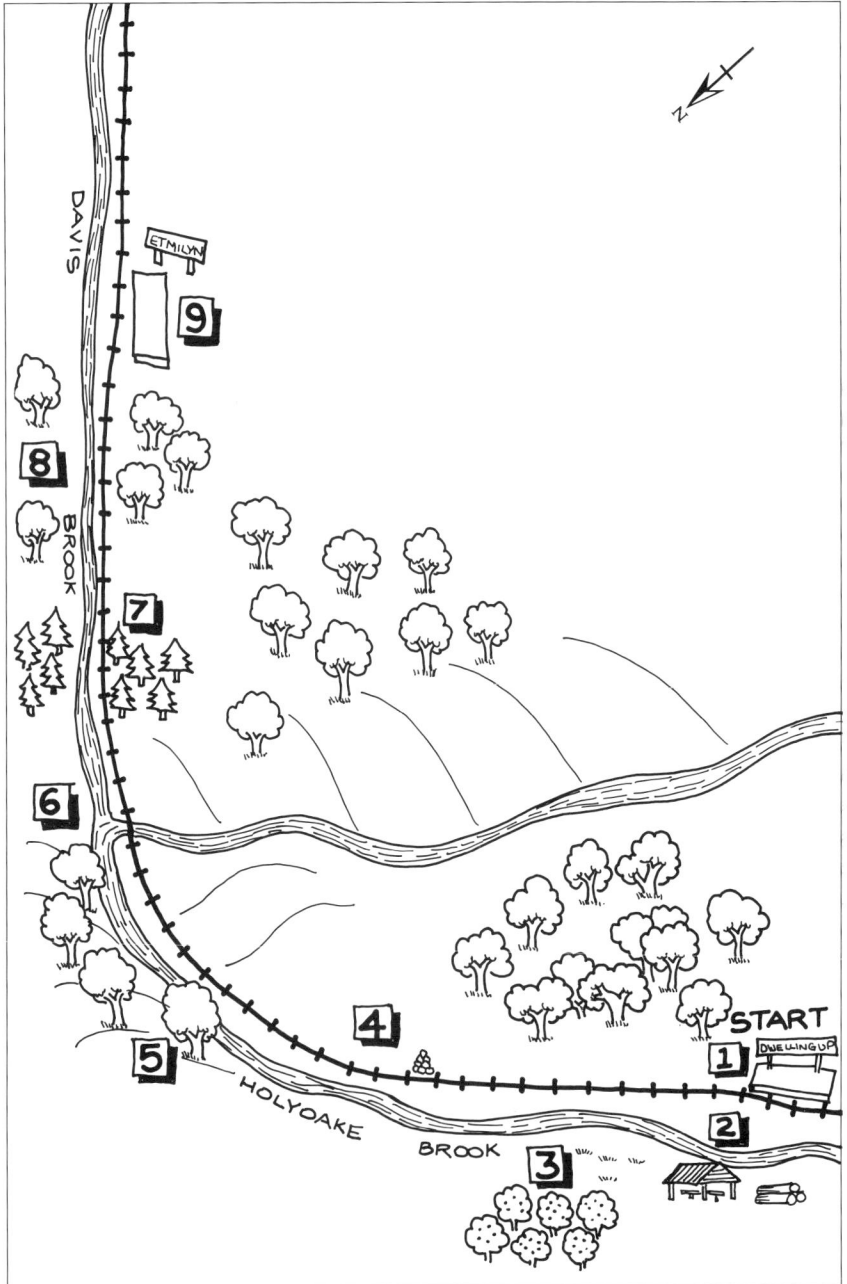

N

DAVIS

ETMILYN

9

8

BROOK

7

6

START

DWELLINGUP

1

4

2

5

HOLYOAKE

BROOK

3

Etmilyn Tramway Trail 　　43

Dwellingup ($)

Length: 12 kilometres return
Grade: 1 (seated all the way!)
Walk time: 1 hour 30 minutes (plus 30 minute stop at Etmilyn Siding)

This is the easiest walk in the book—it involves no walking at all! We have included it because it is the perfect prelude to the Etmilyn Forest Walk and is an integral part of the Etmilyn Forest Heritage Trail. It runs along the Holyoake Brook valley past old and modern timber mills and bush tramways that stretched out in the forests around Dwellingup and what is now the Lane Poole Reserve.

NOTE:

❖ Trains depart Dwellingup at 2 pm every Tuesday, Thursday, Saturday and Sunday.

❖ Trains are steam-hauled on weekends between May and October and during October school holidays.

❖ Check details and times with Hotham Valley Tourist Railway

1 The train departs from Dwellingup Station.

2 On the left is the Coli Jarrah Mill. Beginning on the right is a section of jarrah forest that is regularly low-intensity burned as part of the Dwellingup Townsite protection plan. Dwellingup and many of the surrounding mills were destroyed in a massive wildfire in 1961.

3 To the right, the jarrah forest is still dominant. On the left are orchards of smallholdings. Holyoake Brook is now seen alongside the railway and a small swamp (Quokka Swamp) is visible in the orchards.

4 The old Holyoake townsite was not rebuilt after the 1961 fire. The foundations of the mill are still visible on the left of the track. Just before here, on the right, is a memorial cairn to the original Holyoake residents.

5 The steep valley sides along this section are heavily wooded. Although close to the railway, the steep sides prevented timber being cut from this area and many of the mature blackbutt and jarrah trees are older than 200 years. The oldest jarrah sampled was found to be more than 375 years old.

6 At this point, Holyoake Brook meets Davis Brook, which flows under the tracks and away towards the Murray River. The jarrah forest on the hillside to the right of the track beyond the intersection was heavily cut before the 1920s. High quality regrowth produces sawlogs today.

7   Here, a private pine plantation was recently thinned (1993) and contains radiata pines aged 20 or so years.
8   Blackbutt trees dominate the creekline along this whole section of the tramway.
9   Etmilyn Siding. Here, you alight the train to sit in the forest or walk the Etmilyn Forest Trail (see previous trail). The train returns to Dwellingup station after a stop of 30 minutes.

Tammie Reid

Where is it?: *Dwellingup, 100 km south of Perth*
Travelling time: *1 hour 30 minutes via South Western Highway and South Dandalup Dam (turn off highway at North Dandalup)*
Facilities: *Toilets on train and at Etmilyn Siding*
On-site information: *Brochure available from Dwellingup Station*
Best season: *All year (Check times with Hotham Valley Tourist Railway)*

RED-BACK SPIDER

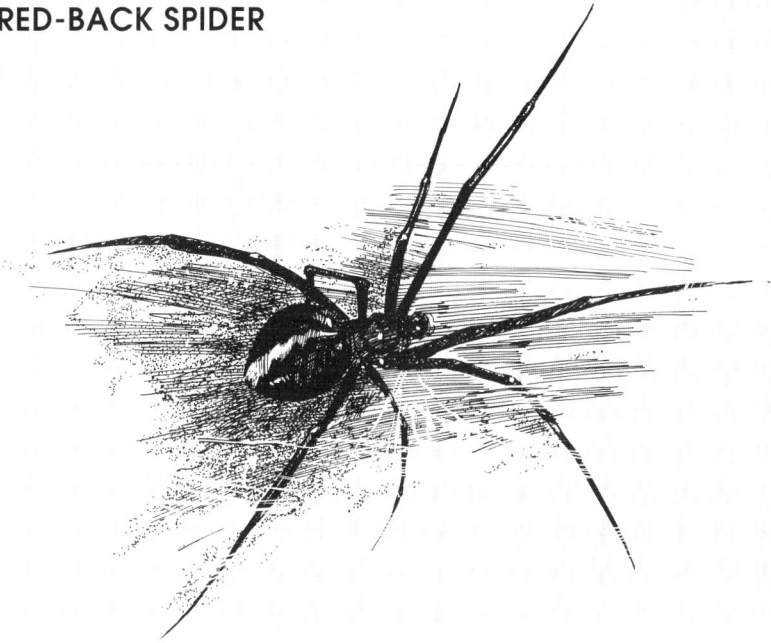

The venomous red-back spider (*Latrodectus hasseltii*) is the most well-known and feared spider in Western Australia. It tends to colonise hot places like stacked building materials, garden sheds, garages, back verandahs and outside toilets. However, these spiders are also found in bushland areas, often tucked away near the base of clumps of vegetation, such as grasses, or under logs and leaf litter.

Large adult females are black with a distinctive orange-red stripe down the middle of the abdomen and a red hour-glass patch on the underside. Their homes are a small tangled web with trip lines, which tell the spider of snared prey. The spider is aggressive and will often rise-up on its hind legs when disturbed. Children accidentally disturbing the spider or its trip lines have been bitten, sometimes fatally. But with care and the correct treatment, this need not happen.

The warm and hot times of the year see these animals thrive. With a large female there is usually a small and potentially harmless male somewhat paler and lacking a red stripe. The male's fangs are too small to pierce human skin. In the female's web are usually found yellow or pinkish coloured egg-sacks.

Details of what to do if bitten by a red-back spider are given on page 13.

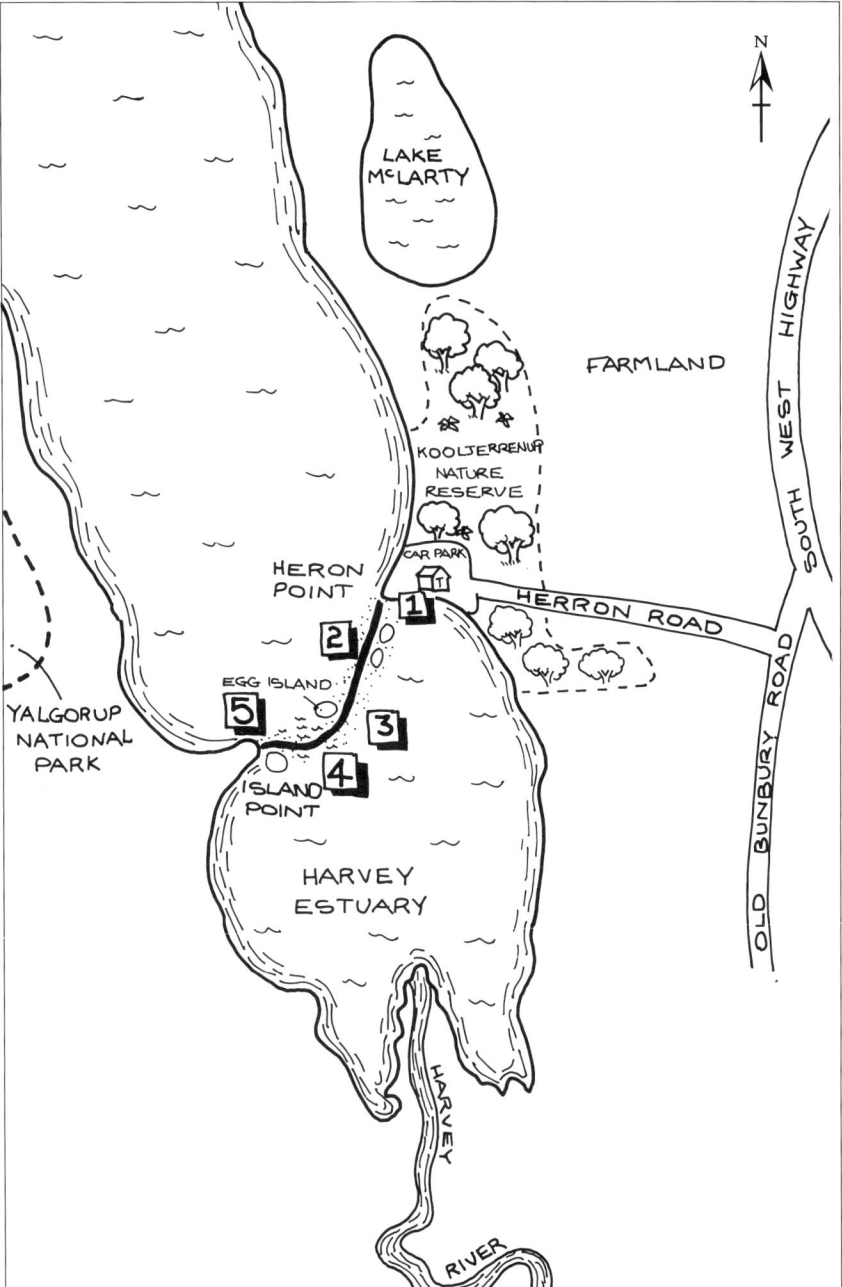

N

LAKE
McLARTY

FARMLAND

SOUTH WEST HIGHWAY

KOOLJERRENUP
NATURE
RESERVE

CAR PARK

HERON
POINT

1

HERRON ROAD

2

OLD BUNBURY ROAD

EGG ISLAND

5

3

YALGORUP
NATIONAL
PARK

4

ISLAND
POINT

HARVEY
ESTUARY

HARVEY

RIVER

Herron Point Causeway Walk

44

Harvey Estuary

Length: *2.5 kilometres return*
Grade: *4 (deep water section)*
Walk time: *2 hours*

This is probably the most unusual walk in the book, as it entails walking or wading through water. It is best done during the summer, when you can wear thongs and bathers, or shorts.

Herron Point to Island Point, on the west side, is a crossing discovered by settlers on horseback who were pursuing an Aboriginal fugitive and saw him ford the estuary at this point. It was marked with a line of poles, but can be picked out by eye. For most of the way it is ankle deep and the sandbar adjoins the little islands. About two-thirds of the way across, there is a channel that is waist deep for a short distance before becoming shallow again.

1   The walk begins at the camping area at the west end of Herron Point Road. The surrounding forest and woodland is Kooljerrenup Nature Reserve, which contains rare orchids.
2   A shallow sandy bar links small islands. Crabs can be seen scuttling along on the sandy bottom. Prawns can be netted here in season.
3   Egg Island. According to Nyoongar Aboriginal tradition, this was the site of a ceremonial ground, the focal point of which was a white egg-shaped stone, a little larger than an emu egg. The egg stone was reputedly moved by two European Australians, but was returned when they fell ill.
4   Deeper channel. This crossing was used by horse and carts. It is part of the Peel-Murray Bridle trail from the Dwellingup forests to Lake Preston. You may decide to cross this channel by wading through it, or choose to return from here.
5   Congratulations! You have reached Island Point. This is also an old Nyoongar camping spot. Rest awhile, then head back across the channel and causeway to Herron Point.

Tammie Reid

Where is it?: *Herron Point Road, Coolup, 110 km south of Perth*
Travelling time: *1 hour 55 minutes via Pinjarra and Old Bunbury Road*
Facilities: *Camping area, carpark, toilets*
On-site information: *None*
Best season: *Best in summer with bathers or shorts and thongs*

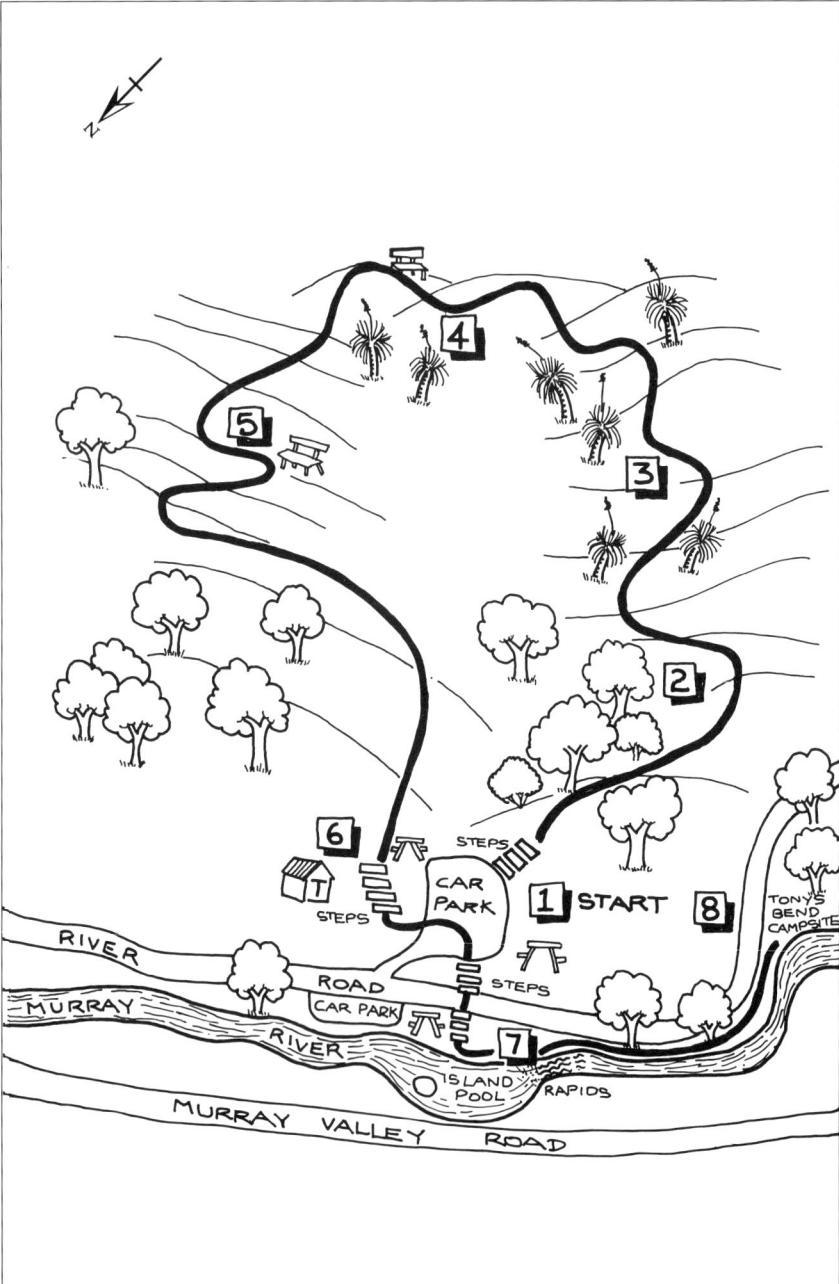

N

4

5

3

2

6

T

STEPS

CAR
PARK

STEPS

1 START

8

TONY'S
BEND
CAMPSITE

RIVER

ROAD

STEPS

MURRAY

CAR PARK

RIVER

7

ISLAND
POOL

RAPIDS

MURRAY VALLEY ROAD

Island Pool Walktrail   **45**

Lane Poole Reserve

Length: *1.5 kilometre loop*
Grade: *3 (some steeper sections)*
Walk time: *45 minutes*

This walk leads up the side of the Murray Valley and, although steep in places, provides excellent views of the valley and river. It passes through tall straight jarrah trees and, further up the valley, a host of balgas (blackboys). The last part of the walk is along the river to Tony's Bend campsite and back to Island Pool. Island Pool is a day-use only site. Overnight camping is available at Tony's Bend, about 100 m upstream—details from CALM's Dwellingup office.

1   The trail leaves the southern corner of the carpark, up a flight of steps and a steep rise through jarrah forest and wattles.
2   At this point, the forest begins to thin a little and the balgas become more numerous. Continue along a more gentle slope up the valley side.
3   Balgas begin to dominate as the trail passes between granite outcrops.
4   You are now at the highest part of the trail. There is a seat where you can rest awhile and take in the views of the valley and the Murray River below. After your rest, begin the descent down a more gentle slope.
5   At this point there is another seat. The track zig-zags for a short distance down a steeper part of the valley side and moves back into jarrah forest.
6   As you cross the carpark, descend the steps to the road. Cross the road and walk down to the river side.
7   The main picnic area is beside the river. There is a rope swing over the water and the small island is clearly visible. This is a popular swimming spot on warm days. From here, walk upstream past a series of small rapids. The riverside vegetation is dominated by flooded gums and blackbutts.
8   Tony's Bend campsite is about 100 m from Island Pool. The area is shaded for most of the day by jarrah and marri forest. Return along the riverside to Island Pool.

John Hanel

Where is it?: *100 km south of Perth, 17 km from Dwellingup*
Travelling time: *2 hours via Dwellingup and River Road*
Facilities: *BBQs, tables, toilets; camping at Tony's Bend*
On-site information: *Triangle symbols along the route*
Best season: *Winter for fast flowing river, spring for wildflowers*

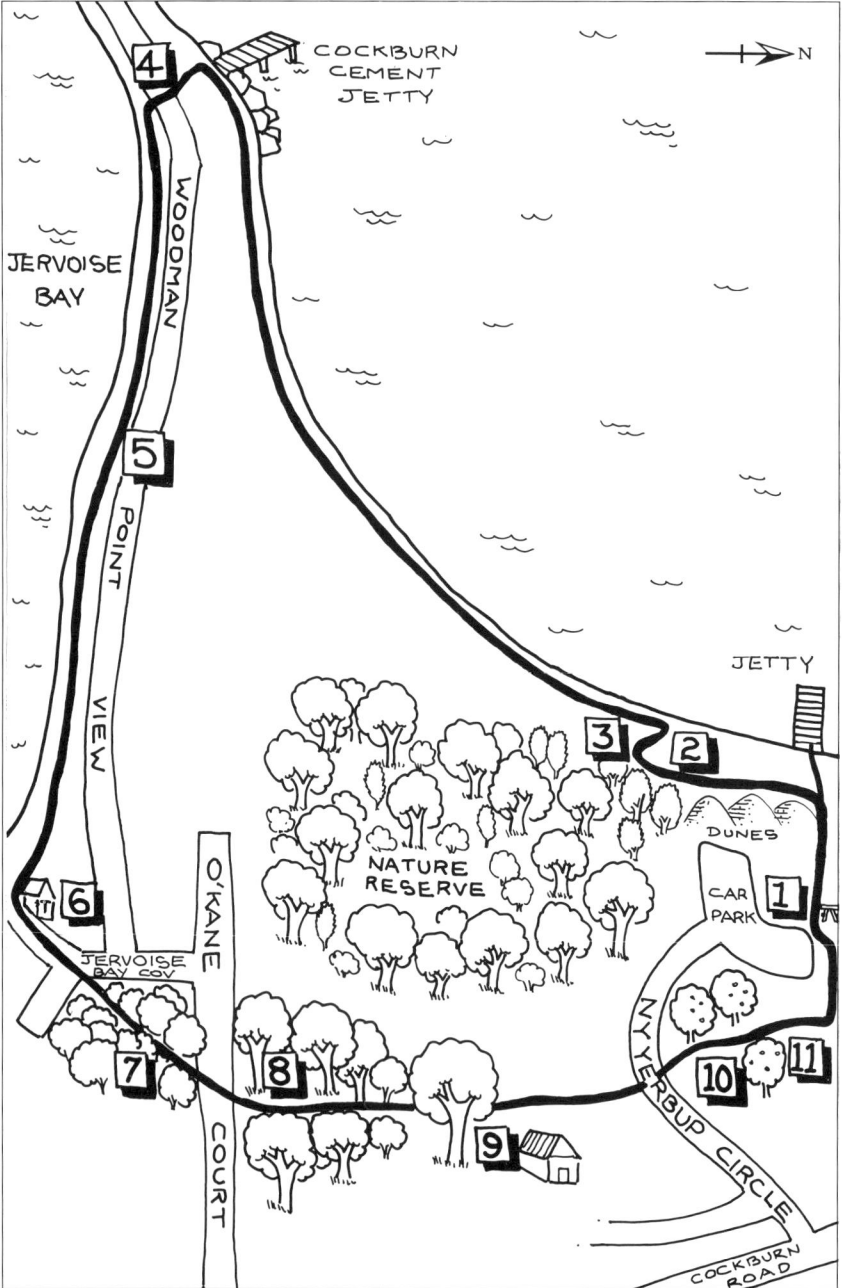

N

COCKBURN
CEMENT
JETTY

4

WOODMAN

JERVOISE
BAY

5

POINT

VIEW

JETTY

3

2

NATURE
RESERVE

DUNES

CAR
PARK

1

6

O'KANE

JERVOISE
BAY COV

7

8

9

NYYERBUP CIRCLE

10

11

COURT

COCKBURN
ROAD

Jervoise Bay Walktrail   **46**

Woodman Point

Length: 4.5 *kilometre loop*
Grade: 2
Walk time: 2 *hours*

Woodman Point Recreation Reserve is a purpose-built recreation area with planted peppermints and some remnant stands of tuart, as well as typical coastal dune vegetation. At the south end is a conservation reserve with stands of Rottnest cypress, tuarts, wattles, basket bush and quandongs.

This walk takes you along the foreshore north of Woodman Point peninsula, beside the reserve and across the isthmus to Jervois Bay, before cutting back along the other side of the reserve and back to the picnic area.

1   Starting from the picnic area, walk towards the jetty. Follow the dual-use path down the second left-hand junction.
2   On the left of the path is the fenced conservation reserve. The reserve is noted for its representations of tuart woodland and Rottnest cypress trees. Here, you will see a stand of cypresses that were burnt in a fire in 1991. These native conifers, once common along the mainland coast, have been largely killed by frequent fire. The only major stands of Rottnest cypress exist at Woodman Point and on Garden Island.
3   At the end of the dual-use path, turn right down the beach access path. Follow the beach south-westwards around the bay.
4   Immediately after the Cockburn Cement jetty, turn left to cross the narrow isthmus to reach the southern side of Woodman Point peninsula and Jervoise Bay.
5   Follow the shoreline with views across Cockburn Sound to Garden Island.
6   At the breakwater, follow the road northwards to rejoin the cycleway. You will find a drinking fountain and toilets close to the beach.
7   On both sides of the path are dense thickets of summer-scented wattle, which flowers late winter to early spring.
8   Immediately after crossing O'Kane Court you will come to some large tuart trees with abundant nesting hollows used by 'twenty-eight' parrots. Other dominant vegetation includes a taller form of summer-scented wattle, as well as *Spyridium globulosum*. Dense tuart woodland can be seen to the left in the reserve, which can be accessed through a swing gate about 400 m west along O'Kane Court.

9   To the right of this point you can see intact explosives storage facilities—a reminder of the area's former use as an explosives reserve.
10 After crossing Nyyerbup Circle you can see quandong trees, which display large green and red berries in late spring to summer.
11 At the next junction of cyclepaths, turn left and return to the picnic area.

Sharon Gray and James Robinson, Friends of Woodman Point

Where is it?: *Woodman Point Recreation Reserve, 22 km south-west of Perth*
Travelling time: *40 minutes from Perth via Fremantle and Cockburn Road*
Facilities: *Picnic areas, BBQs, shelters, toilets, playgrounds, carparks*
On-site information: *Ranger, information boards*
Best season: *All year, little shade in summer*

LOOK, LISTEN, SMELL AND TOUCH

It's not good enough to just visit an outdoor site and simply observe, you've got to immerse your senses in those happenings around you to obtain full appreciation.

When you have arrived at 'the swamp', first realise that you have walked into the living room of all those creatures that live there. This is their domain; you are the trespasser, time to make your peace.

Make for the nearest tuart tree, throw your arms around it, press your face into its rough powdery bark, feel its immense strength and durability. Next take a green leaf; hold it to the sun and see the veins of life and the intricate structure of cells. Then break the leaf, breath deeply and let the pungent odour of its life-blood accost your nostrils. Now you know what a tuart is.

Similarly, for the animal kingdom, listen intently to an orchestra of frogs. Let your ears soak up the sound of a beautiful noise. Then, with shoes off and shirt sleeves rolled up, crawl out into the black water, smell the methane gas as it bubbles up, lower your face to the surface and peer between the dank aquatic vegetation in search of insects. Now you know what a frog is all about, because you've temporarily been one. Magic stuff eh?

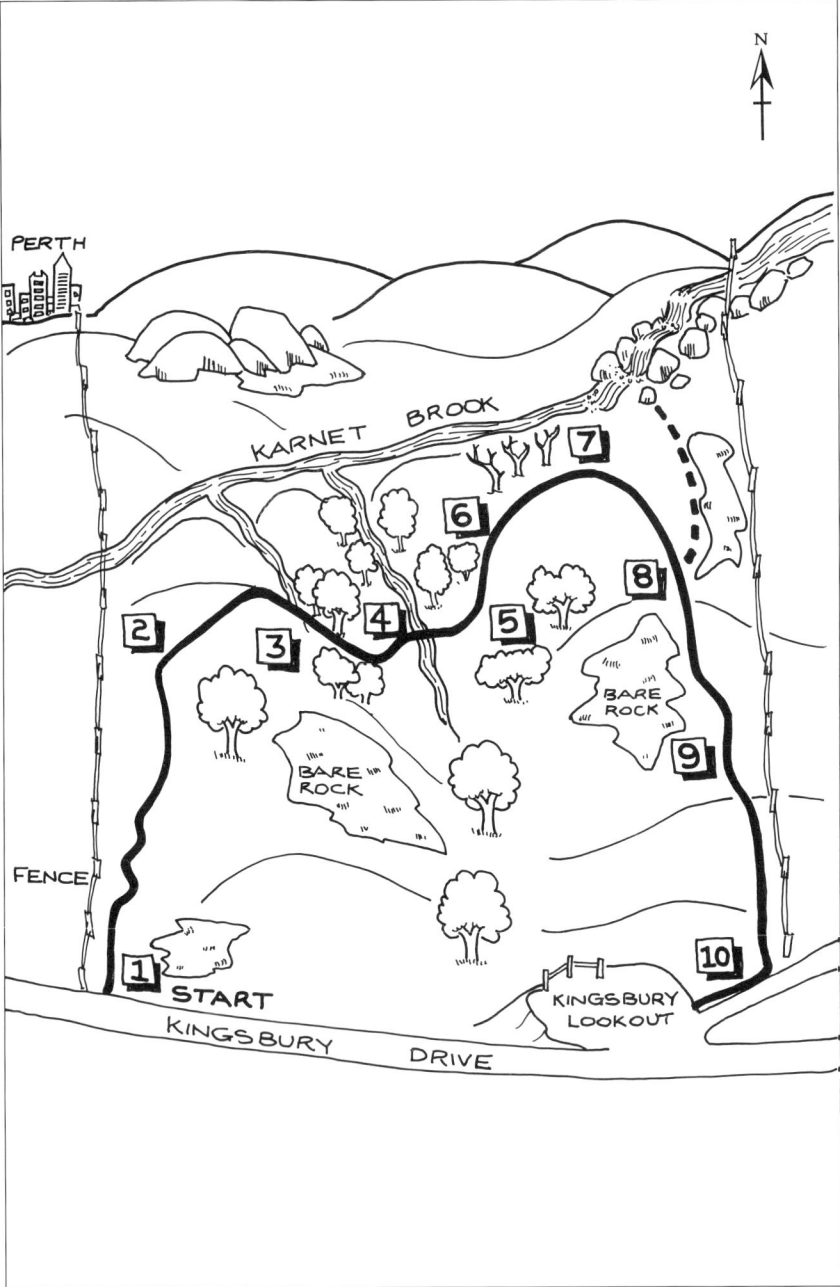

N

PERTH

KARNET BROOK

7

6

2

3

4

5

8

BARE ROCK

BARE ROCK

9

FENCE

1

START

10

KINGSBURY LOOKOUT

KINGSBURY DRIVE

Kingsbury Lookout Walk   **47**

near Karnet

Length: 2 kilometre loop (plus 400 metres optional trek to watercourse)
Grade: 3-4
Walk time: 2 hours

Kingsbury Lookout is located about 2.5 km east along Kingsbury Drive (off South Western Highway), opposite the Buddhist Monastery. The walk takes you down the side of the valley through which runs Karnet Brook. There is an optional section that goes down to a series of small seasonal waterfalls.

After parking at Kingsbury Lookout, you must first walk down-hill (or west) along Kingsbury Drive about 350 m to where a fenceline takes off to your right. Note the small sign 'Loc. 385' on the corner fence post at this site.

1   Here's where you start your walk. Follow the track heading north alongside the fence, with the private property on your left and a view of distant Perth city almost directly ahead. Continue as the track meanders through the rocky scarred break-away country.

2   About 150 m further on you'll be looking directly at an exposed granite rock outcrop on the ridge opposite. Look directly west to take in a view of the Swan coastal plain and the Indian Ocean, on a clear day.

3   Cross the first spring-fed gully and continue down the barren rocky slope to a burgeoning wandoo forest gully.

4   Continue along the contour to find WA Christmas trees (November–December) as you come to the second gully crossing. A steep climb brings you once again to a good viewing level surrounded by the yellow flowering *Acacia pulchella* (spring only).

5   Continue along the contour through open woodland. Look for scattered Darling Range ghost gums uphill on your right.

6   As the view of the coastal plain is obscured behind the first hills of the scarp, you may hear the sounds of waterfalls above the squawking and chirping of birds in the acacia thickets.

7   You are about halfway along your walk from Kingsbury Drive. Here, the nests of meat-ants and the skeletons of fire-scarred wandoos, with their head-high regrowth offspring, dominate your view.

8   Another rocky climb as you start to head back uphill. The fenceline at the top of the hill soon becomes visible. It's at this point that the more adventurous walkers may brave the open rock and scrub to the numerous water falls that flow in the

wetter months. Alternatively, follow the fenceline on your left uphill towards the carpark.

9   Turn around and enjoy the views of the ocean and Garden Island as you stop to catch your breath on the uphill home run.

10 As you reach the gravel 'Y' junction at the top of the hill, turn right (west) to bring yourself back to the Kingsbury Lookout to survey the rugged country you have just successfully negotiated.

Andy Darbyshire

Where is it?: *In State forest 68 km south of Perth*
Travelling time: *1 hour 15 minutes via South Western Highway*
Facilities: *BBQs, tables, carpark, lookout*
On-site information: *Sign at entrance to picnic site*
Best season: *All year, winter for waterfalls*

BUGS, SLUGS AND BEETLES

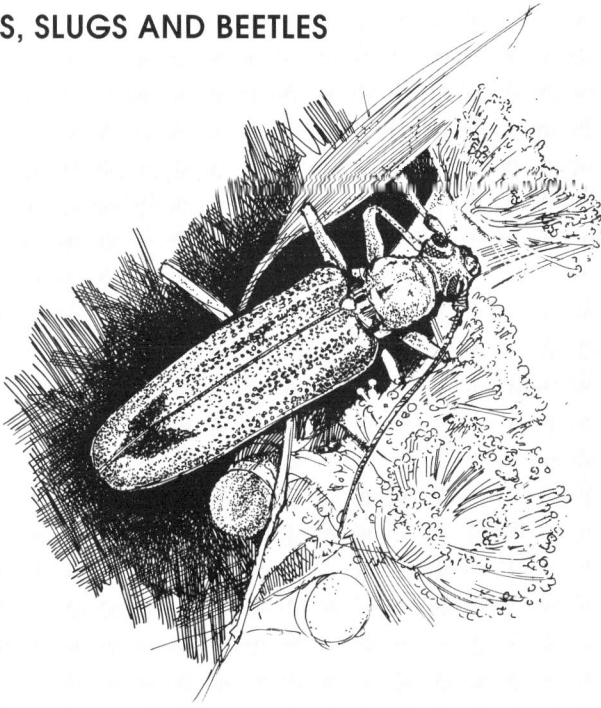

Ant lion larvae are the bugs that create tiny conical funnels in the sand anywhere from outside our front doors to deep in the forests. Adult ant lions resemble dragonflies. They lay their eggs in the ground and the lavae, each only a few millimetres long but equipped with formidable pincers, lies in wait under the bottom of the cone. Unsuspecting ants climb into the cone and are showered with sand until they tumble to the bottom where they are grabbed and their body fluids drained. The satiated ant lion then flicks the empty husk away.

Slugs evolved from snail-like molluscs and are commonly found in moist habitats. As well as helping to break down naturally-occurring organic matter, they can be found at night generously licking clean the household pet's dinner dish, which has been left out on the back lawn.

Beetles are the largest order of insects, with more than 250 000 known species. They are usually easily recognisable because their fore wings are transformed into a pair of hard, thick elytra (wing covers). These meet down the middle of the back, but are held forward when the insect is in flight.

Beetles that have a long snout are actually. The long snout enables them to pierce grains and seeds and extract the flesh.

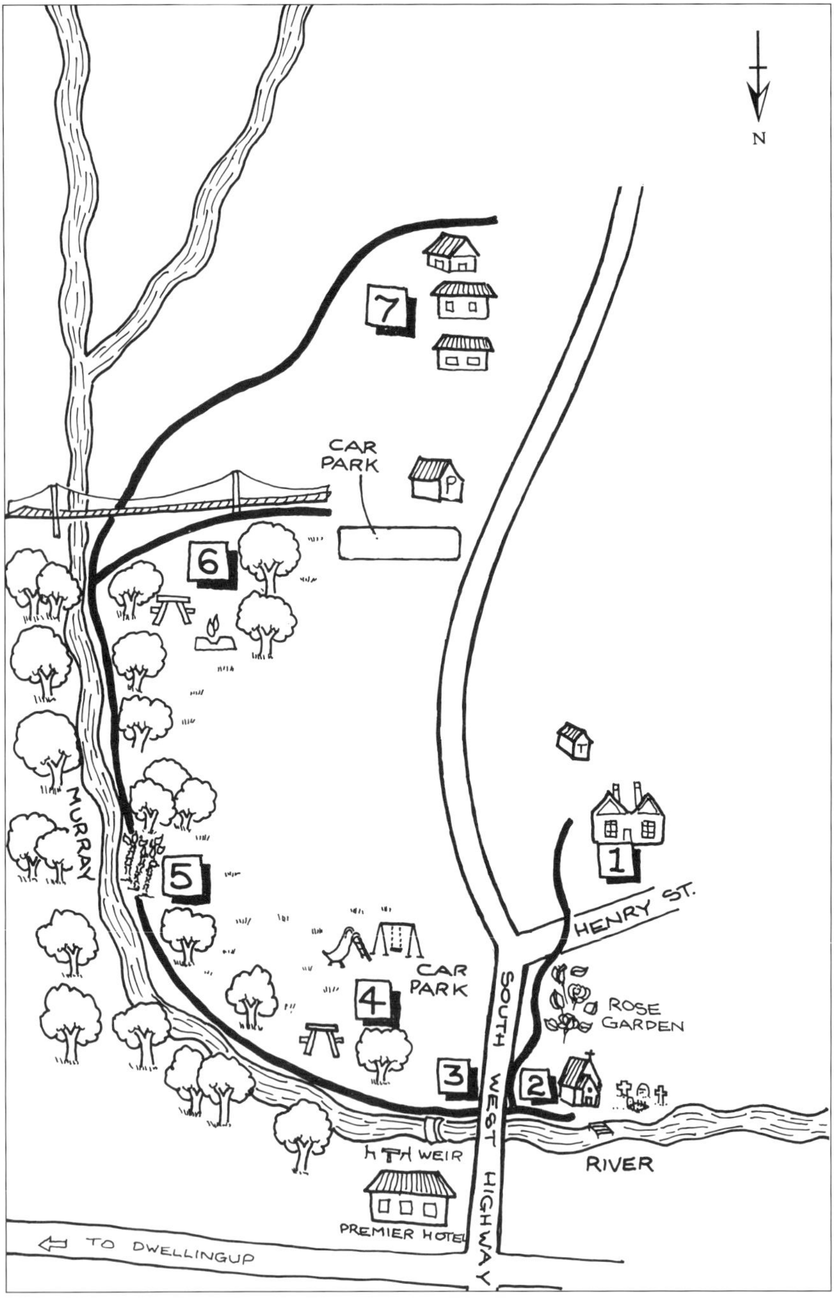

N

7

CAR PARK

P

6

MURRAY

5

CAR PARK

4

3

2

1

HENRY ST.

ROSE GARDEN

SOUTH WEST HIGHWAY

WEIR

PREMIER HOTEL

RIVER

TO DWELLINGUP

Murray River Walk

Pinjarra

48

Length: *1.2 kilometres*
Grade: *1*
Walk time: *1 hour*

This walk retraces the early history of Pinjarra. It features historical buildings and sites, and incorporates the Pinjarra Heritage Trail. Before European settlement, the Pinjarra district was inhabited by Nyoongars of the Bibbulmun tribe who hunted for game and caught fish in the bushland and waters of the Murray River.

1   Begin at the Edenvale complex, which houses the Murray Tourist Bureau, an arts and crafts centre and Heritage Tearooms. Cross Henry Street and pass the Heritage Rose Garden—its oldest rose bush dates back to 1853.
2   St John's Church and Pioneer Cemetery is located beside the Murray River. The first church on this site was built in the 1840s, but was swept away in the 1860 flood. It was rebuilt with locally-baked mud bricks. A wooden platform, next to the cemetery, extends out into the river.
3   Here, the trail goes under the South Western Highway traffic bridge and you can see the massive jarrah timbers underneath.
4   Continue along the sealed footpath to Pioneer Memorial Park and playground. Four large planted hoop pines can be seen nearby.
5   Along this section, the riverbanks are lined with flooded gums. During winter, parrots and wattle birds can be seen and heard squabbling for the blossom.
6   After passing a bamboo patch you will soon come to another grassed picnic area with shady trees. Nearby is a public swing bridge that was built in 1985. This is also the site of the town swimming hole. Ducks congregate here.
7   After the swing bridge, the pathway becomes a little steeper before reaching early municipal buildings that include the Post Office (1895), the Courthouse (1935) and the Road Board Office (1871). Return along the same route or via the shopping area along George Street.

Tammie Reid

Where is it?: *87 km south of Perth*
Travelling time: *1 hour 40 minutes via the South Western Highway*
Facilities: *BBQs, picnic tables, toilets, carpark, playground*
On-site information: *None*
Best season: *All year except hot summer days*

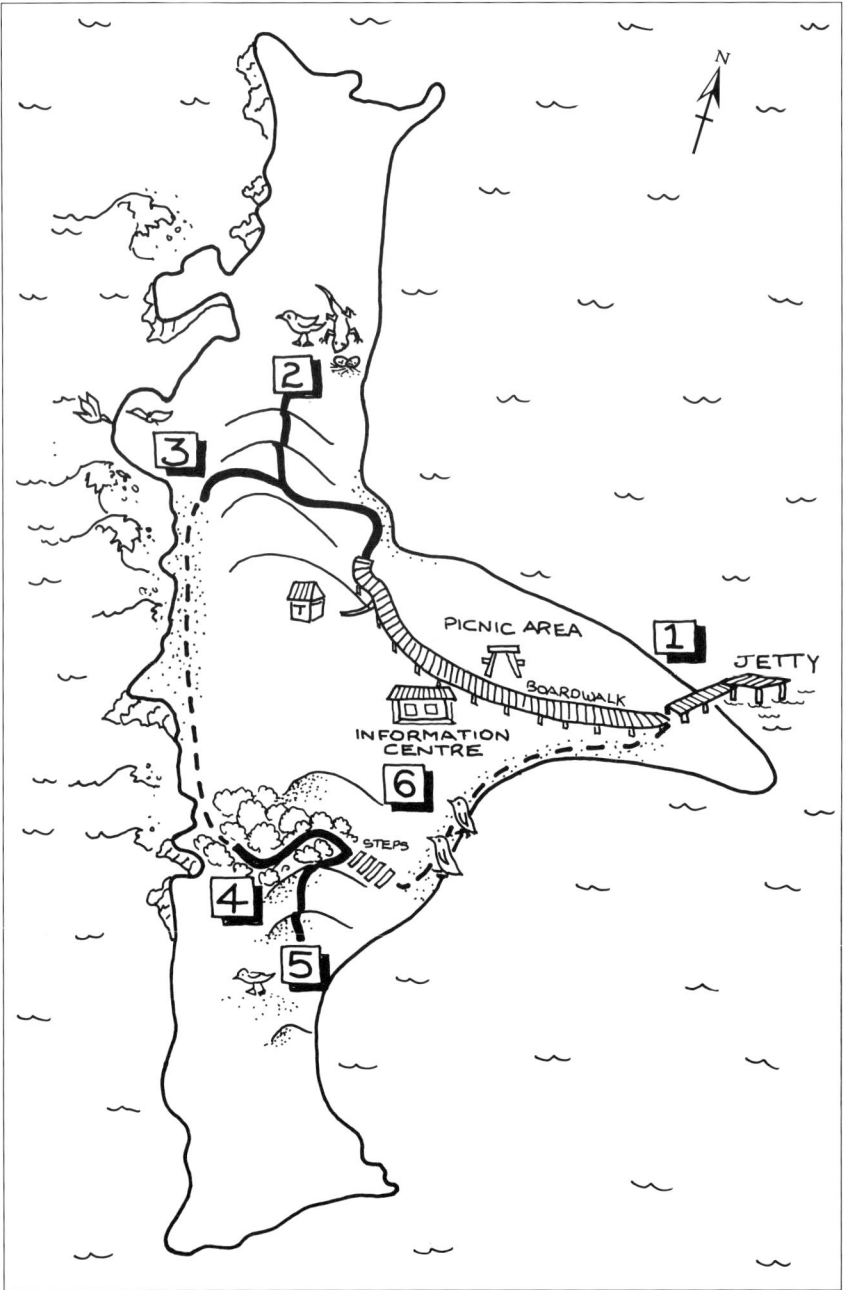

N

2

3

PICNIC AREA

1

JETTY

BOARDWALK

T

INFORMATION
CENTRE

6

STEPS

4

5

Penguin Island Trail   **49**

Shoalwater Islands Marine Park ($ - ferry to island)

Length: *900 metre loop*
Grade: *1*
Walk time: *45 mins*

Situated less than a kilometre from the shore and reached by ferry from the jetty, Penguin Island is the largest of the small islands and rocks in the Shoalwater Islands Marine Park.

The island is covered for the most part by sand dune vegetation and limestone outcrops, among which run the burrows of the largest colony of little penguins in Western Australia. The waters surrounding the island contain an amazing range of marine habitats, including limestone reefs and sheltered seagrass meadows.

1   Follow the jetty down to the island's boardwalk and wind your way over prime penguin breeding and nesting habitat to the information centre and picnic area. At present, the information centre is only staffed on weekends and holidays (1994). This will soon be replaced by a penguin viewing facility.
2   Continue along the boardwalk, past the toilets and up over the headland at the north end of the island. The path here becomes a crushed limestone surface and provides excellent views of nesting silver gulls in (season) and of the magnificent king skinks which raid the nests for eggs. There are also great views of the surrounding islands and waters.
3   Once over the headland, the 'trail' follows the beach. The west side of Penguin Island is the wild side—it's where waves crash onto the beaches and onto the exposed limestone cliffs. Examination of the cliffs will reveal fossilised tree roots thousands of years old. In season, you may also be lucky enough to watch the beautiful bridled terns which fly down from Malaysia to breed.
4   At the southern end of the island, the path winds its way through the vegetation and up over the southern headland.
5   An option exists for climbing the island's highest point. The stunning views of the surrounding marine park are well worth the climb. You may also see Caspian terns nesting on the dune below you.
6   The trail continues along the head and back to the jetty. On the way, keep your eyes and ears open for the little penguins which have made the island famous.

Rae Burrows

Where is it: *55km south of Perth (ferry to Penguin Island leaves from Mersey Point, off Arcadia Drive)*
Travelling time: *45 mins from Perth via Rockingham*
Facilities: *Picnic area, toilets water*
On-site information: *Information centre*
Best season: *Penguin Island is only open outside the penguin breeding season (September–May)*

SPONGES

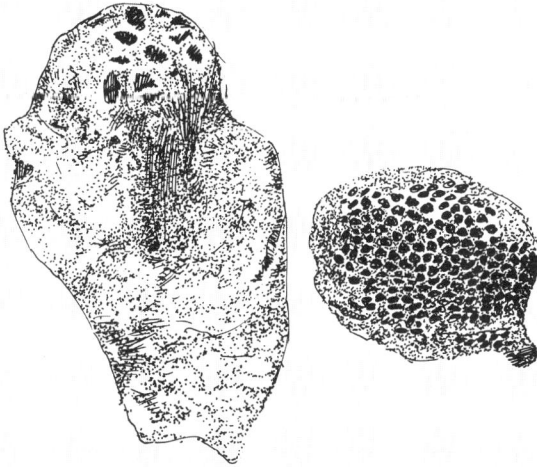

All sponges are aquatic and most of them are marine. The few freshwater sponge species are found in ponds, lakes, streams and rivers. Marine sponges exist in large numbers from mid-tide level on the shore, down to the greatest depths of the ocean. The smallest are about one millimetre high when fully grown and the largest is about equal in size to that of a medium size barrel.

On the shore, they tend to encrust rocks with continuous sheets of various thickness. In shallow or deep seas, the forms are more varied, being spherical, finger-shaped, bushy or tree-like, tubular, cup-shaped, funnel-shaped, or a crust on objects. The texture varies from soft and readily compressible to those that are as hard as stone.

Aristotle was the first to recognise, some 2 000 years ago, the animal nature of sponges. In the sixteenth century, sponges were believed to be solidified sea foam, and in the seventeenth century it was suggested that they were the homes of marine worms. Otherwise, the general impression was that sponges belonged to the plant kingdom.

The characteristic feature of a sponge is that it bears one or more conspicuous rounded openings. These are best described as vents. The rest of the surface under a microscope is seen to be punctured by minute pores. While many sponges are plant like, they contain no cellulose. Some possess true muscle fibres in the outer layers and recent research has suggested that others may possess a rudimentary nervous system. Yet some zoologists contend that sponges are an offshoot from the main animal kingdom.

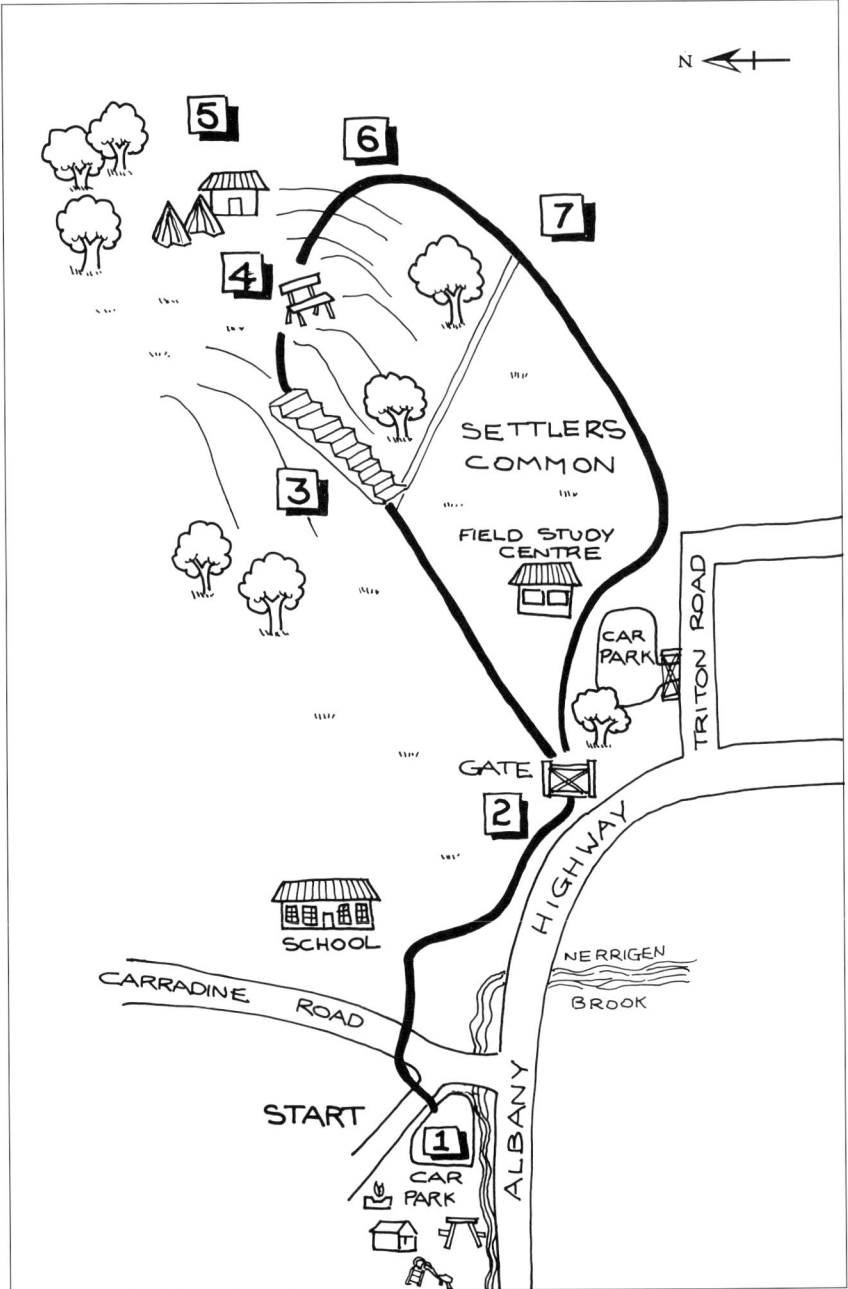

N

5

6

7

SETTLERS
COMMON

4

3

FIELD STUDY
CENTRE

CAR
PARK

TRITON ROAD

GATE

2

HIGHWAY

SCHOOL

CARRADINE ROAD

NERRIGEN
BROOK

START

ALBANY

1

CAR
PARK

Settlers' Common Walk   **50**

Armadale

Length: *2 kilometre loop*
Grade: *3 (some steep steps)*
Walk time: *1 hour (plus extra time if visiting Field Study Centre)*

Settlers' Common is a 383-hectare reserve vested in the Armadale City Council. There is a variety of vegetation types within the common, including jarrah and marri trees, zamias, banksias, parrotbush, orchids, triggerplants and the State floral emblem—the red and green kangaroo paw. There are also many animals, including some 70 species of bird.

This walk begins a little way from the common at a picnic site on the junction of Carradine Road and Albany Highway, Armadale. Dogs are permitted, but **must** be kept on a lead.

1   Starting from the picnic area, cross Angorra Road and Carradine Road towards the school. Instead of walking past the school, go through the carpark to the right, passing in front of the school, and follow the path for about 400 m.
2   An unmarked gate on the left takes you into the area known as Settlers' Common. Here, you can explore the various pathways through the gardens or follow our route straight on towards a flight of steps.
3   On reaching the steps, climb them up to the plateau.
4   At the top is a seat where you can relax and enjoy the panoramic views.
5   Three examples of Aboriginal dwellings have been built here.
6   The path continues down the hill from the opposite side of the plateau.
7   There is a junction with another track that leads back to near the base of the flight of steps. Continue down the hill and make your way to the building set among gardens at road level.
8   The Field Study Centre is open to the public at weekends and has displays. From here, cut back across to the gate and retrace your steps to the picnic area.

June Ellis

Where is it?: *30 km south-east of Perth*
Travelling time: *1 hour from Perth via Albany Highway*
Facilities: *Picnic area, BBQs, playground, toilets, carpark*
On-site information: *Field Study Centre and displays at common*
Best season: *All year, spring for wildflowers*

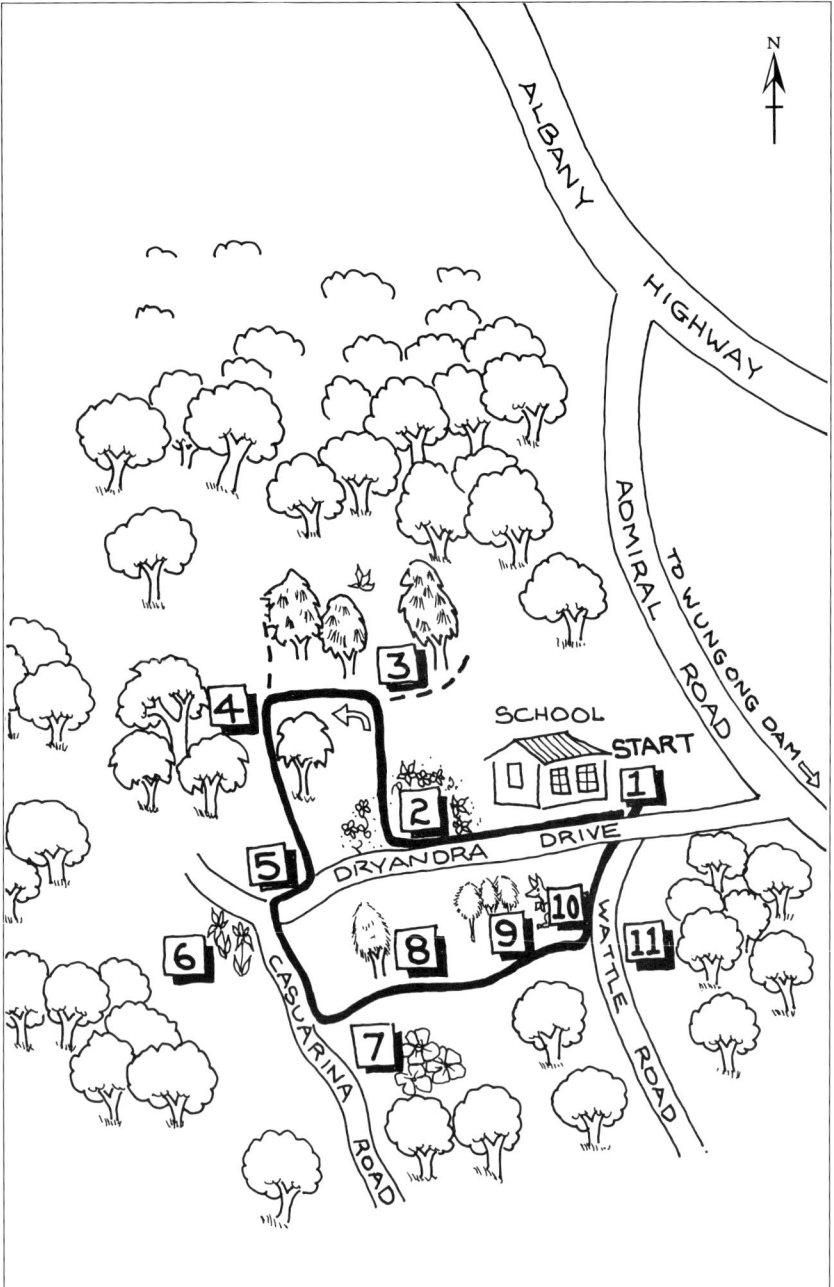

Spinebill Stroll

Bungendore Park

Length: 2.2 *kilometre loop*
Grade: 2
Walk time: 1 *hour*

Bungendore Park is situated on the Darling Scarp, just south of Armadale. It provides sweeping views to the Swan coastal plain. The reserve is home to many trees and shrubs and there are always plants in flower, no matter what time of year. In December, the bright orange-yellow WA Christmas trees burst into bloom.

1 Start at the information bay at the carpark near the school. Follow the markers along Dryandra Drive. Orchids are visible from the roadway (in season).
2 Watch for the right-hand indicator where the walktrail takes you past the western boundary. A profusion of wildflowers are seen here (in season), with hairy jug flowers visible all year round.
3 There is a left-hand turn among the sheoaks which usually host many small birds, including robin redbreasts and grey fantails.
4 At this junction, turn left into a particularly tranquil and sheltered portion of jarrah woodland which has been largely untouched by previous forest activity.
5 At this point, turn right to rejoin Dryandra Drive.
6 Just before the left turn into Casuarina Road, you should spend some time inspecting the species-rich patch of open country on the left.
7 Continue along Casuarina Road until the signs show a left-hand change. Golden hibbertia flourishes along most sections of this track.
8 As you pass over the fine iron-stone gravel, look out for the magnificent specimen of spreading snottygobble to the left of the trail.
9 Here, you will see a stand of upright snottygobbles.
10 Keep a sharp eye open and you could be rewarded with a sighting of the family of black-gloved wallabies that are regular visitors here.
11 Turn left into Wattle Road and head back to the starting point.

David Allen

Where is it?: *Bungendore Park, 31 km south of Perth*
Travelling time: *45 mins via Albany Highway*
Facilities: *Picnic area, carpark*
On-site information: *Trailhead sign, red square direction signs along walk*
Best season: *All year, spring for wildflowers*

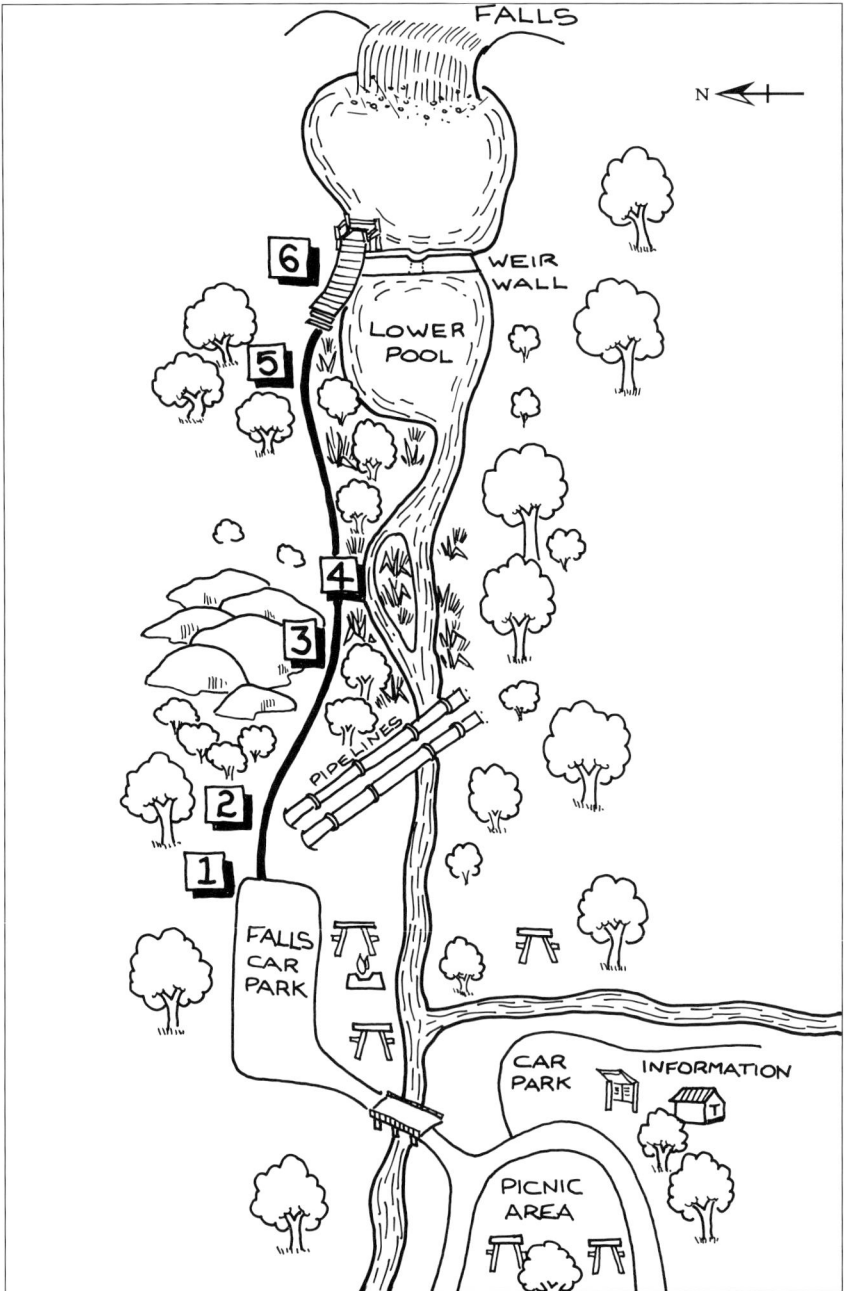

FALLS

N ←+

6

WEIR
WALL

5

LOWER
POOL

4

3

PIPELINES

2

1

FALLS
CAR
PARK

CAR
PARK

INFORMATION

T

PICNIC
AREA

The Falls Walktrail   **52**
Serpentine National Park ($)

Length: *400 metres return*
Grade: *1(accessible by wheelchair)*
Walk time: *15 minutes*

This is one of two walks in Serpentine National Park featured in this book; the other is Baldwins Bluff Nature Trail (page 123). The Falls Walktrail features groves of eucalypts, grevilleas, reeds and wildflowers in season, as well as spectacular views of the falls after winter rains.

1 The walk starts at the Falls carpark along a well-maintained gravel track.
2 These pipes supply water to the Perth metropolitan area from the pipehead dam.
3 The granite outcrops seen here were formed a million year ago and provide a sanctuary for the specialised plants and animals that inhabit them. You may see pincushion plants sprawling over the rocks, or if you are quiet, you may also see a dragon lizard sunning itself.
4 Here, part of the Serpentine River meanders close to the walktrail among the majestic flooded gums and an understorey of reeds, wattles and grevilleas, where splendid wrens, scarlet robins and red-eared firetails nest and search for food.
5 Ghosts of the Darling Range, these gnarled white barked trees, known as the Darling Range ghost gums, are only found in a restricted area between Darlington and Harvey. They mark drainage lines near rocky granite outcrops.
6 A little further on, you come to the lower pool and a raised walkway which leads to a viewing area of the spectacular Serpentine Falls and surrounding hills and vegetation. About 1911, the Public Works Department installed a gauging station and weir to measure the amount of water flowing over the Falls. To date (1994) the station still stands and the weir wall forms the now very popular swimming pool at the base of the Falls.

Wayne Taylor

Where is it: *Serpentine National Park, 50 km south-east of Perth*
Travelling time: *1 hour from Perth via South Western Highway*
Facilities: *Carpark, BBQs, picnic tables, toilets*
Best season: *Autumn, winter, spring for wildflowers*

Common birds of Perth Outdoors

Common Name	Scientific Name	Description	Habitat	Call
Australasian grebe or dabchick	*Tachybaptus novaehollandiae*	A tiny grey-brown water bird.	Freshwater swamps and lakes.	A clear angry chitter; alarm call a sharp *"tik!"*
Australian pelican	*Pelicanus conspicillatus*	Body plumidge white, wing quills black, wing edges, shoulders and area on rump black.	Anywhere where a large body of water and food occurs.	Normaly silent, but some grunt sounds away from breeding areas.
Australian raven	*Corvus coronoides*	Black, with long pointy feathers on throat.	Drier forests and woodlands.	Deep powerful *"aah-aah-aah-aahaaaaahh"* ends with gargle.
Australian wood duck	*Chenonetta jubata*	Male head and neck brown with mane of elongated black feathers, lower back tail covers and tail black, light grey wings. Female generally the same but grey/brown above.	Lightly timbered country near water.	Drawn out mournful *"mew"*.
Banded stilt	*Cladorhynchus leucocephalus*	Head and body white with broad chestnut band across chest, wings black with conspicuous trailing edge in flight.	Salt lakes and brackish estuaries in the south-west of the State.	Yelping notes, *"chowk-chowk"*.
Black duck	*Anas superciliosa*	Dark brown feathers edged with lighter brown. Dark line from bill through eye with pale yellow above and below.	All wetlands and open water.	Loud drawn out *"quack"* for two syllables.
Black swan	*Cygnus atratus*	All black with wing tips white. red bill with white bar.	Predominantly the south west of the State all waterways and offshore in the sea.	Loud trumpet.
Black-faced cuckoo-shrike	*Coracina novaehollandiae*	Medium size, grey with black face.	Open woodlands, parks and gardens.	Rolling phrase in flight; *"chereer-chereer"* at rest.
Carnaby's white-tailed cockatoo	*Calyptorhynchus baudinii*	A large brownyblack bird with white tail.	Forests of the south-west of WA.	Drawn out whistle *"whee-la"*.

Cattle egret	*Ardeola ibis*	Generally white but tinged with orange buff around the head and throat in the breeding season.	Trees and shrubs near water, sometimes seen perched on the backs of cattle.	Croaking calls.
Clamorous reed warbler	*Acrocephalus stentoreus*	Upper parts olive brown, head wings and tail darker brown and under parts pale buff.	Anywhere in reeds, rushes and swamps.	Song is a persistant "*quarty-quarty-quarty*".
Common bronzewing	*Phaps chalcoptera*	A large plump pigeon, upper parts brown and bronze on the wing.	All dryland habitats except wet forests.	Repeated "*oom-oom-oom*".
Darter	*Anhinga melanogaster*	Almost entirely glossy black,head and upper neck brown, buff streaks on upper wing coverts.	Lakes, rivers, swamps and sheltrerd coastal estuaries.	Clicking sounds or a harsh "*klaah*" and hissing near nest.
Eurasian coot	*Fulica atra*	A slate-grey to black waterhen with whitish bill.	Most lakes, wetlands and waterways.	A variety of noisy harsh notes. A sharp "*kyik!*" or "*kyok!*".
Galah	*Cacatua roseicapilla*	A pink and grey cockatoo with a cap-like crest.	Widespread through various habitats.	High-pitched, splintered "*chill chill*" and harsh screeches.
Grey butcherbird	*Cracticus torquatus*	A smaller magpie-like bird with a black hooked beak. Grey and black with white upperparts.	Eucalypt woodlands, forest margins, some parks.	A songster with loud variety of flute-like whistling and musical notes.
Grey fantail	*Rhipidura fuliginosa*	General grey brown above with two small white bars on wings, conspicuous white lines over eye and ear coverts, a permanently fanned tail.	All environments except arid interior along the WA border.	Rapid double or single "*chip*" and a high pitched, melodious, upward soaring song.
Laughing turtledove	*Streptopelia senegalensis*	Light brown and blue-grey.	Cities, towns, nearby cultivated areas.	Soft musical "*cooroocoo-coocoocoo*" with bubbling, laughing style.

Common birds of Perth Outdoors (continued)

Common Name	Scientific Name	Description	Habitat	Call
Little corella	*Cacatua sanguinea*	A pure white crestless cockatoo.	Mallee, tree-lined watercourses, arid woodlands.	Distinctive quick wavering falsetto "*currup*" or "*wuk-wuk*".
Little pied cormorant or shag	*Phalacrocorax melanoleucos*	Black above and white below, white face to above the eye, bill yellow and brown.	On any marine or freshwater environment.	Sometimes "*cooing*" and "*uk-uk*" mostly silent.
Mallard duck	*Anas platyrhynchos*	Male head and neck glossy geen with white collar rest of the body various browns, darker than the female which is dusky brown and chestnut streaked.	City wetlands.	Loud resonant raucous "*quack*"
Pallid cuckoo or rainbird	*Cuculus pallidus*	Medium sized, grey and white.	Woodlands, open forests, other open habitats.	Loud melancholy whistling notes rising up the scale.
Rainbow bee-eater	*Merops ornatus*	Pin tailed slender bird with fine curved black bill. Golden bronze colour.	Open country, forest clearings.	"*pirr, pirr, pirr.*"
Red wattlebird	*Anthochaera carunculata*	dark brown boldly steaked with white, pink-red wattle behind and under the eye.	Forests woodlands and gardens with abundant bottlebrush and similar blossoms.	Loud harsh squawks and laughs.
Red-necked avocet	*Recurvirostra novaehollandiae*	Long-legged waterbird, rusty head with long fine upturned bill and white body.	Coastal estuaries, lakes, swamps, mudflats.	Musical fluty "*toot*".
Rufous treecreeper	*Climacteris rufa*	Rufous brown above with crown and nape grey, face cinnamon-rufous.	Common in the south-west in open woodland and jarrah forest.	'Scolding' notes and a single hard whistle.
Silvereye or greenie	*Zosterops lateralis*	Upper parts generally yellow-green under parts whitish grey, white eye ring.	South western coastal and adjacent areas, suburban parks and gardens.	Call a drawn-out peevish "*cheew*", with a song of a sweet and pleasant warble often repeated.

Singing honeyeater	*Lichenostomus virescens*	Upper parts brown washed olive, but lighter elsewhere and a black stripe running through the eye with a lower yellow stripe.	Southern and west coasts and dry inland, urban gardens with abudant bottlebrush and similar blossoms.	Loud many varied notes mostly not tuneful.
Southern boobook	*Ninox novaeseelandiae*	A small brown bird with pale spots on wings.	Forests, woodlands, parks and gardens.	Falsetto *"boo-book"* or *"morepork".*
Splendid fairy-wren	*Malurus splendens*	The male, cobolt-blue in the breeding season. Otherwise brown, like female.	Forest and woodland scrub undergrowth.	Brisk splintered *"prip, prip".* Alarm, high pitched *"seee".* Song, loud trilling notes.
Spotted turtledove	*Streptopelia chinensis*	Light brown and black neck patch with white spots.	City, parks and gardens.	Musical drowsy *"coo, coo, croo-oo".*
Striated pardalote	*Pardalotus striatus*	Very small, tailess looking, grey, black and white.	Eucalypt forests, woodlands, mallee, watercourse gums.	Constant sharp *"pick-it-up"* or loud *"chip-chip".*
Swamphen	*Porphyrio porphyrio*	Upper parts black brown, face neck, breast shoulders, rich purple/blue, bright red beak and forehead shield.	In swamps and inland waterways.	Loud and harsh screeching calls, resemble *"kee-ouw".*
Western spinebill	*Acanthorhynchus superciliosus*	Upper parts olive grey with broad chestnut collar extending to the throat and breast and a white eyebrow, chest and cheek stripe.	Common and widespread in heath and woodland dominated by banksias.	Loud *"kleet-kleet".*
White-faced heron	*Ardea novaehollandiae*	Two tonned grey with flight feathers being darker, face and stripe on throat white.	Lakes, swamps, estuaries, dams, tidal mudflats and grasslands.	Alarm call a loud *"croak".*
Willy wagtail	*Rhipidura leucophrys*	All black with white chest, underparts and eyebrow.	Parklands and gardens in towns and cities.	Musical notes resembling *"pretty sweet creature"* and a metallic warning rattle.

169

Index by name

171

Walk Name	Location	Region	Walk No
Rocky Pool Walk	Kalamunda National Park	Hills	8
Scented Garden Trail	Kings Park	North	20
Settlers' Common Walk	Armadale	South	50
Shepherds Bush Walk	Kingsley	North	21
Special Valley Walk	Peace Be Still, Chittering Valley	Hills	9
Spinebill Stroll	Bungendore Park	South	51
Swamp Trail	Big Carine Swamp	North	22
Swan River Heritage Trail	Marshall Park	Rivers	35
Syd's Rapids Trail	Walyunga National Park	North	23
10th Light Horse Memorial Trail	Neerabup National Park	North	24
The Falls Walktrail	Serpentine National Park	South	52
Vlamingh Memorial Walktrail	Cottesloe	North	25
Woodloes Walk	Canning River Regional Park	Rivers	36
Yaberoo Budjara Heritage Trail #2	Neerabup National Park	North	26
Yaberoo Budjara Heritage Trail #3	Neerabup National Park	North	27

Index by walk length

Length	Walk Name	Region	Walk No
4.0	Rocky Pool Walk	Hills	8
4.5	Cage in the Bush Walktrail	South	39
4.5	Jervoise Bay Walktrail	South	46
5.0	Swan River Heritage Trail	Rivers	35
6.0	Baldwins Bluff Nature Trail	South	38
6.0	Out & Back Loop Trail	Hills	6
6.0	Rocky Bay Walk	Rivers	34
6.5	Deep Water Walk	Rivers	30
7.0	Piesse Gully Loop Trail	Hills	7
8.0	Mason & Bird Heritage Trail	Hills	4
8.5	Vlamingh Memorial Walktrail	North	25
12.0	Etmilyn Tramway Trail	South	43
13.0	New Victoria Dam Walk	Hills	5
13.4	Yaberoo Budjara Heritage Trail #3	North	27
15.0	Yaberoo Budjara Heritage Trail #2	North	26

CALM offices in Perth Outdoors

State Operations Headquarters

50 Hayman Road PO Box 104
COMO 6152
☎ (09) 334 0333 Fax: (09)334 0466

Regional Office

3044 Albany Highway
KELMSCOTT 6111
☎ (09) 390 5977 Fax: (09) 390 7059

District Offices

Dwellingup:
Banksiadale Road DWELLINGUP 6213
☎ (09) 538 1001 Fax: (09) 538 1203

Jarrahdale:
George Street JARRAHDALE 6203
☎ (09) 525 5004 Fax: (09) 525 5547

Mundaring:
Mundaring Weir Road MUNDARING 6073
☎ (09) 295 1955 Fax: (09) 295 2404

Perth:
5 Dundebar Road WANNEROO 6065
☎ (09) 405 0700 Fax: (09) 405 0777

NOTES

NOTES